Home Renovation:

Making Your Home More Attractive, Modern, and Valuable

Home Renovation:

Making Your Home More Attractive, Modern, and Valuable

Stanley Schuler

RESTON PUBLISHING COMPANY, INC.
Reston, Virginia 22090

A Prentice-Hall Company

Library of Congress Cataloging in Publication Data

Schuler, Stanley.
  Home renovation.

  1. Dwellings—Remodeling.   I. Title.
TH4816.S286   643'.7   74-8769
ISBN 0-87909-347-1

© 1974 by
Reston Publishing Company, Inc.
A Prentice-Hall Company
Box 547
Reston, Virginia 22090

10 9 8 7 6 5 4 3 2 1

Printed in the United States of America.

Contents

Preface

In the 35 years I've been writing about how to renovate homes, there has never been a time when information on the subject was so sorely needed. For one thing, we have reached a point where, purely from the standpoint of family economics, we must do a better job of saving and using and enjoying the houses we have. For another thing, the so-called professionals we have depended on to do this work for us are unwilling and/or unable to do what has to be done at a reasonable price. So one of the purposes of this book is simply to help homeowners solve a problem of growing importance.

The other purpose is to try to clarify what renovation work is within the realm of competence of the average person and what is not. The misunderstanding on this score is considerable and far from uniform. Some people underestimate the difficult jobs and overestimate the easy; others are exactly the reverse. Having learned the ropes of the game entirely by trial and error, I hope to set the record straight.

This is not a book for experts (although there are not many experts on all aspects of home renovation). Rather, it's for the millions and millions who have had little or no experience with tools, but who suddenly find that if they're to have the kind of homes they want, they must be their own contractors.

I wish you success. I don't doubt for an instant that you will have it.

Stanley Schuler

Home
Renovation
Basics

Tom and Ashley Rooney, Bill and Randy Burnett, and Charlie and Cary Hull are three couples I know well. The women are my daughters; the men, their husbands. In a total of 16 years of married life they have renovated or initiated the renovation of five homes.

The number of homes has no significance—but the fact that these particular people did such work does. Until they were married, the girls had never painted, wallpapered, refinished furniture, gardened; and the boys hadn't done much more in the building and repair line. Tom, a research geologist, had hardly raised a hammer—and he felt so strongly about the mere idea that he told Ashley shortly before their wedding, "Don't ever expect me to do what your father does around the house." Bill, a businessman, was only slightly more familiar with tools. He wasn't averse to them or afraid of them, but he knew little about handling them. Charlie, an engineer, was the only one who could claim any understanding of or facility with tools. But when it came to putting them to work on a home repair project, he was still a novice.

Today, all three families are well along in the process of changing from amateur to professional craftsmen. They paint, wallpaper, lay floors, replaster walls, do wiring, refinish furniture, garden with abandon. Charlie has even torn out, rebuilt, and repiped a bathroom. But more important than this, they have changed one tired and three badly run-down properties into attractive, livable, modern homes. (Work on the fifth house is just beginning.) And they have added thousands of dollars to the values of the homes.

These people are not unique. There is no way of determining the actual number of families who renovate their homes in whole or in part during any given year. But having been connected with the housing industry for more than 35 years as a writer, editor, and consultant, I am confident that the majority of American families rejuvenate at least one home during their lifetime as a family. And more and more of them are doing much of the work themselves.

The reason for this do-it-yourself trend is obvious: The cost of hiring professionals to do repair or improvement work today borders on the unbearable—the more so because some workmen have become so elusive and unreliable, so sloppy in their work, and have little pride in the way it turns out.

The once-unregenerate Tom Rooney summed up the situation rather well, I thought, when I was kidding him about all the work he has done on the 110-year-old house he and Ashley bought last year:

> It isn't just that we don't like living like slobs. And it isn't just because we enjoy the convenience and comfort of a well-equipped, well-arranged house. We've made over this house—as we made over the one in Bedford—because it makes sound economic sense.
>
> Don't think I enjoy the work. Ashley does, but not me. Not inside the house anyway. Gardening is something else again. But it's the only way we can afford it. Do you know what one guy asked for refinishing the floor in our little study? $150! I don't want to refinish floors. But at that price you can bet I will. And I wouldn't be surprised if they come out just as well, if not better. It's a cinch, at least, that we'll get them done when we want them done.

WHAT'S INVOLVED IN
RENOVATING A HOME...

Let's get this straight at the outset. Renovate and rejuvenate (I use the words interchangeably) mean to make young again. They involve refurbishing or face-lifting; repairing; remodeling; making improvements. They may also involve making additions, but since an addition by itself doesn't necessarily rejuvenate a house, I am going to limit coverage of this subject to adding on a terrace or deck (Chapter 16) and a garage or carport (Chapter 17). In this modern world, a house without these two features is out-of-date; hence, their addition contributes to renovation and rejuvenation.

Renovating a house can be a major, minor, or medium-size undertaking. For example, my friends the Schweppes are doing it the major way—but then they are old hands at the game, since this is the third house they've worked on. Even so, they wonder every now and then whether they haven't bitten off too much this time.

Both have very successful careers in New York City; the house they're redoing is in eastern Connecticut. It's 200 years old, and though it originally stood strong and proud in its Colonial simplicity, it had been reduced almost to a hovel by successive occupants. But Den and Ellen are determined people. They take delight and pride in restoring antique houses while at the same time adapting them to modern living. What's more, they do almost all the work themselves—not from necessity but because they do it better than the pros. So it's hardly surprising that 18 months after buying the house, they figured they had completed only one-sixth of the project.

By contrast, the renovation of my own home was much simpler, although the house is at least twice as big. When my wife, Elizabeth, and I bought it, it was completely down at the heels; but it was basically sound and up-to-date in plan and appointments. True, we made construction changes in it. For instance, in order to convert a first-floor room to a bedroom, we had to make a study over into a bathroom; and we closed up several doors and cut open several new doors in order to use other rooms in new ways. But I don't count these changes as necessary to the renovation of the house because the house was completely livable without them.

About a year after we moved in, a couple of the middle-aged children of the previous owner dropped by. They had grown up in the place, had loved it, and were frankly curious to see what we had done to it. They were generous in their praise. "It's rejuvenated," one of them said. "Yes," we agreed, "but outside of putting in a new kitchen, we really didn't do that much to it. Basically, all we did was repaint and repaper and refinish the floors."

More often than not, that's all that renovating a home amounts to.

HOW TO DECIDE
WHAT SHOULD BE DONE...

Other friends, John and Happy White, have a positive genius for renovating houses. In the 35 years I have known them, they have taken three of the saddest-looking seaside houses and have turned them into beautiful, functional homes. These were not mere restorations, because in no case was there anything worth restoring: they were major—I'm inclined to say massive—remodelings, and it took a lot of imagination to undertake them.

But while imagination may be essential to the Whites' kind of project, it is not the No. 1 requirement. And it is certainly not the No. 1 requirement for the average project. Determining what should be done to renovate a house requires thoughtful study more than anything else.

Hence, the first rule: *Don't rush.*

Of course it is hard not to rush when you buy a house that needs work, because you want to get as much as you can done *before you move in.* Renovating a house when you're living in it is awkward. On the other hand, the longer you live in a house, the easier it is to see what must be done to it.

Second rule: *Ask and answer the following questions:*

What do we need in our home and what do we want?

As I just said, if you have been living in a house for some time, it is very obvious how well it meets your needs and desires. But when you're buying a house, some of its deficiencies are likely to escape you, unless you have taken the time beforehand to figure out exactly what your family needs and wants in a house. This is not a task to be undertaken lightly. You must do three things:

1 • List your needs in writing—and list your wants separately, also in writing. This not only will clarify your thinking but also will enable you to check off what necessary and desired features the house has. Thus, by elimination, you can readily see what it doesn't have.

2 • Be sure your entire family, including the children, participates in preparation of the lists.

3 • Take care not to ignore the ingrained characteristics and habits of the family members. Many people who are remodeling, building, or buying houses do not do this—with the result that they wind up with features they don't really want, even though they tell themselves they do; or, vice versa, they wind up without features they need, even though they tell themselves they don't. For example, it's silly to say, "We need a big beautiful kitchen," when no one in the family likes to cook. Similarly, it's silly to say, "We can get along without an attic or basement," when the head of the family is a pack rat.

What's wrong with the house?

Here again, it's important to write a list because it eliminates confusion and uncertainty. A list also helps you to decide the order in which the wrongs should be righted. And it sometimes helps to point up the fact that some of the things you first thought were wrong are really not wrong at all.

The wrongs in houses fall into three categories: structural, functional, and aesthetic.

Structural defects include such things as sagging floors, badly cracked plaster, clogged pipes, lack of attic ventilation, etc. Some are minor and can be ignored. But generally these are the first—or among the first—things that should be corrected in a house when it's rejuvenated.

Aesthetic defects or deficiencies are the most obvious wrongs in a house. They leap out at you and offend you. "This room is drab. This one's too dark. This one has a hideous light fixture."

Functional wrongs are the hardest to pinpoint accurately until you have lived in a house for a while. Such things as a badly arranged kitchen and insufficient electrical outlets are easy enough to spot if you are looking for faults. But poor circulation (meaning that you cannot move around the house easily and may have to walk through one room to get to another), lack of zoning (meaning that the rooms are not grouped by their principal uses), and lack of privacy (from the world at large, from neighbors, and from the other members of the family) are not easy to spot.

What is the best way to right what's wrong?

Obviously, if you want your home to be as nearly perfect as possible, you should correct the things that are wrong with it. But when you start thinking about and exploring what should be done, you may find that, for one reason or another, correction is impractical or even impossible. Then your plan of attack must be changed.

Even though they are not essential, what changes will benefit the property?

I am not suggesting that, when you set out to renovate your home, you should throw caution to the wind and make every change that comes to mind. That would be the height of folly. But unless your budget is extremely tight, it would be equally foolish not to at least consider unnecessary changes that would make your home more livable, attractive, or saleable.

For example, two of the things that particularly bothered Randy and Bill Burnett about their first house were the arched openings separating the living room from the hall and the dining room. Actually, there was nothing wrong with the openings, but they dated the house; and when everything else had been brought up to date, they were anachronisms in that particular setting. They should have been squared off before the floor was carpeted, but they weren't. I have since wondered whether they had anything to do with the fact that Randy and Bill didn't get the very reasonable price they asked for the house when they put it on the market. It's possible they did.

Will what we do hurt sales value?

When people renovate a home, they have a tendency to believe that every change they make will increase the sales value. But the reverse effect may occur. This most often happens (1) when the appearance of a house is ruined by the owners' misguided sense of design or (2) when the owner installs features or changes the plan to satisfy peculiar personal requirements.

More will be said later about the importance of using restraint in redesigning and redecorating a house—particularly the exterior. Emphasis here is on the wisdom of not indulging your own idiosyncrasies if you want to sell your house easily and profitably at a later date.

This is not to say that you shouldn't adapt your house to your needs and tastes. After all, you are living in it and you have every right to be happy with it. But don't go overboard. I know a man who put the living room on the second floor of an otherwise conventional two-story house that he built. I have no idea what his reasons were—to him, they were probably the height of logic. But when he put the house on the market, it took months to find a buyer who could envision ways to rebuild the house with the living room where it belonged.

Is renovation of our home the best way to satisfy our housing needs?

This question might be the first you ask yourself. But I put it last because you can answer it better if you first figure out more or less what is to be done to the house.

The point of the question is this: Renovation of a house does not always produce a perfect answer to a family's housing needs. You might be better off to build or buy another house.

Renovation is generally advisable under any of the following circumstances: if you like your home and neighborhood; if it will yield a better home at less cost than you can buy; if it will definitely increase the value of the property.

On the other hand, renovation is generally inadvisable if it costs too much; if your neighborhood is on the skids; if you are rejuvenating the house only in the expectation of selling it, but the changes you make are not enough to increase its marketability to any appreciable extent.

WHERE TO GET HELP IF YOU NEED IT...

Naturally you may feel—and be—quite competent to plan and carry through the renovation of your home without any outside help. But if you are not so blessed with confidence or skill, there are plenty of experts to whom you can turn.

HOUSE INSPECTION SERVICES   Staffed by people who have had considerable building experience, these organizations inspect existing houses, advise on their condition, and recommend what might or should be done to improve them. The larger firms are found only in metropolitan areas, but individuals—usually contractors—who can do the same work are to be found everywhere.

Inspection services charge a flat fee—usually in the neighborhood of $100.

ARCHITECTS   An architect should be your first choice if your project is extensive or complicated, or if you're making a period restoration. Architects not only have design skill but also understand construction; and they are competent to work on both the outside and the inside of a house. Accordingly, they offer a better combination of talents than any other professional.

Architects are most often found in metropolitan areas, but there are many in small towns across the country. All are registered (licensed by the state); no one can call himself an architect otherwise. The majority are members of the American Institute of Architects (AIA)—but this does not mean that those who are not should be avoided since AIA membership is voluntary.

Before hiring an architect you should make sure (1) that he does residential remodeling and is available to work for you; (2) that you take a look at houses he has built and remodeled to ascertain whether you like his style; (3) that you find out from his earlier clients whether they approve of him; (4) that you have a personal meeting with him to get some idea of whether you are going to like him and be able to work with him. A fifth point to check if you're restoring a period house, such as Cape Cod Colonial or Federal, is whether he is truly familiar with the period. If you are then satisfied on all scores, you should enter into a formal written agreement with him.

The amount of work an architect does depends on what you need him for and on how much you are willing to pay him. His work may be limited to drawing up detailed plans and specifications for the changes to be made in your house. Or you may also employ him to help you find and hire a contractor, and then to supervise construction. If the architect does all of these things, his total fee can run to as much as 15 to 25 percent of the actual cost of the remodeling.

INTERIOR DESIGNERS   Also known as an interior decorator, an interior designer is your best choice if the changes in your home are limited mainly to interior refurbishing and involve little, if any, remodeling. This doesn't mean that designers are unable to give you plans for building bookcases and other built-ins and for making simple changes in the structure; but very, very few are competent to do the sort of work an architect does.

Interior designers are much less numerous than architects, and virtually all operate in the vicinity of cities. Some work in interior design firms, others in department and furniture stores. There are also many people who call themselves interior designers or decorators but who have little skill or training, because interior designers are not licensed.

Your best assurance that an interior designer is qualified is to talk to other clients and take a look at the work he has done for them. If he is a member of the American Institute of Interior Designers (AID) or the National Society of

Interior Designers (NSID), this is also some assurance of his qualifications—but not a guarantee that his style will suit your tastes.

Interior designers play various roles. They may simply serve as consultants, recommending what should be done to rejuvenate your home and perhaps giving you plans to follow. Or they may also go out into the marketplace and help you find the materials needed to carry out their suggestions. (In some cases, they actually supply the materials themselves.) Or they may, in addition, provide and/or supervise the workers required to carry out the rejuvenation.

The cost of these services and the ways you pay for them are as varied as the services themselves. Some designers charge a fee; some take a commission on the materials, furnishings, and work you buy; some do both. Whatever the arrangement, you wind up paying more for your interior improvement than you would if you planned the project yourself.

LANDSCAPE ARCHITECTS A landscape architect is your best source of help if you are changing the planting around your house or landscaping the property in any way. I also think he's the best choice if you are building or rebuilding a terrace, but here he gets stiff competition from an architect.

To call himself a landscape architect, one should have a college degree in landscape architecture; but landscape architects are not licensed, and since the landscape architectural societies are not as strong as they should be, one may not be a member. So it's hard to be sure how good a landscape architect is without examining his work and talking to his clients. On the other hand, even though I have a strong personal feeling that a yard should be as well designed as a house, I must admit that if you hire a landscape architect who does less than a perfect job for you, the world is not going to come to an end.

A landscape architect operates like an architect, drawing up detailed plans for improving your property. Then, if you wish, he will go on to supervise the project. In both cases he either works by the hour or charges a flat fee.

All other experts available to you work on a no-charge basis. This is why most homeowners use them. But before you follow suit, you should realize that, as designers, they rank below the professional architects, interior designers, and landscape architects—so what they do for you may not be very inspired.

GENERAL CONTRACTORS A general contractor is the best possible substitute for an architect if you are making major or minor structural changes of several kinds inside or outside your house. True, he himself may not have full knowledge of how all the different parts of a house are best put together—but he has a team of subcontractors who compensate for his deficiencies.

Unfortunately, however, there are a couple of important considerations to be aware of in dealing with general contractors.

In the first place, if you ask a contractor to advise you about what you should do to your home and if you like his ideas, you are morally obligated to let him do the work. This means you have no way of determining whether the price he charges is too high.

Since remodeling of a house is always rather expensive, no one should undertake it without getting at least two or three bids. But if you go to two or three contractors and ask them to suggest what should be done to the house and to tell you what it would cost, you still don't know whether the figures they come up with are fair. Why? Because it is almost a certainty that their suggestions will be different; therefore, the bids are bound to be different.

Here is another reason why it's smart not to go to a general contractor for *advice*: It saves money—but in the end you can't be sure whether it saves money or not. The only way to get the lowest possible bid on a remodeling project is to draw up complete plans and specifications for what you want to accomplish (do this yourself or let an architect do it for you) and give copies to several contractors to study and prepare estimates.

The other consideration in dealing with a general contractor—and this is true whether you go to him for advice or simply ask him to bid on plans someone else has drawn up—is that his honesty and reliability are as important to you as his workmanship. Of course, you can say this about any person you employ. But it's especially true of general contractors because the work they do, as a rule, is extensive and expensive. So if they don't show up for work when they say they're going to or if they cheat in some way, you suffer.

Thus, it follows that before hiring a general contractor, you must check up on him at length. There's only one sound way to go about this. First, call your local Better Business Bureau and ask if they have received any complaints against the contractor. Then call up some of his previous customers and ask what their experiences with him were. Where do you get the names of previous customers? From the contractor, obviously. But on the theory that he is going to give you only the names of contented customers, I recommend that you also call some others. You can get their names by going down to your town building department's office and asking to see the remodeling permits they have issued in the past couple of years. The permits, which are public property, show the names of both contractors and homeowners.

HOME
IMPROVEMENT FIRMS
A home improvement firm is another source of help if you make structural changes in your house; but aside from the fact that they specialize in remodeling work, there is nothing to recommend them over a general contractor. In fact, they may have two strikes against them: (1) Although they give the impression

that they can do any kind of remodeling, many firms actually limit themselves to a few specialized projects. (2) A disproportionately high percentage of home improvement firms are of dubious honesty. Certainly this isn't true of the majority—or anywhere near the majority. But the fact that the national Better Business Bureau has felt it necessary to issue booklets warning specifically against home improvement cheats is evidence that you must be on your toes when hiring one.

KITCHEN DEALERS AND Kitchen dealers and kitchen designers can give you
KITCHEN DESIGNERS   more help with kitchen remodeling than anyone. This
                         is not to say that the plans they draw up are ideal. On
the contrary, some are pedestrian and a few are so unworkable as to be assinine. But no one else, including an architect, can do so well.

Kitchen dealers are actually cabinet dealers, and they make their money by selling you cabinets and countertops. They may also sell appliances and/or make complete kitchen installations. Before hiring one, you should ask several to give you plans and tell you what the cost will be.

Kitchen designers are rare—generally found only in very large cities. They operate like interior designers.

SKILLED   These craftsmen are specialists in different types of
BUILDING CRAFTSMEN   remodeling. They include plumbers, electricians,
                          carpenters, painters, paperhangers, bricklayers,
masons, flooring contractors, and roofers. You can get more practical construction advice from them than from anybody—but don't depend on them for good aesthetic or design sense.

NURSERYMEN   A nurseryman is also a specialist, though he com-
                          monly assumes the role of landscape architect. This
he is not qualified to do. He may be able to select and arrange plants satisfactorily. Indeed, he is often more knowledgeable about what plant will grow where than the landscape architect is. But his advisory skill stops there.

HOW TO WORK WITH
PEOPLE YOU EMPLOY...

Success in rejuvenating a house with outside help depends, first, on finding the best possible help and, then, on working with them in a friendly but businesslike way. This should not be difficult, but for many homeowners it is. Hence, the following rules. Some apply to the people who help plan the renovation, some to those who do the actual work, some to both.

Remember: You're the boss!

Women get into more trouble here than men because they may downgrade their ability to comprehend how a house is built and consequently give up their authority to those they hire. But men as well as women often knuckle under to architects (the worst offenders) and interior designers who adopt a haughty "we know what's best for you" attitude.

In neither case is there any excuse for subservience. The homeowner is always boss; and although you don't have to be assertive, you must make it clear that you are. Otherwise, your home probably won't turn out the way you want it.

Be frank with the planners about how your family lives, how you want to live, how much money you have to spend, etc.!

It may take two or three meetings between you and, say, an architect before he has a clear idea of how you like to live. But don't begrudge the time spent; you will wind up with a better, more livable home as a result.

The job of the professional planner is to tailor a house as closely as possible to you, his client; and he can do this only if he has a chance to study you until he knows you well.

Let the planners have their heads!

Once you tell a planner what you want done, and once he has had a chance to form an impression of you, leave him alone to develop his ideas. That's the only way he can do his best work.

Then when he submits his plans, let him explain his thinking, and don't be hasty in your judgment of what he is suggesting. Upon study, you may find that it is sound. If it isn't, tell him where he's wrong and insist that he try again. As I just said, you're the boss. You are the one who is going to live in the house, so you are the one who must be satisfied.

It must be pointed out, however, that architects are often right when homeowners think they're wrong. A case in point is a small struggle an architect friend of mine had with a client over some windows. Bill is an authority on Colonial design, and he quite properly called for multi-paned double-hung windows in the house he was remodeling for the client. But every time he submitted his plans, he was told by the client that the windows should have single panes. Bill, however, was not about to have an otherwise good Colonial house thus spoiled, and he finally persuaded the client to change his mind.

Understand the work to be done!

One of the aims of this book is to help you understand what is involved in a renovation, even though you don't do the work yourself. Then you can tell when workers are not doing something they should do or are doing something all wrong. Equally important, you may be able to suggest solutions to problems that workers run into.

Be specific with workers about what you want done!

You can't blame them for making mistakes if you haven't spelled out for them what they should do. Blueprints and written specifications are used on large projects. On small projects, when there is any chance for misunderstanding, write out a concise list of things to be done:

> Close doorway between living room and back hall. Hang the door at entrance of blue bedroom and discard present door . . . . Repair ceiling plaster in hall and paint white . . . .

You should also make it clear whether you want the work done quickly, inexpensively, or with attention to all details. This can make a difference in the care the worker takes.

Don't just give directions, however. Review what you want done and give the workers a chance to react. You may find that they see flaws in the project or in your approach to the project, or that they have good suggestions for it.

Supervise the work closely!

You might think that, after going to great lengths to specify what has to be done, you don't have to keep tabs on workers. But no such luck. Contractors and their men often do peculiar things.

In order to get our present house in livable shape in the brief time between when we bought it and when we moved in, Elizabeth and I hired a general contractor to make a variety of changes and repairs. He was well recommended, but we found we couldn't always trust him to do things properly. For instance, we told him to remove an old warm air register in the dining room floor and fill the hole. The floor was made of random-width oak. So imagine our surprise when we discovered he was about to put in narrow strip flooring. On another occasion, just in the nick of time, we found he was about to cover a bathroom counter not with the solid white laminated plastic called for but with a white spangled with gold stars. In both cases, when we asked him why he wasn't using the right material, his feeble excuse was: "I can't find it." But when told to try again, he went to another supplier and did.

In ages past, when builders took more pride in their work, such constant vigilance may not have been necessary. But don't take chances today. Check up on them at least once a day—but stay out of their hair otherwise.

Cooperate with the workers and
insist that they cooperate with you!

This is especially important if you're doing over the house you occupy, because it will quickly become a shambles if you don't. The following simple things should be done:

- At the end of each day, find out from the workers what they will do the next day—and ask what you can do to facilitate their work. Usually this involves nothing more than moving furnishings or perhaps clearing out rooms.
- Keep out of the way as much as possible while the workers are busy.
- Try to insist that the workers use only one outside entrance.
- Definitely insist that finished floors be protected at all times and that the workers clean up after themselves at the end of every day (but I must admit it is hard to enforce the latter).

In a major remodeling of an occupied house,
try to get the workers to finish up in one room
before they go to the next!

Otherwise, the whole house is in an uproar, and you may be forced to move out. It's obvious, however, that work cannot always be scheduled in this way.

If you change your mind about what you want done,
don't order the change to be made without
first finding out from the contractor
how it will affect the price he has quoted!

Roughly 50 percent of all remodelings cost more than the original estimate; and the usual reason is that the owners change their minds while work is in progress, and thus interrupt the flow of work or cause extra work. So it just makes good

economic sense to determine what the effect of a change will be before ordering
it.

The other reason for doing this is to avoid an argument with the
contractor when he submits a final bill that is higher than you expected.

Of course, the smartest homeowner is the one who determines exactly
what work is to be done before he asks for bids, and sticks to his guns thereafter.
But since this is very difficult to do, you might as well face up to the fact that
you won't; and write into agreements with contractors a clause stating (1) that if
you request changes that raise the cost of the project, you will pay for them, and
(2) that if you make changes that reduce the cost, the savings will be deducted
from the final bill.

Be interested and friendly!

That's just plain common sense. You'll never get the best work out of anyone if
you act otherwise.

Don't make final payment until the workers
have completed their jobs satisfactorily!

Admittedly, this can lead to a rip-roaring fight—but it seems to be the only way
that homeowners can protect themselves against irresponsible workers. Before
taking such drastic action, however, make certain that your complaints are valid.
It's a good idea also to have a chat with your lawyer.

WHERE TO GO
TO GET FINANCING...

Commercial banks, mutual savings banks, savings and loan associations, life
insurance companies, and private individuals lend money to people who are
remodeling. You may also be able to arrange financing through a general
contractor, home improvement firm, or kitchen dealer, but the cost is very high.

There are various ways to finance a home improvement, and no one of
them is best for everyone. So talk to several lenders before making up your
mind.

If you own your home and have an open-end mortgage on it, probably the
easiest way to get money for remodeling is simply to ask the mortgage company
for it. True, the amount you can borrow will not exceed the amount by which
you have reduced the principal on the original mortgage. In other words, if you

have reduced the principal on your original $20,000 mortgage by $5,000, you can open-end for no more than $5,000. On the other hand, since you and your home are already known to the mortgage company, there is a minimum of red tape, and the processing charge is small.

Refinancing an existing mortgage is another way to get money, but it is pretty expensive. Furthermore, you lose equity in your home. But if you're unhappy with your present mortgage company, you can refinance with a new one and get out of an unpleasant situation.

If you own a house outright, probably the cheapest way to get money for a major renovation is to take out a conventional mortgage on the property.

If you buy a house that requires immediate remodeling, your best course is to get a conventional mortgage with a construction commitment loan. Under this arrangement, the bank gives you a 75 percent loan on the appraised value of the house as it stands plus the cost of the improvement you make. For example, if the appraised value of the house is $50,000 and you intend to make $10,000 worth of improvements, the bank gives you $37,500 when you take title to the house and $7,500 when the improvements are completed. You pay off the $7,500 construction commitment over the life of the mortgage and at the same rate of interest.

If you don't need a great deal of money, borrowing against the cash value of your life insurance is an ideal solution because the interest rates are low. The alternative, if you haven't built up cash values, is to get a personal loan or a home improvement loan from the bank. Of the two, the latter is the more expensive. You may also be able to get an FHA Title I loan, but this, too, is expensive; and you are permitted to borrow only for permanent improvements that are considered essential.

WHAT YOU CAN AND CANNOT DO YOURSELF...

There's nothing in home renovation that the average, reasonably intelligent, healthy family cannot do after getting used to handling tools. But I am not about to suggest that you should try to prove this statement. There are some things that are best left to the professionals because they are dangerous, complicated, or laborious, or require special tools or long experience. Plastering and wiring are two examples. The others will be covered in later chapters.

Even when you are well able to do a job, however, there may be other reasons why you should not or cannot. One of these is lack of time; the other, lack of muscle.

Unlike many household repairs that can be made in a matter of minutes or hours, it usually takes time to renovate a house. And time is something you probably don't have (1) if one or both of the senior members of the household have a job and (2) if you are already living in the house or anxious to move in. So you are almost forced to go outside for help on at least the most urgent parts of the project. The only alternative is to reconcile yourself to living in a certain amount of disorder, and perhaps discomfort, for several months or a year while you work away at the house on nights, weekends, and holidays.

Rejuvenating a house also requires strength for certain jobs, and if you don't have it, there is no point in risking injury for the sake of the money you can save by doing it yourself. Unfortunately, however, not all back-breaking work is obvious to people who are new to the home renovating field—which is why I list the worst:

Breaking joints in steel plumbing and heating pipes
Moving radiators
Planting shrubs and trees
Laying large flagstones
Installing large kitchen wall cabinets
Installing cast-iron tubs
Covering ceilings with gypsum board
Mixing concrete
Moving fill

Work that is unusually tiring, even though it isn't back-breaking, includes:

Installing any kind of 4 x 8-ft. panels
Sanding floors with electric sanders
Laying bricks
Installing roofing
Working in a cramped space
Digging

SETTING PRIORITIES...

There are undoubtedly some families that have done over their homes in one fell swoop. But I don't happen to know them. Most homes—even those that are completely remodeled in a couple of weeks—are done over in a series of steps. One common reason for this is that the owners lack the money, time, or energy to do the whole job at once. The other common reason is that, in order to make their lives reasonably comfortable and convenient, the owners decide to finish up certain rooms or installations before they go on to the next.

Deciding the order in which to renovate a house is not a very difficult task, but there are several things you should and shouldn't do.

**Don't ask someone outside
the immediate family for suggestions!**

That's almost fatal, because what they consider important is not necessarily what you think important. I remember that, after we first saw what the Schweppes are doing to their house, Elizabeth said, "I don't know why they're going at it that way. I think I'd have done the living room first." But Ellen's reason, volunteered some time later, makes perfect sense: "We did the powder room first so people wouldn't feel reluctant about paying a call."

Find out what the different jobs will cost!

Ascertaining such costs in advance is patently essential if you don't have an unlimited budget to work with.

Find out roughly how long the different jobs will take to complete!

As a general rule, you don't want to undertake a very long job before a short job because it delays maximum use of the house. For instance, you can probably suffer with a kitchen that will take two weeks to remodel if, in the same period, you can redo three bedrooms.

Take into account the work involved and where it's to be done!

One of the worst eyesores in the Hulls' house was the stairway and second-floor hall, and the Hulls were tempted several times to redecorate this area as soon as possible. But Charlie wisely held off until he had rebuilt the second-floor bathroom, because it was obvious he couldn't get the old fixtures and piping out and the new ones in without damaging the stairway and hall walls. On the other hand, there would have been no reason for delay if the bathroom work involved nothing more than painting, papering, and tilesetting.

If you are moving into a house while it is being overhauled, consider the furnishings that are going into the rooms!

For example, one of the first things Ashley and Tom Rooney did to their old house before moving in was to repair the plaster, apply paint, and build a closet in their bedroom. Reason: They have a king-size bed that would have been extremely difficult to work around after they moved in.

**If your home needs major work,
try to do some of the quick-and-easy jobs first!**

The improvements made boost your morale and whet the appetite to get on to the other, tougher tasks.

2

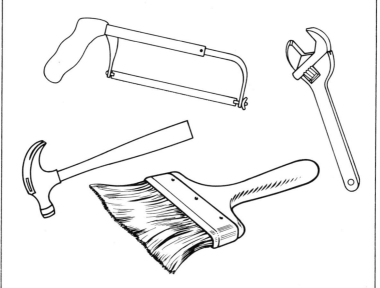

Tools
for the Job

One of the most useful and unusual wedding presents I ever heard of was a large kit of carpentry tools a friend of mine gave to a young couple entering matrimony without benefit of golden spoons. Very few families, however, start life so well equipped. There are very few, in fact, who are so well equipped when they buy their first home, and this presents problems if and when they attempt to work on it.

Tools are a must when you renovate a home—and it's pretty hard to make do without the right ones. I have tried to cut boards at a right angle for Tom Rooney when he didn't have a square; and I've tried to rip boards for Charlie Hull with a crosscut saw; and I've tried to nail down flooring for Bill Burnett with a 12-oz. hammer he bought at the five and dime store—and all I can say is "Murder!"

But good tools are costly and I can't blame you if you don't want to load up on them before you have a crying need for them. So what's the answer? I'm not sure but I believe it's this:

1 • Rent the power tools that you need only occasionally. They're nice to own, but people got along without them for centuries and you can, too—especially in view of their cost. Renting is cheap and the tools almost always are of top quality.

2 • Borrow—if you can—the specialized hand tools that you may use only once or twice.

3 • Buy at the outset the tools that are basic to the work you plan to do. The following will take care of most jobs.

TOOLS FOR
CARPENTRY WORK...

Some of these are used only for carpentry. But a number are needed for other types of remodeling and repair work. These include a hammer, electric drill, level, pocketknife, putty knife, sawhorses, square, workbench, clamps, screwdriver, and a 6-ft. rule.

AWL   This is an icepick-like tool with a short blade (Fig.
                                    2-1). It is very useful for making starting holes for
screws and other threaded gadgets, and for marking cutting lines on wood.

Fig. 2-1   Awl.

CLAMPS   Clamps are necessary in many gluing operations and
                                    are also used to hold things in place while you
assemble or work on them. There are various designs and sizes to choose from.
As a starter, get a pair of 5-in. C clamps, so called because they are C-shaped
(Fig. 2-2).

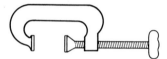

Fig. 2-2   C clamp.

CLAW HAMMER   Take time in buying a hammer, ask for advice from
                                    the hardware dealer, and don't skimp on the price. A
first-class hammer will last a lifetime, and make your work easier and your
workmanship better than a cheap tool.

The hammer should weigh 16 oz. and feel nicely balanced when you grasp
the end of the handle and swing it. The face (hammering surface) should be
"bell-faced"—slightly convex so you can drive a nail flush with a wooden surface
without denting the surface. The claw should be curved for efficient nail-pulling
(Fig. 2-3). Straight claws will also pull nails, but not as well; they are designed
primarily for ripping things apart. Whether you buy a hammer with a wood,
fiberglass, or steel handle is up to you.

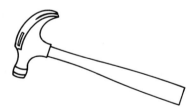

Fig. 2-3   Hammer.

ELECTRIC DRILL   An electric drill (Fig. 2-4) is the only power tool
generally considered essential. It's amazing how often
you need it for drilling holes, and you can use it also for rough sanding,
wire-brushing, buffing, and even cutting.

Electric drills are categorized according to the capacity of their chucks.
The commonest size is called a 1/4-in. drill because it will take drills with shanks
up to 1/4 in. in diameter. The next larger size is 3/8 in. The only other basic
difference between the two is that the smaller size operates at higher speed.

I favor the 1/4-in. drill because it is thoroughly efficient for most
jobs—and very economical. Even discount-store models that sell for less than $10
are good, although naturally they have a shorter life than more expensive
models. A 3/8-in. drill becomes necessary only if you do a lot of drilling in
masonry.

When electric drills were a new idea, the largest bit you could use in a
1/4-in. model bored a 1/4-in. hole. Today, however, you can buy a wide variety
of bits that fit a 1/4-in. chuck but will make holes up to 1-1/2 in. across. Since it
is not often that you must bore holes larger than this, there is no need to buy a
brace and bit. Borrow it from someone else.

Fig. 2-4   Electric drill.

LEVEL   Also called a carpenter's level or spirit level, this tool
resembles a narrow board with a glass vial filled with
alcohol in the middle of one of the long edges and another vial set in a round
hole at one end (Fig. 2-5). Made of either wood or metal, it is used to determine
whether a surface is absolutely horizontal (level) or absolutely vertical (plumb).
This is indicated by a bubble in the alcohol.

Glass Vials

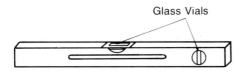

Fig. 2-5   Level.

Since good construction requires that most surfaces such as floors and walls be either level or plumb respectively, you cannot get along without a level. But there is no need to invest in the fanciest models on the market. A simple 2-footer is good enough.

MITER BOX   In order to cut wood accurately to a 45° angle—as when you install moldings in a corner—you require an inexpensive wooden miter box (Fig. 2-6). This is nothing more than a small square trough with several slots in the sides to hold a saw blade.

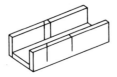

Fig. 2-6   Miter box.

NAILSET   A nailset is a short steel rod with a tapering end that has a cupped tip (Fig. 2-7). It is used to countersink finishing nails (drive them beneath a surface).

Nailsets are made with tips of different sizes for countersinking everything from small brads up to the biggest finishing nails—but you can get by with just one if it has a 1/16- or 3/32-in. tip.

Fig. 2-7   Nailset.

PLANE   The only plane I have used for years is a 6-in. block plane (Fig. 2-8), which is operated in one hand. Unlike other planes, it smooths wood across as well as with the grain, and you can work it into tight places.

Of course, if you get into carpentry that calls for shaving many boards lengthwise to size, a junior jack plane which is used in two hands will prove helpful. But limit yourself to a block plane at the start.

Fig. 2-8   Plane.

POCKETKNIFE   Get a sturdy jackknife with two or three blades. If you don't use it for anything else, you can at least sharpen pencils. But I find it indispensable for shaping, whittling, smoothing, scraping, and cutting everything from wood to the insulation on electric cable to screen wire.

PUTTY KNIFE   This is needed for filling holes with putty, spackle, etc., and also for scraping paint and setting window panes. Buy the best you can find—preferably one with a wooden handle and a not-too-flexible blade (Fig. 2-9).

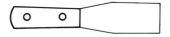

Fig. 2-9   Putty knife.

RULE   A 6-ft. folding rule made of wood is rigid enough that you don't have to rest it on a flat surface when making a measurement. I happen to prefer it—but many workmen favor the compactness, durability, and easy opening of a tape rule, which is a thin ribbon of steel that slides into a neat case. Take your pick or buy both.

Note that tape rules come in several lengths up to 25 ft. The longest is especially good for measuring long pieces of lumber or for laying out a new wall.

SAW   For cutting boards across the grain, a 26-in.-long crosscut saw (Fig. 2-10) with eight teeth (called points) to the inch is best to start with. You will probably find soon you need a rip saw to cut lumber with the grain unless you rent a portable circular saw. In both cases, buy the best: Your descendants will use them a hundred years hence.

A keyhole saw (Fig. 2-11), though less essential, is required for cutting large holes inside the borders of walls, floors, doors, etc.

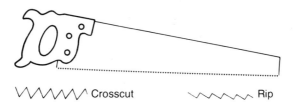

Fig. 2-10   Saw.

SAWHORSE   You need two—not just for carpentry but also for paperhanging and many other jobs. Build them

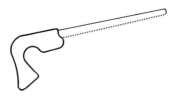

Fig. 2-11   Keyhole saw.

yourself out of 2 x 4s and four steel sawhorse brackets available from a hardware store or by mail order. For each sawhorse, cut four legs 22 in. long and nail them into the brackets. Make the horizontal cross rail, which connects the pairs of legs and on which you rest your work, 36 in. long, and fit it into the tops of the brackets (Fig. 2-12). The resulting sawhorse is about 25 in. high—a good working height when you are carpentering but a little low for wallpapering.

Hinged sawhorse brackets are also available. You can fit in the cross rail when you need a sawhorse; and remove it and store the sawhorse parts in a small space at other times.

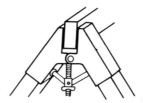

Fig. 2-12   Sawhorse.

SCREWDRIVER   You can use a lot of screwdrivers—they are needed so often that it's convenient to store them here and there around the house as well as in your toolbox. And since cheap screwdrivers are, to all intents and purposes, as good as expensive ones, the cost is low.

Buy conventional screwdrivers with blades of several lengths and widths. You should also have a Phillips screwdriver with a star-shaped tip of about 3/16-in. diameter.

SHARPENING STONE   Get a 2 x 7-in. stone with coarse grit on one side, fine grit on the other. Coat both sides with No. 30 engine oil before using.

SQUARE   A square is really an L-shaped tool made of rigid steel or aluminum. There are several types, but you can do all you have to do with a single framing square that has 24- and 16-in. blades, called the body and the tongue, respectively [Fig. 2-13(a)].

However, a combination square is handy to have, too. This has a handle that slides along the blade and is shaped so you can mark 45° as well as 90° angles [Fig. 2-13(b)].

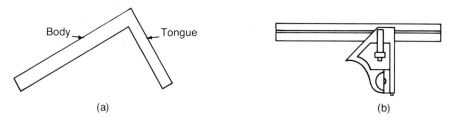

Body   Tongue

(a)   (b)

Fig. 2-13   (a) Framing square; (b) Combination square.

SURFORM TOOL   This new gadget has a blade with hundreds of tiny, sharp cutting edges. It's used for shaving down and shaping wood and plastics. In this respect it is like a rasp, but it is more than a substitute for that tool because it cuts faster and is more versatile.

Several types of Surform tool are made. The most useful has an adjustable handle that permits you to operate it either as a plane or as a rasp (Fig. 2-14).

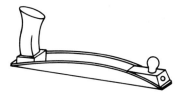

Fig. 2-14   Surform tool.

WOOD CHISEL   Used primarily for cutting holes and recesses in wood, this seems like a rather specialized tool, but when you need it—which is surprisingly often—you can't do without it. For general purposes buy a standard chisel with a 3/4-in.-wide blade (Fig. 2-15). This should be all you need until you start hanging lots of doors; then a butt chisel with a 1-1/2-in. blade comes in handy.

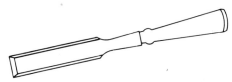

Fig. 2-15   Chisel.

WORKBENCH   It's cheaper to make than to buy one. The plan in
                             Fig. 2-16 shows a simple but more than adequate
design. Install a woodworker's vise at one end under the front edge.

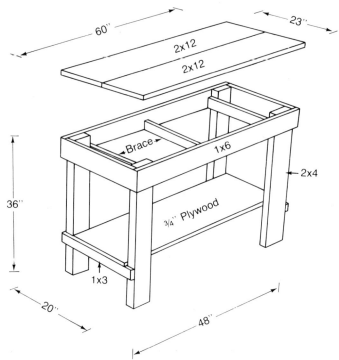

Fig. 2-16   Workbench layout.

ADDITIONAL TOOLS
FOR PLUMBING WORK...

What you need here depends on whether your house is plumbed with steel or
brass pipe or with copper pipe. Houses built before World War II generally have
steel or brass—sometimes plus a little copper which was added in recent years.
Post-war houses generally have copper.

HACKSAW   A hacksaw is a somewhat squared-off steel bow with
                             thin interchangeable blades made specifically for
cutting metal (Fig. 2-17). You need several coarse-toothed blades for thick
metals, such as steel pipe; fine-toothed blades for thin metal, such as copper
tubing.

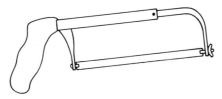

Fig. 2-17   Hacksaw.

There are handier tools for cutting pipe, but with a hacksaw you can do the job well enough—no matter what the metal. And you will use the saw occasionally for cutting bolts, BX cable, etc.

PROPANE TORCH   This is the handy modern substitute for a blow torch (Fig. 2-18). It's required for soldering joints and opening soldered joints in copper pipe. You can use it also for burning off paint on siding.

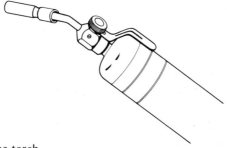

Fig. 2-18   Propane torch.

SLIP-JOINT PLIERS   Needed not merely in plumbing work but also for many other jobs around the house, these pliers are designed so you can quickly adjust the width of the jaws to grasp everything from a pencil to a pretty large pipe (Fig. 2-19). A pair 6 to 8 in. long is a good size for most work.

Fig. 2-19   Pliers.

WRENCHES   A monkey wrench with smooth jaws shaped like a square C is needed with all kinds of pipe and will allow you to open and close pipe joints and faucets of all sizes [Fig. 2-20(a)]. A

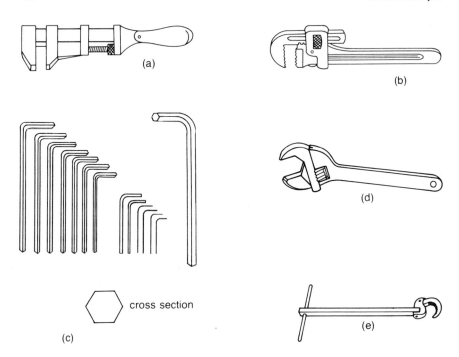

Fig. 2-20   (a) Monkey wrench; (b) Stillson pipe wrench; (c) Allen wrenches; (d) Adjustable angle wrench; (e) Basin wrench.

pipe wrench—also called a Stillson wrench—with toothed jaws is required only for steel or brass pipe so you can grasp the pipe in a vise-like grip [Fig. 2-20(b)].

In a house piped with copper, two monkey wrenches with 3-in. capacity will permit you to take care of most problems. In a house with steel or brass pipe, get a 4-in. monkey wrench and a 4-in. pipe wrench.

The only other wrenches you need are hex, or Allen, wrenches. These are very small L-shaped devices made of hexagonal steel rods [Fig. 2-20(c)]. They are used for tightening and loosening setscrews with hexagonal openings in one end. Such screws are found in modern faucets, plumbing fittings, and doorknobs; and there is nothing you can do about them if you don't have the wrenches. Buy a set—it is very inexpensive.

An adjustable angle wrench, with smooth jaws opening from the end of a handle, is useful in plumbing work and also for tightening and loosening bolts, spark plugs, etc., up to 2 in. across [Fig. 2-20(d)]. It is not essential if you own a monkey wrench, but a 1-in. size is good to have because it's small and easy to handle.

The alternative to an adjustable wrench is a set of rigid open-end wrenches. The cost is about the same, but it's easy to lose some of the wrenches in a set, and, if you don't use them often, you're likely to fumble around trying different sizes before you hit on the right one.

A basin wrench may be required if you are replacing the faucets on a lavatory or sink [Fig. 2-20(e)]. It's designed so you can reach up under the bowl, and loosen and tighten the nuts clamping the faucets to the fixture. Sometimes this job can be done with an angle wrench; if not, a basin wrench is the only answer.

ADDITIONAL TOOLS
FOR ELECTRICAL WORK...

LINEMAN'S PLIERS   These are designed for cutting wires and for twisting and tightening operations. You must have them for all electrical work. A 7-in. size is adequate.

ADDITIONAL TOOLS
FOR MASONRY WORK...

COLD CHISEL   This heavy, hardened-steel chisel (Fig. 2-21) is required for opening cracks in masonry, breaking out old masonry, chipping concrete off bricks and stones, and cutting bricks, stones, and concrete blocks. It is also used to cut the heads off bolts and to break steel and iron pipes when you can't remove them otherwise. A single 1/2-in. chisel is usually all the homeowner needs, but you can get other assorted sizes at low cost.

Fig. 2-21   Cold chisel.

MASON'S TROWEL   This is a large, flat, more or less diamond-shaped trowel for placing and smoothing concrete (Fig. 2-22).

Fig. 2-22   Mason's trowel.

POINTING TROWEL   This is a small version of a mason's trowel. It's used
                       for packing mortar into joints and smoothing it off.

ADDITIONAL TOOLS
FOR GYPSUM BOARD
AND PLASTER WORK...

WALL SCRAPERS   Get both 4- and 6-in. sizes (Fig. 2-23). The blades
                       should be flexible. Use them to apply gypsum board
joint compound over joints between panels and to patch plaster in large holes.
You may use them also in combination with a razor blade to cut wallpaper
around doors and windows.

Fig. 2-23   Wall scraper.

ADDITIONAL TOOLS
FOR TILESETTING...

ADHESIVE SPREADER   A spreader is a flat piece of thin steel with a handle.
                       The straight bottom edge is notched to place nu-
merous thick beads of adhesive in parallel rows on the wall to be tiled (Fig.
2-24). The same spreader is used to apply adhesive for resilient flooring, various
types of wall panel, etc.
        Another, more useful type of adhesive spreader has two edges—one
notched, the other smooth.

GLASS CUTTER   This is a straight piece of steel with a little cutting
                       wheel in one end and notches in the side (Fig. 2-25).
It is used for cutting large ceramic tiles as well as for cutting window glass and
mirrors.

WINDOW-WASHER'S   If you don't already have one for washing windows,
SQUEEGEE   get a 6-in. size to spread grout into the joints between
                       tiles.

Adhesive spreader

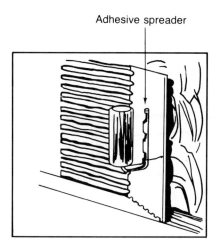

Fig. 2-24   Adhesive spreader.

Fig. 2-25   Glass cutter.

ADDITIONAL TOOLS
FOR PAINTING...

SCRAPER   The commonest type has a narrow, straight steel
blade clamped more or less at right angles to the end
of a straight handle (Fig. 2-26). If the blade is sharp, the tool works well on dry
varnish and other clear finishes, but you usually must soften paint before you
can scrape it off.

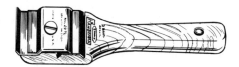

Fig. 2-26   Wood handled scraper.

ELECTRIC   This hand-held gadget has a 3 x 6-in. heating
PAINT REMOVER   element in the base (Fig. 2-27). When you hold it
                            over a painted surface, it rapidly softens the paint so
you can remove it with a stiff wall scraper. It is safer than a propane torch and
faster than a liquid paint remover.

Fig. 2-27   Electric paint remover.

BRUSHES   As long as you use a roller to paint large surfaces, you
                            need only the following: 2-in. and 3-in. trim brushes
for alkyd enamel, a 3-in. trim brush for latex paint, and a 1-in. sash brush for
alkyd enamel. A 4- or 5-in. wall brush is also advisable if you refinish floors.

It doesn't make much difference whether the brushes have hog or
synthetic bristles. I like the former, but many expert painters prefer the latter.
The important point in either case is to buy top-quality brushes. You may pale
at the price, but you won't be sorry. Such brushes last for years, flow paint on
more smoothly, and hold their bristles.

ROLLER AND   Unless you're striving for a very smooth finish—in
ROLLER PAN   which case you should use a brush or spray gun—use a
                            roller to paint walls and ceilings. I also like a roller to
paint the larger flat surfaces on doors and woodwork because the work goes fast
and easily.

Buy a 7-in. or, better, 9-in. roller. One model is about as good as another,
but be sure to get one with a threaded socket in the end of the handle so you
can screw in an extension handle for painting ceilings. The soft roller covers that
actually apply the paint are short-lived. I recommend a top-quality cover for
latex paint, because the paint can be washed out with water and the roller cover
used again and again. But because other paints are difficult to remove from a
roller cover, use cheap covers for them and throw them out after your job is
finished.

Roller pans last forever. Buy one wide enough for a 9 in. roller. Pans that are made of reasonably stiff metal are best because they don't get out of shape.

DROP CLOTH   You can cover a floor with newspapers, of course; but they're unsatisfactory because they don't stay put. A fabric drop cloth is much better. (But never use a plastic cloth because it doesn't absorb paint splatters.) A 12 x 12-ft. size is about right. Bigger sizes are heavy, hard to handle, and bulky to store. Old mattress pads are excellent substitutes for a real drop cloth.

ADDITIONAL TOOLS
FOR PAPERHANGING...

SCRAPER   Scrapers made specifically for removing old wallpaper have a thin, sharp, 4-in.-long blade attached to a rigid handle at an angle of about 75° (Fig. 2-28). They work like a charm—it's rarely necessary to wet the wallpaper. If the blade breaks at a corner—as it sometimes does—you can reverse it; then, after it breaks again, replace it.

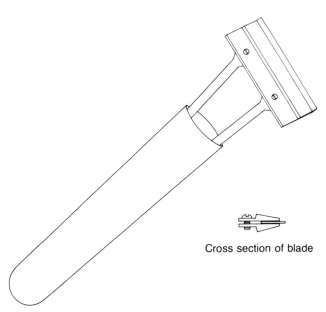

Cross section of blade

Fig. 2-28   Paperhanger's scraper.

PASTE TABLE   All you need are three straight, smooth pine boards 1 ft. wide and 6 ft. long. Lay these over your sawhorses. When you're through hanging paper, wash the boards well, store them in a clean place, and don't use them for anything else.

PASTE BRUSH   Get an 8-in. width (Fig. 2-29). Use it also for sizing walls.

Fig. 2-29   Paste brush.

SMOOTHING BRUSH   This is a short-bristled brush 12 in. wide (Fig. 2-30). It's needed for smoothing down wallpaper.

Fig. 2-30   Smoothing brush.

SEAM ROLLER   This is usually a 1 in.-wide wood or plastic roller for flattening seams between adjoining wallpaper strips (Fig. 2-31).

Fig. 2-31   Seam roller.

BUCKETS   One for paste and another for water—but buckets used for other household chores are plenty good.

SHEARS   You can get by with any type, but that's just making trouble for yourself. If you expect to do very much wallpapering, get a pair of 12-in. shears.

PLUMB BOB AND LINE   The bob is a steel weight with a point on the bottom end and a hole in the upper end to receive the line. The latter is a 6-ft. piece of ordinary cotton cord (Fig. 2-32). You must have them to make sure wallpaper hangs straight.

   Actually, professional paperhangers normally use a spirit level because it speeds work somewhat. But a 4-ft. size is required, and this is more expensive and larger than you need for carpentry and masonry work.

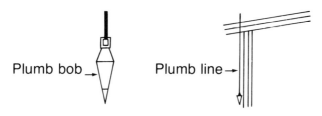

Fig. 2-32   Plumb bob and line.

SINGLE-EDGE   Buy them by the hundred from the wallpaper dealer
RAZOR BLADES   and use them for making straight cuts in paper. Along with paint roller covers, they are the only tools recommended here that are expendable.

LADDERS   Ladders are essential for making many home improvements and also for simple repair work. But the only one you have to buy is a stepladder. A 5- or 6-footer is the most useful size. It can be made of aluminum or wood: The former is lighter, more durable, and more rigid; but the latter is less slippery to climb on and doesn't have the tendency to "walk" that makes aluminum stepladders a bit frightening.

   As a rule, extension ladders don't get enough use around the home to justify their purchase (at a rather high price). You can rent one at any time. You can also probably borrow one from a neighbor.

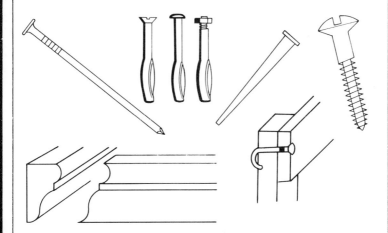

3

How To
Fasten
Things
Together

Fastening—the one operation common to almost all building work—is done in many ways with many different kinds of fasteners. Even though you may never have occasion to use some of these, you should be aware of all the possibilities because there are times when you must try several methods before your purpose is accomplished.

The simple wooden straight chair which I am sitting in as I write is an example. Over the years the two rungs between the back legs have come loose repeatedly. For a long time I tried to stick them back in place with white PVA glue, but without success. Then I shifted to epoxy glue. No luck. By then one of the mortises had become enlarged by wear and I tried jamming toothpicks into it around the epoxy-coated rung. Still no luck. Now I realized that one of the loose legs had become slightly warped, and this was why the glued joints kept breaking. I considered driving a nail through the leg into the end of the looser rung but concluded that the rung didn't stick into the mortise far enough for the nail to hold. So I gave up making a proper repair, forced the rungs into the legs as far as they would go, and looped a heavy wire tightly around the legs. The repair doesn't look pretty—but it has worked like a charm. And I feel less ashamed of it since I noticed some months ago that about half the chairs in the huge main reading room of the Boston Public Library are also held together with wires.

NAILING...

The commonest way to hold things together in a house is with nails. Most are made of steel. As a rule bright steel nails are used inside the house, but they should never be used outside because they are too likely to rust—even though you countersink the heads and cover them with putty. Use galvanized nails instead—or aluminum, if you are nailing down aluminum flashing, gutters, or leaders.

43

"Penny" and the letter "d" are used to describe the size of most nails. For example, a 1-in. nail is described in conversation as a two-penny nail or in writing as a 2d nail. Other standard-length nails are identified as follows:

Table 3-1

NAIL SIZES

Length (in.)	Size	Length (in.)	Size
1	2 d	3	10 d
1 1/4	3 d	3 1/4	12 d
1 1/2	4 d	3 1/2	16 d
1 3/4	5 d	4	20 d
2	6 d	4 1/2	30 d
2 1/4	7 d	5	40 d
2 1/2	8 d	5 1/2	50 d
2 3/4	9 d	6	60 d

Nails over 6 in. are called spikes, and their size is indicated in inches. The diameter of both nails and spikes increases gradually with their length.

Various types of nails are used around the home.

COMMON NAILS These are the basic construction nail [Fig. 3-1(a)]. They have thick shanks and big, flat, round heads that are normally left exposed. For this reason, they are used mainly in concealed locations, such as in the framing of a house. But because of their strength, they are also used to attach wood siding to the sheathing, and in this case the heads may be countersunk and covered with putty.

Common nails are available in all standard sizes except 5d, 7d, and 9d.

WIRE NAILS Wire nails look like tiny common nails and are used for fastening thin materials where you don't care whether the heads show. They are available in sizes from 5/8 in. to 1-1/2 in., and are sold by the inch.

BOX NAILS These also resemble common nails but have very thin shanks. They come in various sizes up to 20d. You should use them in situations where common nails might split the wood.

SHINGLE NAILS Shingle nails are short, sharp-pointed common nails
AND ROOFING NAILS which are always galvanized. Roofing nails are even shorter and have extra large heads; they are also always galvanized.

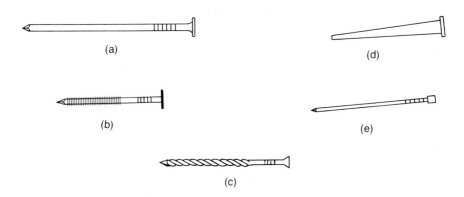

Fig. 3-1   (a) Common nail; (b) Annular-ring nail; (c) Screw nail; (d) Cut nail; (e) Finishing nail.

ANNULAR-RING NAILS   Also called ring-grooved and ringed-shank nails, they look like common nails with concentric grooves on the shanks [Fig. 3-1(b)]. The grooves give the nails unusual holding power. Consequently, the nails are used mainly in sheet materials, such as gypsum board, that have a tendency to pull loose from the framing of the house.

SCREW NAILS   Screw nails also have unusual holding power because the shanks have a steep, spiral thread [Fig. 3-1(c)]. The heads are small. Screw nails are used mainly for laying wood floors.

CUT NAILS   Also flooring nails, the shanks are rectangular and taper upward from a blunt point to a rectangular flat head [Fig. 3-1(d)].

DOUBLE-HEADED NAILS   These are common nails with two heads, one about 1/4 in. above the other. They are designed for putting together structures, such as scaffolding, that you intend to take apart. The upper head, protruding above the surface, is easy to grasp with a hammer.

FINISHING NAILS   Because they have thin shanks and very small, more or less globular heads, finishing nails can be easily countersunk beneath the surface with a nailset [Fig. 3-1(e)]. They are available in 3d, 4d, 6d, 8d, and 10d sizes, and are used in trim, built-ins, cabinets, etc.

BRADS   Brads are tiny finishing nails ranging from 1/2 to 1-1/2 in. long. They are used to fasten thin pieces of wood, as in latticework.

CASING NAILS   These are so similar to finishing nails that you
                          probably can't detect the difference. However, they
have slightly thicker shanks; the heads are cone-shaped, making them even easier
to countersink; and they come in 4d, 6d, 8d, 10d, and 16d sizes.

An important point to note about the last three nails is that, because of
their small heads, they may be pulled right through a piece of wood if the piece
warps outward or if you put the claw of a hammer under it and pull outward.
This means that these nails are less reliable fasteners than those of the common
type.

Choosing the best nail for a job is the first step in nailing, though the
decision is not always crucial. For instance, finishing and casing nails are
interchangeable. Similarly, if I need a short common nail, I don't hesitate to use
a shingle nail. On the other hand, it's a mistake to put down wood flooring with
anything other than a cut nail or screw nail. And one of the worst mistakes in
building—perpetuated, unfortunately, by many contractors—is to put up gypsum
board with anything other than annular-ring nails.

Choosing a nail of the proper length is more difficult unless you are told
what to use (as is often the case in the chapters that follow) or watch what a
carpenter uses. But as a rough rule of thumb, if you are nailing boards, plywood,
hardboard, gypsum board, and the like to the framework of the house or any
other solid base, the nails should be at least three times longer than the thickness
of the boards, plywood, etc. Even longer nails should be used if you're fastening
something to the end of a board or timber because nails do not hold well in
end-grain.

On the other hand, if after you nail two things together you will be able to
see or feel both sides (for instance, if you nail lattice strips together in a trellis or
if you nail moldings around the edges of a countertop), you should ideally use
nails that will not go quite all the way through. This, however, does not produce
a very secure joint unless you use a great many nails. For maximum security, if
you don't object to the appearance, you should use a nail that projects about
1/2 in. beyond the back side, and hammer the projecting end down flat. This is
called clinching or clinch-nailing (Fig. 3-2).

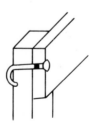

Fig. 3-2   Clinching nails.

Four other methods of nailing are called face-nailing, concealed nailing, nailing on the diagonal, and toenailing:

1 • Face-nailing means to nail through the exposed surface.

2 • Concealed nailing is nailing in some way—usually diagonally through the edge of a board—so the nailhead is hidden.

3 • Nailing on the diagonal may be done through the face or edge of a board. If done through the face, the purpose is to increase the nail's holding power.

4 • Toenailing is done when you butt the end of one board or timber to the side of another board or timber. The nails are driven diagonally through the edges and end of the butted piece into the side of the other piece.

SCREWING...

Although screws are harder to drive than nails, they get the nod over nails (1) when you need to fasten two things together very securely and/or (2) when you want to be able to take the things apart easily without damaging them.

STANDARD WOOD SCREWS   The screws most often used around the home are called wood screws because they are driven into wood. (Machine and sheetmetal screws are found only in appliances, heating plants, and sometimes fireplace equipment.) Standard wood screws, which have a single, straight slot in the head, are made of steel, brass, bronze, and aluminum in three designs:

1 • Flat-head screws [Fig. 3-3(a)] have a head that is flat on top and wedge-shaped underneath so the flat top can be driven down flush with the surrounding surface.

2 • Oval-head screws [Fig. 3-3(b)] are similar except for the fact that the top of the head is oval and projects slightly above the surrounding surface.

3 • Round-head screws [Fig. 3-3(c)] have a semicircular head that projects entirely above the surrounding surface.

PHILLIPS-HEAD WOOD SCREWS   These are exactly like standard screws except that they have crossed slots in the head and can therefore be installed only with a special Phillips screwdriver. They are less common than standard screws but are easier to drive because the screwdriver cannot slip out of the slot.

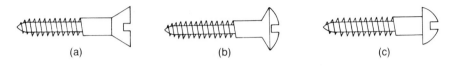

(a)   (b)   (c)

Fig. 3-3 (a) Flat-head screw; (b) Oval-head screw; (c) Round-head screw.

LAG SCREWS Lag screws have square heads without slots and are turned with a wrench. These very large, heavy steel screws are sometimes used to join large timbers.

Wood screws are made in countless sizes. Lengths range from 3/16 to 5-1/2 in. The diameter of the smooth part of the shank ranges from 5/64 to almost 3/8 in. (The diameters are expressed in gauge numbers starting at 0—approximately 1/16 in. in diameter—and running to 24—approximately 3/8 in. in diameter. Most screw lengths are made in several gauges—but no single type of screw is made in every length and every gauge.

Screw selection is pretty much a guessing game. The choice of metal depends on whether the screw is to be exposed to moisture, whether it must resist unusual stresses (steel screws are strongest), the metal with which it will be in contact (if any), and the appearance desired.

The screw should be long enough so that the threaded portion of the shank will penetrate for almost its full length into the wood at the point of the screw, but the point should not go all the way through unless it will be concealed. For example, if you are fastening two 1-in. boards together (they are actually only 25/32 in. thick), you should use a 1-1/2 in. screw for maximum strength. You might also use a 1-1/2 in. screw for attaching a 1-in. board to a 2 x 4, but a longer screw would be better if the board is subjected to unusual weight or stress.

The gauge of the screw should be suitable to the thickness of the wood into which it is driven and also to the size of the screw hole provided in whatever metal object you may be fastening down. For example, you obviously cannot drive a large-diameter screw into the edge of 1/4-in. plywood or through the screw holes in the average brass coat hook. On the other hand, you should not use a screw of very small diameter to install a coat hook (or anything else) because the head might not be big enough to guarantee that the hook could not be ripped off over it.

The other thing to consider in selecting the gauge of a screw is how strong a joint you need. The higher the gauge number, the deeper the threads and the better they hold. If possible, large-diameter screws should always be used when they are driven into the end-grain of wood and when they are driven into wood that is too thin to permit use of a long screw.

Finally, you have to consider the shape of the screw head. If you're joining wood to wood, the best choice is a flat-head screw because it can be set flush with the surface or countersunk. Flat-head screws are also used in mounting some pieces of hardware; but oval-head screws are used for many others, such as keyhole escutcheons and coat hooks, because the slightly rounded head conforms better with the surface of the hardware. Round-head screws are used primarily to fasten metal objects that do not have screw holes with beveled sides.

To drive a screw into a soft wood such as white pine, fir, or basswood, all you have to do is make a starting hole with an awl. But it facilitates matters to bore a hole with a drill. This is a necessity in hardwood. Known as the pilot, the hole should be almost as deep as the screw is long and a little narrower than the threads. In hardwood, it is then customary to drill a shank hole the same diameter and depth as the smooth shank of the screw. Finally, if you are putting in a flat-head or oval-head screw, you should drill a wide, shallow hole with a countersink bit for the screw head.

Electric drill bits that make all three holes simultaneously are available in hardware stores. They are known as combination drills and countersinks. If you intend to cover a screw with a wood plug, as in a plank floor, you can also buy a combination drill, countersink, and counterbore that makes all four holes at once.

BOLTING...

Nuts and bolts are the answer when you need an exceptionally strong joint that can be taken apart at any time. There are four kinds to choose from.

STOVE BOLTS   Stove bolts [Fig. 3-4(a)] have heads like flat-head screws and shanks that are threaded for their entire length. They range from 3/8 to 6 in. in length and 1/8 to 1/2 in. in diameter. They are tightened with a screwdriver and wrench. The heads should be countersunk.

MACHINE BOLTS   These bolts have square or hexagonal heads that are turned with a wrench [Fig. 3-4(b)]. The shanks are threaded for only part of their length. Sizes range from 3/16 to 1-1/4 in. in diameter, 3/4 to 39 in. length. When installed, both the bolt head and the nut protrude above the surface.

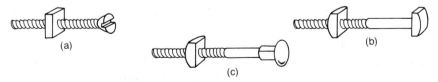

Fig. 3-4   (a) Stove bolt; (b) Machine bolt; (c) Carriage bolt.

CARRIAGE BOLTS   Carriage bolts [Fig. 3-4(c)] have smooth, oval heads
                             with short, square collars beneath. The shanks are
partially threaded. Lengths are 3/4 to 20 in.; diameters, 3/16 to 3/4 in. The
purpose of the collar is to keep the bolts from turning. If used in wood, the bolts
are hammered down until only the heads protrude above the surface. In metal or
other materials, a square hole must be made for the collar.

CONTINUOUS   These are actually threaded rods up to 3 ft. long and
THREADED BOLTS   3/4 in. in diameter. You can cut them to any length
                             and bend them to a special shape. They are held
firmly in place with nuts at both ends.

Bolts are normally made of steel but are available in noncorrosive metals.
Use lengths that protrude just far enough through the bottom piece being joined
so that you can tighten the nuts securely.

To install a bolt:

1 • Drill a hole the size of the shank all the way through the things you
    are fastening together, and insert the bolt and screw the nut on the
    end.

2 • If the material under the nut is metal, a lock washer should be
    slipped onto the bolt ahead of the nut to keep the nut from coming
    loose.

3 • If the material under the nut is wood that you do not wish to
    damage, install a flat washer against the wood, then a lock washer,
    and finally the nut.

A flat washer may also be used under the head of a machine bolt if you
don't want the head to damage wood underneath. Flat washers also enable you
to fasten things together with a bolt that is of much smaller diameter than the
hole provided.

TACKING AND STAPLING...

Tacks and staples don't look alike, but they are used for many of the same
purposes—usually for fastening a flexible material, such as screen wire,
upholstery, or carpet, to wood.

Despite differences in design, one type of tack can be substituted for
another in most situations. It is important to know only whether you should use
steel, copper, or aluminum and how large a tack is required. The smallest size is
3/8 in. long; the largest, 7/8 in.

Three kinds of staples are found in houses. All are made of steel:

1 • A large electrician's staple used to fasten cables to studs and joists.
2 • A small insulated staple for fastening down extension cords.
3 • The third resembles the wire staples used in an office; it is the most useful of all—provided you have a workshop stapler to drive it.

The workshop stapler is held in one hand and operated by squeezing the handle. It drives staples up to 9/16 in. long deep into wood. You might find it handy for replacing the wire in window screens; installing asphalt shingles, insulation, building paper, or polyethylene vapor barriers; and covering chair seats.

GLUING...

Adhesives have been so greatly improved over the years that they are being depended on more and more to fasten things together. The best of the general-purpose types that you might use in renovating your home are the following:

EPOXY GLUE   This is a very strong, moisture-resistant adhesive, but since it is fairly expensive, I reserve it for jobs that other glues can't do—for example, putting together a chair rung that is broken almost straight across. In addition to being a good wood glue, it is excellent for bonding other dense materials such as metal, glass, and stone.

Epoxy is called a two-part glue because it comes in two tubes. The contents are mixed together in equal proportions just before use.

POLYVINYL-ACETATE   Commonly called white wood glue or PVA glue, it is
GLUE   a rather thin, white liquid that becomes colorless when dry. Although only moderately strong, it is an excellent material for most wood-to-wood gluing jobs. But it should be used indoors only because it is not very resistant to moisture.

RESORCINOL GLUE   This is the outstanding glue for bonding wood that will be exposed to moisture. It consists of a red liquid and a powder that are mixed together as you need glue. When dry, it leaves a dark red stain.

SILICONE RUBBER   A thick, rubbery adhesive made in several colors, it
ADHESIVE   can be used to glue almost any material except wood. Its unusual feature is that it will securely fasten things

that do not fit together perfectly. It can, in fact, bridge a gap almost 1 in. across. For this reason, it is widely sold as a caulking material.

All general-purpose adhesives are used in pretty much the same way:

1 • Thoroughly clean the surfaces to be glued—removing all old glue, paint, varnish, rust, wax, grease, etc.—and let them dry.

2 • Plane and sand the wood smooth.

3 • Apply the glue in a thin coat to one surface. Don't leave gaps.

4 • Fit the pieces together properly and clamp them. (This does not apply to silicone rubber adhesive.) Use C clamps if possible, but be sure to place pieces of thin plywood under the jaws to keep them from denting the surface. The plywood also helps to spread the force of the clamp over a larger area.

On round and irregular pieces, a web clamp, consisting of a long nylon tape and steel fastener, is ideal. Lacking a web clamp, tie a cord around the glued piece and twist it tight, windlass-fashion, with a stick of wood or screwdriver. Padding is needed under the cord so it won't cut the surface.

If the glued piece defies clamping because of its size or shape, weight it down. Use a bag of sand or a plastic bag full of water if a rigid weight won't stay put.

5 • Clean off glue that squeezes out of the joint after clamping.

6 • Let the glue dry for 24 hours.

Adhesives used primarily in building operations are of three types: mastics, contact cements and wallpaper pastes.

MASTICS   These heavy, thick adhesives are used to fasten down
                                 such things as resilient flooring, asphalt roll roofing, ersatz plastic bricks, gypsum board, hardboard paneling, and ceramic tile. Always use the type specified by the building material manufacturer.

In cases where a mastic must be applied to every inch of a large surface such as a floor, it is usually put on with a notched spreader that leaves parallel ridges of mastic about 1 in. apart. The spreader should be held at an angle of about 45° to make ridges of ample size. The valleys between the ridges should be almost bare.

When wall panels are glued directly to studs or furring strips, mastic is applied in thick beads with a caulking gun.

And sometimes when the mastic should be put down in thin ribbons, as for roofing, it is spread with a putty knife or wall scraper.

CONTACT CEMENTS These are rubber-based adhesives used primarily to apply laminated plastic sheets to plywood or to particleboard to make countertops. They are also used to some extent to install plastic panels on bathroom walls. They are very strong and waterproof but difficult to work with.

The cement is applied with a paint brush to both pieces being fastened together, and allowed to dry. The pieces must then be very carefully aligned before they are stuck together because the cement forms an instantaneous bond that cannot be broken.

WALLPAPER PASTE Wallpaper paste is produced to several formulas that may or may not be used interchangeably to apply wallpaper, vinyl wall covering, grasscloth, fabric, felt, burlap, and other flexible materials. As in the case of mastics, you should use the type recommended by the wallpaper manufacturer.

Some pastes are sold as a dry powder that is mixed with water as you need it; others are viscous liquids. Application is usually made with an 8-in. paste brush, but some pastes are best applied with a paint roller.

SOLDERING...

Because you are not likely to solder metals together during remodeling except when you install copper piping, directions for how to solder are given in Chapter 10.

JOINING WOOD TO WOOD
WITH MISCELLANEOUS DEVICES...

CORRUGATED Also known as wiggle nails, these are small strips of
FASTENERS corrugated steel with sharp teeth on one edge [Fig. 3-5(a)]. They are made in straight pieces and rings. Used to fasten boards that are butted together at the ends or sides, they are placed across a joint and hammered down flush with the surface. Window screens and picture frames are often joined at the corners with corrugated fasteners; and when boards are used instead of plywood to make deep shelves in closets and cupboards, they are joined along the sides with the same fasteners.

SKOTCH FASTENERS These serve the same purposes as corrugated fasteners. They have long, sharp prongs projecting down from a horizontal strip of steel [Fig. 3-5(b)].

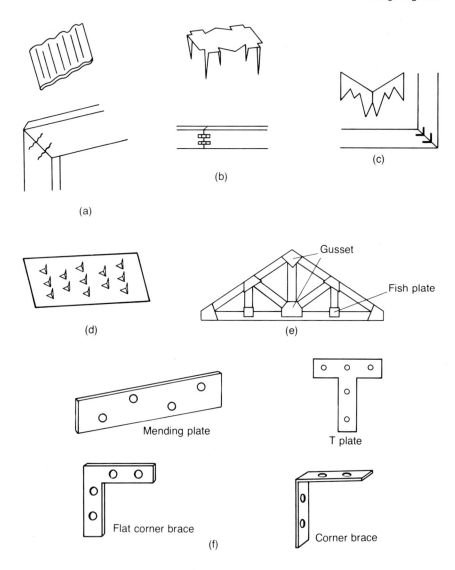

Fig. 3-5   (a) Corrugated fastener; (b) Skotch fastener; (c) Chevron fastener; (d) Connector plate; (e) Gusset; (f) Plates and braces.

CHEVRON FASTENERS   Chevron fasteners are small, L-shaped devices with points along one edge [Fig. 3-5(c)]. They can be substituted for corrugated and Skotch fasteners when you join boards in a mitered corner.

CONNECTOR PLATES   These have a general similarity to Skotch fasteners, but because they are much bigger and have several dozen teeth projecting from the bottom, they are used for joining larger pieces of lumber [Fig. 3-5(d)].

GUSSETS AND   Gussets and fishplates are, to all intents and purposes,
FISHPLATES   the same thing. They are small boards or pieces of plywood used to fasten timbers in a framework such as a roof truss [Fig. 3-5(e)]. After the timbers are butted together, two gussets are placed over the joint on opposite sides and nailed to the timbers. For extra strength, bolts may be substituted for nails.

MENDING PLATES   These flat steel or brass plates are screwed across a joint to hold it together or add strength. Four types are used [Fig. 3-5(f)]: One is a straight strip known only as a mending plate. Another, shaped like a T, is called a T plate. Another, shaped like an L, is called an angle iron or flat corner brace. The fourth, also L-shaped, is designed to fit inside a corner formed by pieces of wood instead of being placed flat. It is called a corner brace or angle iron.

Brass mending plates are small, but those of steel measure up to 10-in. long. All are installed with flat-head screws; small stove bolts can also be used.

FASTENING THINGS TO WALLS...

Frequently all you need is a nail. But there are times when these marvelous devices are of little or no value because (1) the wall is made of masonry or (2) it is hollow at the point where you want to attach something. Then you need a special fastener.

TOGGLE BOLTS   Toggle bolts are made for attaching things to any kind of hollow wall such as a stud partition or a wall built of concrete blocks. Although slender, they are capable of supporting considerable weight and of resisting most efforts to tear the objects down.

The commonest and most useful type of toggle bolt has a round, flat screw head and a shank up to 6 in. long which is threaded from end to end. The nut has two wings that open and close automatically and give the bolt its name—spring-wing toggle bolt [Fig. 3-6(a)].

The bolt is very easy to use:

1 • Drill a hole through the wall. It should be just wide enough to receive the nut (minimum diameter is 3/8 in.).

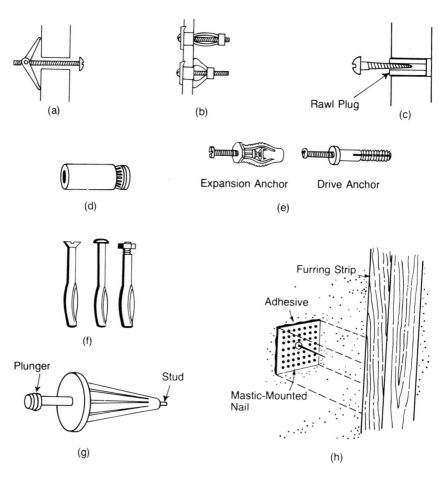

Fig. 3-6   (a) Toggle bolt; (b) Hollow-wall screw anchor; (c) Fiber anchor; (d) Machine-screw anchor; (e) Nylon anchors; (f) Drive anchors; (g) Stud; (h) Mastic-mounted nail.

2 • Insert the bolt through a hole in whatever you are hanging and screw the nut on the end a little way.

3 • Push the nut through the hole in the wall. When it enters the hollow space, the wings spring open.

4 • Pull the bolt back so that the wings of the nut press against the inside wall surface and tighten the bolt as much as you can with your fingers. Then use a screwdriver to complete tightening. (The bolt can be removed at any time—but when it is, the nut falls to the bottom of the wall space.)

**HOLLOW-WALL
SCREW ANCHORS**
Also called Molly screws, these can be used in place of toggle bolts except in very thick walls because the longest anchor is only 3 in. The device consists of a slender bolt that is screwed into a cylindrical sleeve, thus forcing the sleeve to mushroom outward against the inside surface of the wall [Fig. 3-6(b)]. One type of screw anchor has a hard, sharp point so it can be driven through gypsum board with a hammer. The more common type, however, is installed in the following way:

1 • Drill a hole through the wall the same diameter as the sleeve.

2 • Unscrew the bolt from the sleeve and slip it through a hole in whatever you are hanging.

3 • If the wall is covered with ceramic tile or other dense material, file off the two pointed lugs on the sleeve. But if the wall has a fairly soft surface, leave the lugs alone: They are designed to bite into the wall and keep the sleeve from revolving.

4 • Screw the sleeve all the way onto the bolt.

5 • Push the sleeve through the hole in the wall and tighten the bolt with a screwdriver until the hung object is firmly held. Should the sleeve turn in the hole during this operation, hold it with the tiny wrench which should be given to you when you buy a screw anchor. (If you subsequently remove the bolt, the sleeve stays in place in the wall.)

**PLASTIC AND FIBER
ANCHORS**
These simple little gadgets are used to fasten lightweight objects to masonry, plaster, and ceramic tile. The size of the anchor you need is determined by the size of the screw that is required. Buy the two together.

To install an anchor:

1 • Drill a hole of the same diameter and just a little bit longer.

2 • Tap in the anchor until it is flush with the wall surface.

3 • Slip the screw through the object, and then drive it into the anchor. This forces the anchor to expand and grip the sides of the hole [Fig. 3-6(c)].

LEAD SHIELDS
Lead shields—also called lead anchors—are larger than plastic and fiber anchors, but work in the same way. They are used to fasten large objects to masonry walls. Lag screws are used in the biggest shields.

**MACHINE-SCREW
ANCHORS**
These are used to replace lead shields when the latter fail to hold securely. Consisting of a rather complex anchor and bolt-like machine screw, they expand

with exceptional force against the sides of the hole in which they are used [Fig. 3-6(d)].

The length of the screw used with a machine-screw anchor is critical. It must be exactly equal to the thickness of the object you are hanging plus the length of the anchor. And the hole drilled in the wall must be the exact length of the anchor.

NYLON ANCHORS Nylon anchors are all-purpose fasteners because they can be used in masonry walls, conventional hollow walls, and hollow walls covered with only a 1/4-in. thickness of plywood or hardboard [Fig. 3-6(e)]. One kind of anchor is designed to hold a screw; another is used with a screw-like nail that is driven in with a hammer. Though both are small, they are capable of supporting surprising weight.

DRIVE ANCHORS Drive anchors are used in solid masonry for fastening heavy objects. Made of spring steel, they are designed so that when you hammer them into a drilled hole of the proper diameter, they are forced against the sides of the hole so hard that it is next to impossible to remove them [Fig. 3-6(f)]. Three head styles are available: round, countersunk, and stud. The latter is threaded for a nut so you can remove whatever you hang.

STUDS These nail-like fasteners, made of heat-treated steel, are driven into solid masonry either with a special stud driver that you hit with a hammer or with gunpowder in a "pistol" [Fig. 3-6(g)]. Their main advantage is that no holes need be drilled for them; consequently, they can be installed very rapidly. Their principal use in the home is for attaching wood furring strips to basement and other masonry walls.

Several styles of stud are available. Rent the tool for installing them.

MASONRY NAILS Made of zinc-coated, hardened steel, masonry nails are hammered directly into mortar joints between bricks, concrete blocks, and stones. One type is an angular cut nail; a better type has a round shank with spiral threads. Neither is as reliable as the various fasteners already described.

MASTIC-MOUNTED
NAILS These odd-ball gadgets are used for fastening furring strips to masonry. They have enormous flat perforated heads that are stuck to the wall with heavy mastic [Fig. 3-6(h)]. The furring strips are then pounded down over the shanks and the points are clinched.

MAKING JOINTS IN WOOD...

Knowing how to form the joints between pieces of wood is as important as knowing how to fasten them. Fortunately, the homeowner who does his own carpentry does not need to master as many joints as a woodworker who builds furniture. Neither does he need as many expensive tools.

BUTT JOINTS   Butt joints [Fig. 3-7(a)], though rather weak, are very common in the structure of a house because they are quickly made. In this joint, the end of one piece of wood is placed against the end or side of a second piece, and the two are then fastened together with nails, screws, corrugated and similar fasteners, mending plates, gussets, or wood blocks. Various ways of making a butt joint are illustrated in Fig. 3-7(a).

MITER JOINTS   Miter joints [Fig. 3-7(b)] are a form of butt joint, though they are never known by that name. The ends of the two boards being joined are cut at an angle—usually of 45°. The pieces are then fastened together with nails, screws, angle irons, or corrugated, Skotch, or chevron fasteners.

LAP JOINTS   Lap joints are easily made joints in which the wide surface of one board is laid on the wide surface of another board, and the two are held together with nails, screws, or bolts. The result, known as a simple lap joint, is utilitarian but ugly. Half-lap joints [Fig. 3-7(c)] are stronger and more attractive. In these, identical notches to half the depth of the wood are made in the two pieces; and the pieces are then fitted together and fastened.

RABBET JOINTS   Rabbet joints [Fig. 3-7(d)] may be used to join boards side by side or end to end to form a corner. To cut rabbets (rectangular grooves) in the sides of boards, however, almost requires an electrically driven router—so it's not a joint for the average handyman. The corner joint, however, can be made with a saw alone or with a saw and chisel. All you do is cut a rabbet in the end of one board and set the squared end of another board into it.

HOUSED DADO   A housed dado joint [Fig. 3-7(e)] is formed by
JOINTS   cutting a groove across one board (but not at the very end) and slipping the end of another board into it. Held together with nails, screws, or glue, it is considerably stronger than a butt joint.

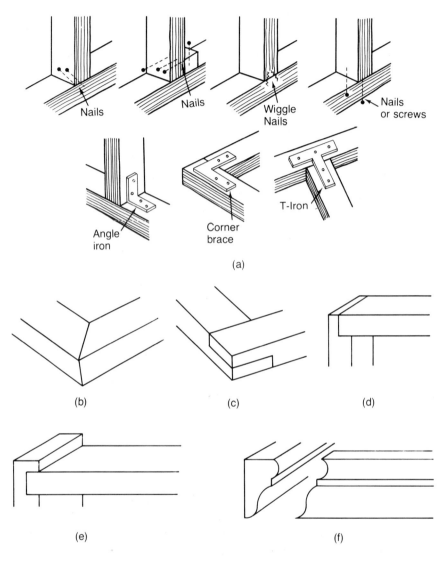

Fig. 3-7   (a) Butt joints; (b) Miter joint; (c) Half lap joint; (d) Rabbet joint;
(e) Housed dado joint; (f) Coped joint.

COPED JOINTS   A coped joint [Fig. 3-7(f)] is used to join moldings at
the inside corners of a room. The end of one molding
is cut away to conform to the contoured side of the adjoining molding and is
then butted to it. You must have a coping saw with a slender, fine-toothed blade
to make the joint.

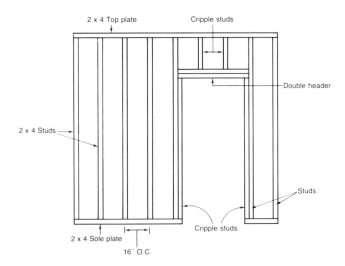

2 x 4 Top plate

Cripple studs

Double header

2 x 4 Studs

Studs

2 x 4 Sole plate

Cripple studs

16″ O.C.

Interior Walls and Ceilings

I very much doubt that anyone who has renovated a home has not done something to the interior walls and ceilings. Because they are the largest, most prominent surfaces in the house, you can't help being afflicted by them if they are dirty, scarred, or dreary. And once afflicted, you soon take steps to correct the situation.

There is an amazing number of things you can do—so many, in fact, that I recently wrote a book as long as this one that is devoted entirely to interior walls. I commend it to you if you're looking for the unusual. But the usual is thoroughly covered right here.

REPAIRING PLASTER
WALLS AND CEILINGS...

I learned something a while ago from Tom and Ashley Rooney's paint dealer. The plaster in several rooms of the Rooneys' new ancient house was crisscrossed with long, jagged cracks; and when I pushed it, I found it was loose from the lath, yet none of it had fallen. I had never seen anything like it and put it down as an oddity. But evidently it's a common problem in the Boston area—and probably elsewhere—because the paint dealer gave Tom an immediate, cheap solution. "Just drill holes through the loose plaster and pull it up tight to the laths with ceiling buttons; and then cover the buttons with gypsum board cement," he told Tom.

It worked like a charm.

The buttons are metal disks about the size of a nickel with a center screw hole surrounded by smaller holes. You install them with flat-head screws that are long enough to go through the plaster and the wood laths behind. (They don't work if the plaster is applied to metal or gypsum lath.) Try them if you have the same problem; and if you can't find them for sale, either take a trip to Boston or use ordinary flat steel washers instead.

I still think, however, that loose sheets of plaster that refuse to fall are not a widespread problem. But other problems are.

CRACKS   Whatever the cause of cracks—shrinkage of the plaster or settlement of the house—all are treated in the same way.

1 • Scrape them open with a beer can opener, screwdriver, or anything else that's handy. If they are very wide, try to make the sides straight up and down or, better, bevel them backward so the patching material will be "keyed in". Then blow out all crumbs.

2 • Fill small cracks with spackle or gypsum board joint compound. In both cases, the prepared pastes that come in cans are superior to the dry powders that you must mix with water. They stick well to any dry surface. Apply them with a putty knife.

3 • Large cracks should first be brushed or sprayed with water. Then with a putty knife pack them tight with patching plaster. Because this is a very fast drying material, mix it with water in small batches just before you use it.

4 • When the patching material is completely dry, sand it smooth with medium sandpaper.

SHALLOW HOLES   Fill with spackle or gypsum board joint compound. When sanding, take care not to remove more filler in the center of the holes than around the edges. Wrapping the sandpaper around a wood block helps to prevent this.

DEEP HOLES   If they are not large, you can fill them with spackle or joint compound. But for large holes, start with patching plaster. Cut the sides of the hole straight or bevel them backward, and wet them with water. Then fill the holes almost to the top. The plaster should be fairly stiff; otherwise, it will sag. When dry, fill the holes the rest of the way with joint compound.

If a deep hole is extremely large, filling the bottom with a prepared plaster mix—preferably one containing wood fibers—is better than working with patching plaster because the former sets more slowly. When dry, complete the job with joint compound, and draw the edge of a straight board or a carpenter's framing square across it to make it level and flush with the surrounding wall.

HOLES ALL THE WAY   Cut a piece of cardboard a little bigger than the hole,
THROUGH THE LATH   poke a hole in the center, and pull a string knotted at one end through it. Wet the edges of the hole with

water; then push the cardboard through it. Holding the string, center the cardboard behind the hole and pull it up tight against the back of the plaster. Fill the hole part way with patching plaster, and hang onto the string until it sets. Then snip off the end of the string and add more patching plaster to just below the wall surface. Finish with gypsum board joint compound (Fig. 4-1).

If the hole is huge, cut it back at the sides to the centers of the studs. Fit a piece of gypsum board or metal lath to the hole and nail it to the studs. Then fill it like an extremely large deep hole.

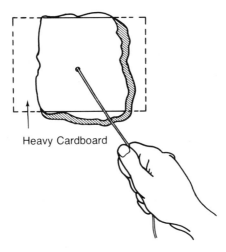

Heavy Cardboard

Fig. 4-1   Closing holes in plaster walls.

BULGES AND HIGH SPOTS   These should be cut out if they are not sound. Otherwise conceal them by covering them with a thin skin of gypsum board joint compound and extending the compound far out to the sides. Use a wide wall scraper to apply the compound, and when it is dry, sand thoroughly.

This is the way Tom Rooney concealed his ceiling buttons. Even on such small objects as those it is necessary to make several applications of compound, spreading each farther to the sides than the one before. But when you are all done, you will be amazed to see what a smooth, apparently level wall or ceiling you have.

POWDERY PLASTER   In an old house, crumbling, powdery plaster is usually the result of a water leak. So stop this before doing anything else. Then scrape out all the weak plaster—even if you have to go clear down to the lath—and fill it like a hole of corresponding depth and size.

REPAIRING GYPSUM
BOARD WALLS AND CEILINGS...

NAIL POPS   Nail-popping is the worst problem with gypsum board. It occurs when the nails holding the board work loose from the studs or joists, and the heads then blister or actually pop right through the surface of the gypsum board.

To correct the condition, drive the nailheads down again and drive a new annular-ring nail alongside. Then cover the heads with gypsum board joint compound.

CRACKS   These occur only at joints between panels. Open them slightly with a beer can opener or screwdriver and fill with spackle or gypsum board joint compound. If you find in scraping the joint that the paper tape covering it comes loose, remove the tape by making cuts with a sharp knife on either side and lifting it out with a putty knife. Smear joint compound in the gap and smooth a new piece of tape firmly into it. Then cover the tape with one or two layers of compound.

HOLES   Use joint compound or spackle in small holes. Through-the-wall holes about the size of outlet boxes are filled like those in plaster.

Larger holes all the way through the wall should be trimmed back in a square or rectangle, as shown in Fig. 4-2.

1 • Out of a scrap piece of gypsum board cut a patch 2 in. wider and 2 in. longer than the hole. Turn the patch upside down and draw the outline of the hole in the center. The margins between the edges of the patch and the pencil lines should be 1 in. wide.

2 • With a knife, cut entirely across the patch on each of the four lines, and bend the margins backward to break the plaster core. Then carefully cut the plaster from the back of the heavy paper on the face of the gypsum board. This gives you a flat plug with flanges.

3 • Apply gypsum board joint compound around the sides of the hole. Fit the plug into the hole and press the flanges into the compound. Then cover the entire patch well out beyond the edges of the flanges with joint compound, and sand smooth when dry. An additional coat of compound may be needed to conceal the patch completely.

If you have an extremely large hole to contend with, cut it back along the sides to the centers of the studs. Then cut across the top and bottom of the hole at right angles to the studs. Toenail pieces of 2 x 4 to the studs under the top and bottom edges of the hole. The edges should be centered on the 2 x 4s.

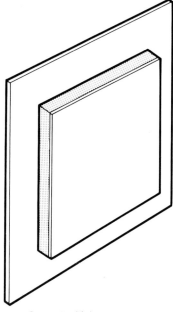

Step 1: Make gypsum board plug to fit hole.

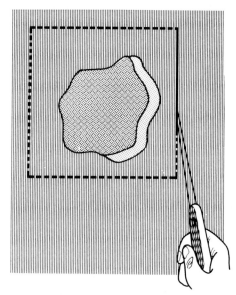

Step 2: Cut hole in wall to same size as plug.

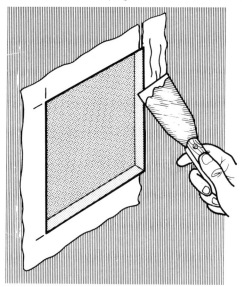

Step 3: Apply joint compound around opening.

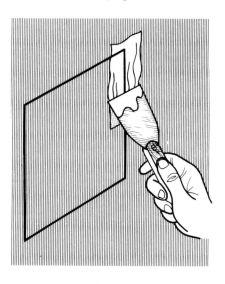

Step 4: Install patch and cover edges with joint compound.

Fig. 4-2   Repairing large holes in gypsum board walls.

Then cut a patch of gypsum board to fill the hole and nail it in on all four sides. Complete the joints according to directions given under "Covering Walls and Ceilings with Gypsum Board" later in this Chapter.

REPAIRING FIBERBOARD
WALLS AND CEILINGS...

This is likely to be a lost cause. I have struggled with every type of fiberboard and have always got very makeshift results.

One of the most ornery boards, which was widely used in houses of the 1920s and 30s, is named beaverboard. It is a thin, relatively hard board with several bad habits. Even though installed properly, it warps and ripples badly. It also pops nails and pulls loose sideways from the nails around the edges (which are always covered with wood battens).

Popping nails can be reset as in gypsum board. But it is often impossible to fasten down loose edges because they have pulled away from the studs and also because the board becomes brittle with age. The rippling and warping can be made less noticeable by troweling on gypsum board joint compound, but you need such gobs of the stuff that I doubt whether the cure is very sensible.

Soft fiberboard—the kind generally called insulating board—is less cantankerous. However, the joints contract and expand badly; and the boards pull loose from the nails. Holes and gouges can be filled in a sort of way with spackle, but they are still prominent because the spackle is smoother than the board. And if anyone kicks a hole in the board—which is about as easy as kicking a hole through a newspaper—you're a goner.

In other words, if you are cursed with fiberboard walls, the best way to repair them is to rip them out and put in something else.

REPAIRING WOOD PANELING...

When Elizabeth and I took possesssion of our house, the dining room was paneled with creosote-stained boards which looked as if they had been salvaged from crates. We coated them with a stain-killer to keep the stain from bleeding through the finish paint and also to establish a good base for spackle. (When using spackle or gypsum board joint compound on wood, always prime the wood first.) And then I used up two pints of spackle filling knotholes, nail holes, cracks, splits, roughness in the wood, and the end joints between boards. Two coats of paint followed.

Today, most visitors think the paneling is handsome—which goes to show how well you can repair damage in wood paneling, as well as in doors, windows, trim, baseboards, and other woodwork.

But paneling with a natural finish is something else again because there is no filler that exactly matches wood in color and texture. Plastic wood comes as close as anything. One manufacturer claims to produce it in all popular wood colors; even so, when sanded smooth, the patch still looks like a patch. Under the circumstances, my best recommendation is to leaves holes and cracks and bad scratches alone. Small scratches can be made less obvious—though they cannot be removed—by rubbing with the meat of an oily nut or with furniture polish.

If paneling and woodwork with a natural finish become dirty or blemished by skin oils, clean with the white appliance wax that is used in the kitchen. If the paneling has been waxed, and the wax rather than the wood is dirty, scrub it off with a wax remover or benzine. In either case, you should then go over the paneling with furniture polish or—for a really tough finish—with paste floor wax.

WATERPROOFING AND REPAIRING CONCRETE AND CONCRETE BLOCK WALLS...

Interior walls are sometimes made of exposed concrete blocks, but exposed blocks are usually found only in the basement. And poured concrete is strictly a basement-wall material. But this is no reason for ignoring these materials, because basements very often benefit by renovation; and a renovated basement definitely benefits the entire home.

WATERPROOFING   All basement waterproofing projects start outside the house, where the water comes from.

First, make sure that the ground around the house slopes away from it for a distance of 6 ft. or more. The slope does not have to be acute, but it must be definite so that ground water will flow away.

If there is a steep hillside on any side of the house, cut diversion ditches across it to channel water around the house. If this isn't possible, establish a definite ditch at the foot of the hill so that down-rushing water will not push up the sloping ground next to the house. In some situations, it may even be necessary to install catch basins and drains.

The second step is to carry roof water as far away from the house as possible. Many architects dislike gutters and leaders (downspouts), but there is no better way to divert the rain on the roof away from the foundations. Ideally, the leaders should empty into 4-in. drains which, in turn, empty into a city storm sewer or a stream or pond or low place well removed from the house and neighboring properties. The equally good alternative is to pipe the water from the leaders into the footing drains that empty into the storm sewer, etc. Still another good idea, if the soil in your garden is very porous, is to empty the leaders into perforated drain pipes that run through the yard about 6 to 12 in. beneath the surface. This gets rid of the water and at the same time irrigates the lawn and garden.

Four-inch drains are inexpensive and easy to put in because the pipes are made of lightweight composition material in long lengths which are fitted together with tight sleeves. But if you balk at using them, you won't be the first person who did. Don't, however, be foolish enough just to let the leaders dump water on the ground right next to the foundation walls. The least you can do is to put underneath each of them a concrete or plastic trough that slopes away from the house several feet. Or fasten to the end of each leader a hose that automatically rolls out when filled with water and rolls back in a small coil when the rain stops.

If you live in a house without gutters, diversion of roof water is more difficult. The best solution is to build shallow concrete or brick troughs in the ground under the eaves and lead them away from the house. Another possibility, which is more attractive but somewhat less reliable, is to dig a trench a foot wide and a foot deep under each eave. Lay in the bottom a row of perforated drain pipes that leads to a storm sewer, etc.; and then fill the trench with pebbles or crushed rock.

WEEPING WALLS   This problem is especially common in concrete block walls. There are no really active leaks; the walls just ooze. An effective and inexpensive way to control the problem is to apply a thick cementitious paint that comes as a powder and is mixed with water.

The walls must be clean and unfinished (except with cement paint). Spray with water if they are not already damp. Then scrub the paint into the pores with a stiff bristle brush. Let it dry for 24 hours and scrub on a second coat. Usually this stops the leakage; if not, keep applying paint.

Special epoxy coatings are also excellent on weeping walls, but they are more expensive. And because they remain in workable condition for only a short while after mixing, you cannot cover very much territory at one time.

ACTIVE LEAKS IN   If you can, wait until the leak stops. Then cut open
WALLS AND AT THE   the area around it with a cold chisel. If using ordinary
BASE OF WALLS   portland cement, open the crack to a width of at least
                           3/4 in. and to a depth of 3/4 in. Make the edges as
straight up and down as possible or bevel them backward, and dampen them with water. Mix 3 parts clean builder's sand with 1 part cement and enough water to make a workable mixture, and pack it into the hole with a putty knife or small pointing trowel.

Leaks between the floor and wall are handled in the same way. Or you can use a special cement such as Top 'n Bond or Watta Bond. In the latter case, simply scrape the cracks open and blow out the crumbs. Dampen the area around them. Then plaster the cement over the cracks at a 45° angle to the wall and floor. It should be about 1-1/2 to 2 in. thick directly over the crack (Fig. 4-3).

If a leak is always active, you need hydraulic cement. Open and clean out the crack. Then mix the cement according to the directions on the package, force it into the crack with your hand, and hold it until it sets.

Fig. 4-3   Repairing leaks between the wall and floor.

SERIOUS LEAKAGE OVER This is a job for a masonry contractor—and a costly
LARGE WALL AREAS one for you. Trenches must be dug around the house
down to the footings (Fig. 4-4). Perforated 4-in. drains are laid next to the footings and covered with about 8 in. of crushed rock. The drains are sloped into a run-off drain leading to a storm sewer, etc. The walls are then covered completely on the outside with cement plaster, followed by two coats of asphalt waterproofing compound. If the walls are in extremely bad condition, a membrane of building paper goes between the coatings of asphalt.

BASEMENT FLOOR This is hardly a wall problem but while we're
LEAKS IN MANY PLACES discussing leaks in basements. . . . Hire a masonry
contractor to coat the floor with asphalt waterproofing compound and then to cover it completely with 2 in. of concrete.

NON-LEAKING HOLES Open them with a chisel and fill with latex or vinyl
AND CRACKS cement which is sold in small packages. These are
special cements that stick tight to concrete, concrete block, wood, and plywood, even when troweled to a feather edge.

If portland cement is used, the holes and cracks must be cut open to about 3/4 in. in width and depth.

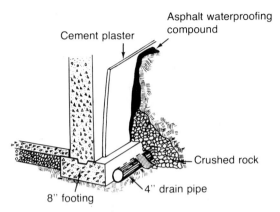

Fig. 4-4   Waterproofing outside walls below grade.

PAINTING
WALLS AND CEILINGS...

Most people cut their do-it-yourself teeth by painting walls. That's how easy the work looks—and it is.

PAINT FINISHES   Of the many types of finish available, only three can be called essential, and only five more need to be mentioned here.

Latex paint   This is the No. 1 interior paint because it can be used on walls and ceilings in all rooms except the kitchen and bathrooms. It dries so fast that you can apply two coats in a day. All clean-up work at the end of the day is done with water. The durability and washability of the final finish are good. Touched-up spots are usually invisible. And the almost-odorless paint can be applied to new plaster and concrete as soon as they are hard and dry.

Latex paint is ideal for application to gypsum board, plaster, and masonry surfaces; but it is not good on wood, plywood, or hardboard, despite manufacturer's assertions. Maybe some day—but not right now.

I have the same feeling about semi-gloss and gloss latex paints. You can get better results with alkyd enamel. But latex does give a superb flat finish.

When painting new gypsum board, plaster, or masonry, apply a latex primer and follow with one or two coats of latex finish paint. The primer is unnecessary for repainting jobs. Just brush or roll on one or two coats of finish paint. There are only two precautions to take: (1) Don't paint when the temperature is under 45° or over 85°. (2) Don't try to spread the paint out too much.

Alkyd enamel
Alkyd or oil-base enamel is the No. 2 interior paint only because it isn't used to cover so many square feet of the house. But you can't do without it for painting all walls paneled in wood, plywood, or hardboard; all doors, windows, and woodwork; and kitchen and bathroom walls. It's attractive and tough; the newest enamels dry in a few hours.

Select the type of alkyd finish with care. Flat enamel is much less washable than semi-gloss; and semi-gloss is less washable than gloss, but the difference in this case is not great enough to warrant use of gloss unless you like the high shine it gives. In other words, use semi-gloss enamel on kitchen and bathroom walls and on all doors, windows, and woodwork throughout the house because these surfaces are exposed to dirt and grease and need fairly frequent washing. But you might use flat enamel on wood, plywood, and hardboard walls that need little, if any, washing.

To use alkyd enamel on an unfinished surface, apply an alkyd primer first and sand it lightly when dry. Then put on one or two coats of the enamel. If you are changing the color of a painted surface, follow the same schedule. But if you're not changing color, omit the primer.

My observation indicates that most homeowners shy away from applying alkyd enamel with a roller because it is difficult, bordering on the impossible, to clean the roller well in mineral spirits. But if you want to make life easy for yourself, use a cheap roller cover; keep it soaking in the roller pan in mineral spirits until your painting project is finished; and then toss it into the trash.

Varnish
Varnish is the best clear finish if you want to protect wood or plywood from soiling and to make them easy to clean. As long as it is not exposed to a great deal of sunlight, it is durable and washable, and produces a soft glow. But on the negative side, it deepens the color of the surface to which it's applied and also gives it a yellowish cast; and when it is scarred, you can't touch it up invisibly.

For most indoor jobs, interior varnish is preferred. But if you need an exceptionally tough finish, use urethane varnish. You can buy flat, semi-gloss, or gloss finishes; but the last is so shiny it's objectionable and should be toned down with very fine steel wool.

Varnish must always be applied to a clean, well-sanded surface in a warm, dust-free atmosphere. Don't stir the can before use. Load your brush well and flow the varnish on liberally with the grain; then smooth off across the grain, and finish with the grain. One coat is generally enough on wall paneling; two are better on woodwork that people touch.

Oil stain
This transparent, pigmented liquid is used to change the color of wood and plywood without concealing

the grain or texture. You can apply it with a brush or rag. Smooth it out evenly and let it stand for about five minutes; then rub off the excess with clean, dry rags. If you want a darker color, apply a second coat immediately. When you finally get the proper tone, let the stain dry for 48 hours before applying varnish or other final finish.

There are two things to remember when using stain: (1) The color you achieve with any given stain depends on the wood species. That is, pine treated with mahogany stain is not exactly like mahogany treated with the same stain. If you want uniformity in a paneled wall, therefore, you should use the same wood for the trim and the paneling. (2) Before using a stain, try it out on a scrap of wood or plywood like that on the wall. Keep track of how many minutes it sinks in before you get the desired color. Then give it approximately the same sinking-in time on the wall.

Stain-killer   Stain-killer is a white-pigmented shellac that is applied to knots in softwoods to stop the resins from bleeding through and staining a final paint finish. It is also applied to wood that has been treated with creosote stain (now no longer used, but encountered in old houses) or old-fashioned varnish stains that have a tendency to bleed.

Because stain-killer has an alcohol base, it can also be used to prime wood or plywood in houses that are too cold to permit use of other primers.

Stain-killer is thin and runny and, therefore, a little troublesome to apply. But since you don't have to be careful about its final appearance, you can brush it on quickly. It dries in about 30 minutes, but give it an hour to be safe; then sand lightly and apply the final finish.

Sanded paint   This consists of latex paint mixed with real or imitation sand to give a sandpaper-like finish. Its principal purpose is to conceal flaws in the surface to which it's applied—and that's why people who do a sloppy job of building gypsum board walls and ceilings like it. Apply it with a brush or roller—two coats for complete coverage.

(P.S. You can give any paint a sand finish simply by mixing in well-washed sand or a material named Perltex.)

Textured paint   Textured paint is used for the same reason as sanded paint or just because you want walls or ceilings to have a definite texture. It is a thick latex or oil-base paint available in white and light pastel shades. If you need a dark color, the best way to achieve it is to apply any available textured paint and then go over it with ordinary paint of the same type.

Brush textured paint on a small area and immediately texture it with a stiff brush, comb, sponge, or roller made to produce a special pattern. One coat is usually enough.

The principal drawback of textured and sanded paints is that, once you put them on a wall or ceiling, they are permanent. Removal is extremely tedious.

Block filler   Block filler, a very thick, white latex primer, is used to fill the voids in concrete blocks and other masonry surfaces. Thus, it gives the surface a smoother-than-normal finish, and it also cuts down on the amount of paint required for the finish coats. Apply it with a brush or roller.

ESTIMATING PAINT   Figure the square footage of the total area to be
REQUIREMENTS   covered, and multiply by the number of coats required. Then divide by the number of square feet that a gallon of the paint you intend to use covers. This figure is normally printed on the can. If not, the paint dealer should be able to give it to you.

As a rough rule of thumb, the amount of paint needed for doors, windows, and trim is one-quarter of that needed for the walls.

Overestimating your paint requirements by a little is far better than underestimating—particularly if you have the paint mixed to a special color. This is because many paint dealers do not keep a record of exactly how they mixed paint the first time; consequently, it's touch and go whether they can mix it the same way if you happen to run out.

PREPARING TO PAINT   First, move out everything you can; pile what you
A ROOM   can't in the middle of the room, and cover it well.
                                        Take off the plates over electric outlets, door knobs and their escutcheons, key escutcheons, window locks, etc.

Remove wallpaper and similar coverings. (See the section on "Hanging Wallpaper" below.) However, if the covering is over gypsum board and will not come off without taking the paper face on the board with it, leave it alone. Stick down all loose edges with wallpaper paste and paint it.

Wash the walls and ceiling where they are dirty or greasy with detergent solution or trisodium phosphate (sold under such trade names as Soilax and Spic 'n Span). The entire kitchen must be washed. Rinse well and allow to dry. If a wall is mildewed, a strong solution of chlorine bleach will usually clean it; but if the wall is also very dirty, use 1 cup bleach, 2/3 cup trisodium phosphate, 1/3 cup household detergent, and 3 qt. warm water.

Remove floor wax on baseboards with one of the prepared wax removers used on kitchen floors or with benzine.

Repair all wall and ceiling surfaces, also the woodwork. Spot-prime patched areas with any latex paint or primer; otherwise, they will look lighter in color than the surrounding area. Also spot-prime knots in wood or plywood with a stain-killer.

Scrape off loose paint and sand carefully. If the remaining paint is badly scarred but sound, you can take it off by softening it with a paste-type paint remover and then scraping. But it is far and away easier to spread a thin layer of gypsum board joint compound over the surface with a wide wall scraper and sand with medium sandpaper when dry. An electric reciprocating sander is especially handy for this work.

To remove sanded or textured paint, use a sanding disk on your electric drill. It has a much more aggressive action than a reciprocating sander, but even it may not do the trick. In that event, you'll have to use paste-type paint remover and a scraper. Finish by sanding the surface with medium sandpaper.

Cover the floor with drop cloths. If you don't think your hand is steady, apply masking tape to door and window trim, floors at the edges of baseboards, etc., to keep paint off them. If you have good-looking brass or chrome door hinges that you don't want to paint, cover them with masking tape, too.

Check the directions on the paint can carefully. If the paint is new, it should have been shaken up for you by the dealer. If it is not new and has settled, mix slowly up and down as well as round and round with a clean stick of wood. Should the can be very full, pour part of the paint into another clean can or paint bucket, and mix each one separately before recombining them.

If the paint is old and has a skin on the surface, cut carefully around the edges with a knife, grasp the center of the skin in your fingers, and lift it out. If the skin breaks or if you find the paint has lumps, stir it thoroughly and strain through screen wire or cheesecloth into another can.

If the surfaces to be painted were mildewed, it's a good idea—even though you washed them with bleach—to stir a mildewcide into the new paint. But, unfortunately, this chemical has been outlawed in many places.

PAINTING THE ROOM   Paint rooms in this order: (1) ceiling, (2) walls, (3) doors, windows, trim, and woodwork, (4) baseboards. But if you're using the wall paint on the doors, etc., you can paint them all at the same time.

To paint a window, start on the mullions, progress to the sash frames, and finish with the jambs and casings. On doors, paint the edges, then the panels or louvers, then the rails and stiles surrounding the panels or louvers, and then the jambs and casings.

Use a roller on ceilings and walls. The type of roller cover required depends on the type of paint and on how smooth the surface is. If the roller has an extension handle, you can paint a ceiling from the floor. This eliminates climbing and moving a stepladder, but you still need a ladder to paint the edges of the ceiling and the very top of the walls.

Do the corners between walls and ceiling first. Use either a brush or a special cutting-in roller. (Cutting in means to paint along a joint in a surface.)

For some reason, I have never thought much of the latter. On the other hand, brushed-on paint has a noticeably different texture from rolled-on paint. This means that, if you use a brush in the corners, you must take pains when you follow with your big roller to work it in as close to the corner as possible.

To use a 7- or 9-in. roller, fill the tray about half full and roll the roller down into it until the cover is evenly coated. Then roll back up over the corrugations in the tray to remove excess paint. When transferring the paint to the ceiling or wall, don't roll too fast or use too much pressure, because this causes the roller to cover you with a fine mist and also leaves thick ridges on the ceiling at the ends of the roller.

Roll on the paint in any direction in a strip about 3 ft. wide. The strip should run the narrow way on the ceiling, from ceiling to floor on the walls. Thus, when you go back to paint the next strip, the edge of the first will still be wet and will blend into the new paint. (If the edge is allowed to dry, you get a distinct line between strips.)

Start each new roller load a short way from the previously painted area and roll toward that. After applying about three loads, go back over them, rolling in one direction. Be sure to work out any ridges left by the roller ends.

When painting up to a door, window, baseboard, or corner of the walls, you run into the same problem you have when painting the corner between wall and ceiling. You cannot use a large roller tight into a corner or against trim or moldings; instead you must cut in either with a brush, which leaves a narrow strip of brush marks, or with a cutting-in roller, which is hard to use.

When you come to a ceiling light, loosen it and paint underneath. If the fixture isn't heavy, let it dangle while the paint dries. But a heavy fixture must be held while you paint and refastened at once. Wall lights, regardless of weight, must also be refastened as soon as you paint behind them.

After painting a fairly large area, inspect it for skips, sags, ridges, lumps, insects, etc., and correct them while the paint is still wet. At the same time, make sure you haven't spattered the floor; and wipe off wet gobs on the drop cloth since you may step in them and track them through the house.

CLEANING UP　　　　　When the whole job is done, inspect it once more. It's a lot easier to fix up mistakes before you clean your painting equipment than afterwards. Then wash rollers and brushes that have been in latex paint in water. I like to put them, in the roller tray, into a bathtub or kitchen sink under a running stream. Roll the roller back and forth in the tray until it is clean. Then roll it over newspapers and stand it on end to dry. Hang the brushes to dry or lay them flat.

When using alkyd enamel, clean the roller tray with a paper towel and pour in mineral spirits about 1-in. deep. Roll the roller through this and then let it soak until the next day. It need not be submerged. Brushes should be worked up and down in a can of thinner, and then hung in the thinner by sticking a wire through the handles and placing it across the rim of the can. Never let a brush stand on its bristles.

When you are completely finished with a painting project, take extra pains to get all the paint out of brushes. Work the bristles between your fingers. Then wash the brushes in a strong household detergent solution, rinse well, wipe on newspapers, and let air-dry. Store them either by hanging by the handles or by wrapping in brown paper or a plastic bag and placing them flat in a drawer.

The final step in a painting project is to mark on the top of the paint can the room you painted and the date. If the label has been obscured, write down the type of paint. This will eliminate a lot of guesswork the next time that you rummage through your paint shelves for the same or another paint.

HANGING WALLPAPER...

When you try paperhanging for the first time, you'll be happily surprised how easy it is. And you'll be delighted with the lift the paper gives your home because there are no two ways about it—modern wallpaper is beautiful. You will find so many excellent patterns in your favorite paint and wallpaper store that you will be hard put to decide which one to use.

Obviously, I can't pick patterns for you—but I do strongly urge that, until you have done quite a lot of paperhanging, you stick to pre-trimmed machine-printed papers because they are less expensive and less fragile than other types, and they eliminate the not-too-easy trimming step. It's also a good idea to do your first job with a washable paper since it takes more scrubbing than a nonwashable paper and since you may need to scrub it to remove paste you get on the surface.

If you want to hang prepasted papers, fair enough; but buy them because you like the pattern, not because they are easier to hang. They're not—that is, they're not if you follow the manufacturer's directions for rolling the paper into a box of water to wet the paste. They are messy and hard to stick down, and are difficult to slide on the wall when you are butting joints. You should use prepasted papers only if you hang them like unpasted wallpaper.

So much for what to use when you are learning to hang paper. Just to keep you out of trouble, let me add the papers you should not use because they are difficult to handle or require special care in handling: hand-prints, flocks, sand-finished papers, scenics, strippable wallpapers.

ESTIMATING YOUR NEEDS   Despite the fact that wallpapers are made in various widths, a single roll of one covers about the same area as a single roll of another—approximately 30 sq. ft.

To estimate the number of rolls you need, measure the height of the walls (from the top of the baseboards to the ceiling) and their total length, and multiply the figures. Then find the square footage of each door and window; total the figures, and subtract from the wall area. Divide the answer by 30 to find how many single rolls you need.

You will pay for your order by the single roll. But the odds are that the paper that is delivered to you from the factory via the dealer will be put up in double rolls.

All of which is confusing, but that's the way the wallpaper industry operates.

PREPARING
THE ROOM

Move out all the furniture you can, and put the rest in the middle of the room. But don't forget to leave plenty of space for your paste table.

Remove the plates on electric outlets, heating registers, and surface-mounted and recessed medicine cabinets. Also remove mirrors hung in clips or channels, and metal bathroom fittings such as paperholders, towel racks, etc. Mark the location of the screwholes for these with carpet tacks stuck into the holes head first. The points should protrude a little so they will poke through the paper.

If you are papering new walls or ceilings of gypsum board, prime them with latex paint. Should you fail to do this, you will never be able to remove the wallpaper without taking off the paper covering on the gypsum board.

If an old wall is painted, wash it as necessary to remove grease, dirt, pencil and pen marks, etc. Remove mildew with chlorine bleach. Rinse well in both cases. Old calcimine must be removed completely with warm water and steel wool. Sand glossy paint.

Remove the roughness from textured and sanded paint with a disk sander and/or paint remover. The most feasible alternative is to hang a very heavy paper with a pronounced texture, but even with this it's advisable to put a lining paper underneath.

Old wallpaper can be left on the walls only if you are positive it is pasted down tight and after you sand the joints where they lap. However, there is still no assurance that the moisture in the new paste will not seep through the old paper, loosen the old paste, and cause blisters in both layers of paper.

Complete removal, in other words, is advisable. And it isn't very hard if you buy a strip-off wallpaper scraper. Work the blade under the old paper and push. The wallpaper usually zips off in long strips even when dry. If not, soak it with a sponge.

That fiendish old tool, a wallpaper steamer, is rarely necessary today. But if your scraper doesn't work, there is no other alternative. Rent an electric steamer from your wallpaper dealer, fill the tank with water, and bring it to a boil. Then hold the perforated metal plate connected to the tank by a hose against the wall. The steam emerging quickly loosens the paper so you can scrape it off.

Whatever the method used to take off wallpaper, wash the wall with water after you're through to remove all scraps of paper and paste.

The final step in preparing the walls is to repair cracks, holes, popped nails, etc. Wallpaper will not conceal such defects. Neither will it keep an unsound wall from falling apart.

MIXING PASTE Use wheat paste that contains size. Size is a glue that makes paperhanging easier, and it is needed on all walls except those covered with old wallpaper. If your paste does not contain size, it is necessary to apply size in a separate step before starting to hang paper.

Mix fresh paste every day in a clean bucket. Slowly add about 1/4 lb. of paste powder to a little more than a quart of water and mix until all lumps are dissolved. The paste should be about the consistency of potato soup. If it's too thin, add more powder; if too thick, add water. Later during the day when the paste thickens, you can add more water.

To provide a rest for your paste brush while you hang paper, tie a strong string across the top of the paste bucket.

MORE PREPARATIONS
1 • Unroll all the rolls of paper and check the "run numbers" on the back. If you have a roll with a number different from the others, turn all the rolls pattern-side up and see whether the oddball matches the others perfectly. If it doesn't take the whole batch back to the store and demand a new set of rolls.

2 • If you're hanging a nonwashable wallpaper, swab water on a corner of the pattern to test whether the colors fade or run. If they do, be extra careful about keeping paste off the face of the paper.

3 • Examine the pattern and decide how it should be positioned on the wall. If the paper is plain or if the pattern is made up of many small elements, it makes no real difference what goes where. But if the pattern has a very large element, that should be positioned an inch or two below the ceiling.

4 • Decide on your starting point. Generally this is beside a door or window or in a corner. But certain formal and bold patterns should be started in the center of the most prominent wall.

5 • Decide where the last strip of paper will be hung. You can hang paper in one direction all the way around a room; in that case the last strip will wind up next to the first strip. The alternative is to paper in opposite directions from the starting strip and end up

somewhere else in the room. It makes no difference which course you follow; but you must always hang the last strip in an inconspicuous part of the room because the pattern will not match the strip it abuts. In other words, finish the job in a corner out of the main line of view or possibly over a door or window.

6 • With a carpenter's level, draw a horizontal line around the room a few inches below the ceiling. This will show whether the ceiling is level. If it is, hang the paper to it. If it isn't, use the pencil line to control the positioning of the paper up and down the wall; otherwise, with some patterns, you will tend to hang each strip at a slightly different height with the result that your last strip may wind up one or two inches higher or lower than the starting strip.

7 • Cover the floor with drop cloths. Set up the paste table with the paste bucket and a bucket of water underneath.

CUTTING AND PASTING WALLPAPER Measure the wall height from ceiling to baseboard. Then make sure which is the top of the paper. It isn't always obvious. But there should be arrows on the back pointing to the top.

Remove the curl from the paper by unrolling it about 3 ft., grasping the roll in one hand and the loose end in the other, saw the paper, pattern up, around the front edge of the paste table. Then do the next 3 ft., and so on.

Lay the paper pattern up on the paste table with the top at your left. Find the point where it will hit the ceiling, measure up 2 or 3 in., and cut across the paper at a right angle with a razor blade and framing square. Then from the ceiling mark, measure down the wall height plus 2 or 3 in. and cut the paper there. The extra 4 to 6-in. of length will allow you to trim the strip exactly to the ceiling line and baseboard. All other strips should be oversized in the same way.

After taking out the curl, roll the roll of paper out alongside the first strip and match the pattern carefully (Fig. 4-5). Put a pencil mark at the bottom of the new strip opposite the bottom of the first strip, and then cut a second strip from the roll. Don't be surprised if the new strip is longer—perhaps much longer—than the first. This is simply because of the way the pattern is laid out. If the difference in length is only a couple of inches, leave it that way. But if the difference is greater than this, trim the top back to within 2 or 3 in. of the point where the strip will hit the ceiling. It will be easier to handle when you hang it.

If there is a huge difference in the length of the two strips—say a foot or more—it obviously means that a lot of the paper is going to be wasted. But here's a professional's trick to reduce waste: Instead of cutting all strips in normal sequence out of a roll of paper, cut all odd-numbered strips out of the first roll and mark them with an O, and cut all even-numbered strips out of another roll and mark them with an E.

Fig. 4-5   Matching pattern and length of wallpaper strips.

Match and cut four or five strips of paper at a time and pile them in sequence with the first at the bottom and the last at the top. Then flop over the entire pile. The backs are now facing upward; the tops are still at your left and should be aligned with the left edge of the paste table.

Push all but the top strip a little toward the back of the table. Align the front edge of the top strip with the front edge of the table. Hold it firmly and spread a thin, even coat of paste over the portion resting on the table (Fig. 4-6). Cover every inch, working mainly across the paper. Take special care to cover the edges with crosswise—never lengthwise—brush strokes. Along the far edge, let a little paste spread on to the strip underneath; but along the front edge, try not to get any paste on the table. You can avoid this by lifting the paper with your free hand a little. If you do get paste on the table, wipe it off with a damp rag.

Fold the top half of the pasted portion down over the bottom half. Align the edges of the fold, and smooth the paper down—but don't put too much pressure on the crease.

Push the bottom strips a few inches further toward the back of the table, and pull the strip you are pasting to the left until it is all the way on the table, with the bottom edge aligned with the right edge of the table. Align the front edge with the front edge of the table.

Finish pasting the strip. Then fold the bottom edge up to meet the top edge, and smooth the fold down (Fig. 4-7).

You can hang the strip immediately or paste two or three more strips in the same way before starting installation.

HANGING THE PAPER   If you are starting the first strip alongside a door or window, measure the width of the wallpaper minus

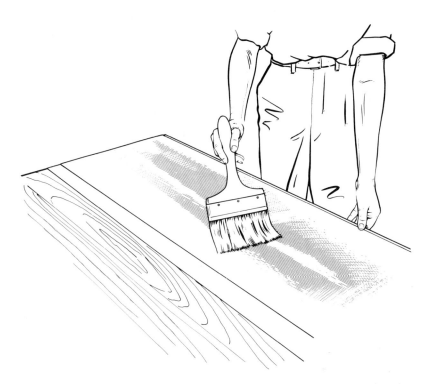

Fig. 4-6 Pasting wallpaper strips.

1 in. to the side of the door or window, and strike a plumb line. If you are starting in a corner, measure 1 in. out from the corner and strike a plumb line. If you are starting in the center of the wall, find the exact center, measure half of the width of the wallpaper to either side and strike a plumb line.

"Striking a plumb line" means to establish a vertical line on a wall or other surface. This can be done with a long carpenter's level or a plumb line and bob. When using a line and bob, the usual practice is to run a piece of blue chalk over the line. Then a nail is tied to the top of the line and driven into the wall. When the line stops swinging, hold the bob against the wall with one hand, grasp the center of the line with the other, pull the line straight out a few inches, and let it snap against the wall. This makes a blue line. The trouble with this method of striking a plumb line, however, is that the chalk is easily erased and may smear the wallpaper. A better procedure is simply to let the plumb line stop swinging; then make five or six pencil marks directly behind it up and down the wall.

To hang the first strip, face the wall squarely. Hold the top corners of the strip in your two hands. The folds should be facing the wall. Pull the top edge loose a few inches; raise your arms and let the paper unfold of its own weight.

Fig. 4-7   Folding pasted wallpaper strips.

Be prepared to stick out a foot to catch it in case it comes down with too much of a rush.

Align one edge of the strip with the plumb line and press the strip to the wall at the ceiling line (Fig. 4-8). Smooth the top down a few inches with a hand. Then take your smoothing brush out of your hip pocket, and smooth down the upper 3 or 4 ft. of the strip. If it doesn't align perfectly with the plumb line, pull it loose most of the way to the ceiling and try again. When you're new at the game, you may have to do this several times. You may even find that the strip is so crooked that you must pull it completely off the wall and start over again. But with a little practice you'll be able to hang strips accurately almost every time.

Once the upper part of the paper is positioned and smoothed, unfold the bottom part and smooth it down. Then go over the entire strip with your smoothing brush to assure tight adhesion to the wall and also to brush out bubbles and wrinkles. Should any of these persist, pull off the paper back to that point and smooth it down once more.

Now brush the paper tight into the corners at the ceiling line and baseboard, and sharpen the creases by drawing the unopened points of your shears lightly across them. Pull the paper partly off the wall, cut along the

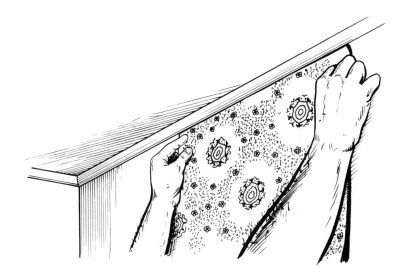

Fig. 4-8   Hanging wallpaper strips to the ceiling line.

creases with shears (Fig. 4-9), smooth the paper down again, and wipe every speck of paste off the ceiling and baseboard with a damp rag.

Cutting strips at top and bottom with shears is the recommended procedure for beginners because there is little chance of straying off the crease lines. But a faster procedure which you will probably soon adopt is to use a single-edge razor blade and a wide wall scraper. Push the straight edge of the scraper blade into the corner and hold the side of the blade against the wall. Then draw the razor blade along the scraper's edge. Proceed thus across the entire strip (Fig. 4-10).

Still later, you will probably give up the scraper and use a razor blade alone. But remember—*no matter how you use a razor blade, it must be very sharp to produce a perfect cut.* That's why professionals buy blades by the hundred and use each one for only two or three cuts.

The last step in hanging the wallpaper strip is to go over it with a clean damp rag to remove paste on the surface.

All succeeding strips are hung in the same way. But four additional steps must be taken:

1 •   Match the pattern of each new strip carefully to the previous strip; but don't be upset if you don't get an exact match near the bottom of the strip when you have labored to get one at the top. This just happens sometimes. It's annoying—but no one will ever notice it because it will probably be hidden by furniture.

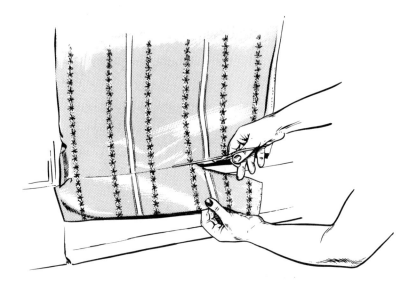

Fig. 4-9   Cutting wallpaper strips at the bottom.

2 • Always butt the edges of the adjoining strips. In the old days
      paperhangers often lapped the edges, but this made ugly joints and is
      no longer accepted practice. Anyway, butt edges are just as easy to
      make.

      Hang each strip as close to the previous strip as you can.
      Then before you smooth it down tight, slide the edge against the
      adjacent edge. Use your brush as much as possible to move the
      strip—not your hands, which may be dirty. And work from the
      center of the strip, not just along the edge. This helps to protect
      against tearing the paper.

      If you fail to get a perfect butt joint, it is probably because the
      wall isn't level. Just don't allow a gap between strips because it will
      stand out like a sore thumb. A slight lap is better. But a big lap
      should be eliminated by centering the edge of a framing square over
      it and cutting through both layers of paper with a new razor blade.
      Remove the slivers and press the paper down.

3 • After a joint has dried for about 15 minutes, run your wallpaper
      roller up and down over it. Use light pressure: enough to assure that
      the edges of the strips are stuck down but not enough to squeeze
      paste out of the joint or dent the paper.

4 • Hold your plumb line along the edge of every fourth or fifth strip to
      make sure you're still hanging the strips straight.

Fig. 4-10   Trimming wallpaper strips around doors and above baseboards.

Hanging wallpaper
around an inside or
outside corner

An example that helps to clarify this technique is illustrated in Fig. 4-11. Assume you are hanging wallpaper that is 21 in. wide around the room from left to right.

Measure the distance from the corner to the edge of the strip just before the corner. Since corners in houses are rarely straight, measure near the top and bottom of the wall. The distance at the top is 10 in.; at the bottom, 9-1/2 in.

Paste and fold the corner strip on your paste table. Align the edges of the folds very carefully. Your next step is to cut the strip lengthwise into two pieces so the strip will be easy to hang and, more important, so it will hang straight on the second wall without bad wrinkles or bubbles in the corner.

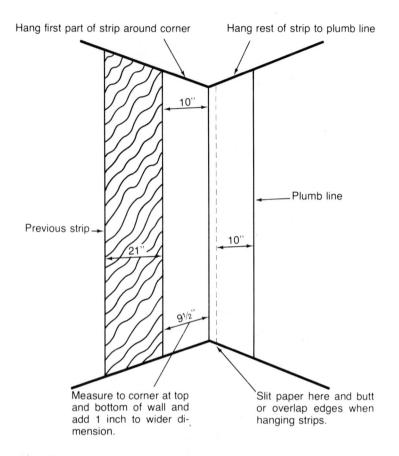

Hang first part of strip around corner   Hang rest of strip to plumb line

10"

Plumb line

Previous strip →

21"

10"

9½"

Measure to corner at top
and bottom of wall and
add 1 inch to wider di-
mension.

Slit paper here and butt
or overlap edges when
hanging strips.

Fig. 4-11   Hanging wallpaper around a corner.

Measure 11 in. (1 in. more than the wider wall measurement) from what
will be the left edge of the corner strip when you hang it. Make and mark this
measurement at both the top and bottom folds. Then lay a *straight* board on the
marks and slice both layers of paper in two with a razor blade.

Hang the 11-in.-wide strip on the wall beside the previous strip and smooth
it into and around the corner. Press it tight into the corner and try to remove
any wrinkles in the narrow flap on the second wall. (Actually, there should be a
very few, if any, wrinkles. That's the reason for splitting the paper: so that it
laps around the corner such a short distance that there is little chance of
wrinkling.)

When the strip is smooth and trimmed at top and bottom, drop your
plumb line along the edge of the flap and mark the point that is closest to the
corner. From here measure 10 in. along the wall and strike a plumb line.

Hang the 10 in. wide strip to the plumb line. It probably will overlap the 11 in. strip to a certain extent; but since this occurs in a corner, it will not be very noticeable.

Handle outside corners in the same way. But if the partial strips overlap at the corner, check whether the cut edge of the top strip stands out prominently. If it does, lap the bottom strip over the top.

Hanging wallpaper
toward a door

Assume that you are still hanging 21-in. paper from left to right. Measure from the top and bottom of the door frame to the edge of the previous strip, as shown in Fig. 4-12. If the wider space is 18 in. or more, hang the new strip in the usual way; press it tight against the side of the door frame, and with your shears, snip it at the top of the frame so the 3-in.-wide flap can be smoothed down on the wall. Then cut the strip along the side of the frame. Use a new razor blade and wall scraper in the manner described for cutting paper at the ceiling and baseboard.

The preceding technique for hanging paper toward a door should be followed only if the strip overlaps the door frame 3 in. or less.

Assume the measurement from the door frame to the previous strip of paper is 8 in. at the top of the frame, 8-1/4 in. at the bottom. Add 1 in. to the wider measurement and transfer the total—9-1/4 in.—to the pasted and folded strip on your paste table. Cut the strip in two lengthwise at that point.

Hang the 9-1/4-in. strip alongside the previous strip and smooth it to the wall and tight against the door frame. Snip across the top of the frame and smooth the flap to the wall above the door. Then with a razor blade remove the paper flap alongside the door frame.

Measure from the ceiling to the top of the door frame, and cut the remaining 11-3/4-in. strip to a length exceeding the measurement by several inches. Paste it to the wall over the door. Because it's such a short piece, it is hard to hang straight. The best way to check whether it is straight is to compare the pattern at the ceiling line with the pattern of a full strip.

Hanging wallpaper
away from a door

This is the reverse of the foregoing procedure, and is illustrated in Fig. 4-13. Measure 21 in. (the width of your paper) from the edge of the short strip over the door and strike a plumb line on the wall. Then measure to within 1 in. of the side of the door frame—say, 15 in.

Cut a full-length strip lengthwise to this measurement. Shorten the 15-in. piece to fit over the door and paste it down.

Hang the 6-in. strip to the plumb line, snip it to fit over the door, and cut it along the side of the door frame.

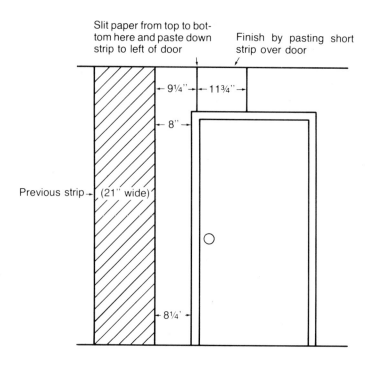

Fig. 4-12 Hanging wallpaper toward a door.

Hanging wallpaper around a window

Follow the directions for papering around a door. The job is somewhat harder, however, because the sill projects beyond the frame. And because of difficulties in aligning short strips above the window with those below, it may be necessary to lap a joint or two. If so, make the lap below the window rather than above.

Hanging wallpaper around electrical switches and outlets

Smooth the paper right over an outlet. At a switch, poke a hole through the paper for the toggle; then smooth down the paper. Cut away the wallpaper around the inside edges of the box. For safety, use a sharp knife with a handle insulated from the blade. Or use a razor blade and turn off the current at the fuse box.

Press the paper firmly to the wall around the switch or outlet.

Hanging wallpaper around a light fixture

Turn off the light some time before you get to it. The bulb should be cool. Unscrew the fixture from the wall and let it hang from the wires if it is not heavy; have someone hold it otherwise.

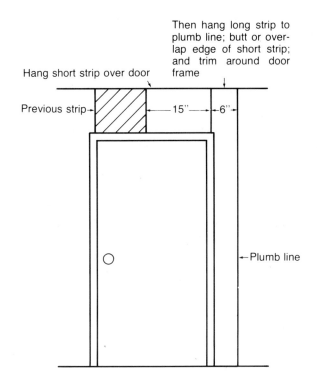

Then hang long strip to plumb line; butt or overlap edge of short strip; and trim around door frame

Hang short strip over door

Previous strip→

Hang the strip in the usual way and smooth it to the wall above the light. With shears, make a straight cut in from the nearest edge of the paper to the center of the light; and snip out a 2-in. hole for the wires. Fit the slit edges around the wires. Then smooth the paper to the wall the rest of the way down. Butt the slit edges.

Hanging wallpaper around a recessed medicine cabinet	Take the cabinet out of the wall, paper right over the hole as you do for electrical outlets, and then cut out the paper and reset the cabinet.
Hanging wallpaper behind a radiator	Don't try. Remove the radiator first by loosening the nuts connecting it to the pipes. This is a minor chore as compared to smoothing the paper down behind the radiator.
Hanging wallpaper in a dormer	It's impossible to match the wallpaper on the triangular walls in the dormer with the paper on the slanting walls in the room. So don't try. Use a plain

Fig. 4-13   Hanging wallpaper away from a door.

pattern, a busily confused one, or one with an overall design. The mismatching will not be too obvious.

However, if the wall below the dormer window is in the same plane as the room walls, it is papered in normal sequence with the room walls.

If you have a deep walk-in dormer, the entire thing should be papered separately from the rest of the room.

Hanging wallpaper on a slanting wall and knee wall

A knee wall is the short wall below a slanting wall. Hanging a single long strip of paper on the two walls is more exasperating than complicated because the top of the paper keeps peeling off the wall just when you think you have it stuck. The only way to solve this problem is to be as stubborn as the paper.

To make sure the strip is vertical, draw a line on the slanting wall and then part way down the knee wall with a carpenter's level.

If the corner between the walls is not horizontal—and it is quite likely not to be—the strip will hang crooked on the knee wall. To correct this, pull it loose from the knee wall and brush the upper end of the paper firmly into the corner. Then cut along the crease with a razor blade. Raise the knee-wall strip a fraction of an inch and paste it down along the vertical line. The top edge should overlap the bottom edge of the slanting-wall strip very slightly. To make the lap less noticeable, rearrange it with the bottom edge of the slanting-wall strip over the top edge of the knee-wall strip.

Hanging wallpaper in a stairway

This is similar to hanging paper in a room. Start with the longest strip simply because it's the hardest to handle and it's nice to get it out of the way. You may need an assistant to help you lower and align the strip with your plumb line.

Hanging wallpaper on a ceiling

This is not as difficult as you might think. Nevertheless, I suggest you attempt it only if the ceiling is low or you are very tall. Running back and forth on planks suspended between a couple of wobbly stepladders while you are looking over your head is a good way to end up in the hospital.

Paper a ceiling before the walls. The paper should extend 1 in. down all the walls that are to be papered. Paper across the ceiling, not lengthwise.

Before pasting the first strip, measure out from the wall it will parallel the width of the paper minus 1 in. Coat a long string with blue chalk, tie the ends to nails, nail the string to the ceiling over the measurement marks, and snap a line on the ceiling.

Cut the wallpaper strips 2 in. longer than the width of the room. Paste and fold them like strips for walls.

Face the wall the strip will parallel. Start at the right end if you're right-handed, the left if you're left-handed. Support the strip on a roll of wallpaper held in your left hand if you're right-handed (Fig. 4-14). Open the end of the strip with your right hand and smooth it to the ceiling along the chalk line. Shift as soon as possible to your smoothing brush. Work out wrinkles and get the strip well stuck down section by section. When the whole strip is in place, smooth it into the corners and down the walls.

Hang succeeding strips in the same way. Butt the edges.

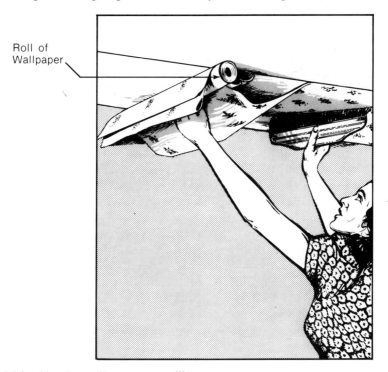

Roll of
Wallpaper

Fig. 4-14 Hanging wallpaper on a ceiling.

COVERING WALLS AND CEILINGS WITH VINYL WALL COVERINGS These once drab wall coverings have soared in popularity since manufacturers started turning them out in the same kind of beautiful patterns and colors that are available in wallpaper. The explanation is obvious: Vinyl is tough. You can scrub it—not just wash it. It resists most stains. And it withstands hard wear and considerable abuse.

If you can hang wallpaper, you can hang vinyl; it's done in almost exactly the same way. If you haven't hung wallpaper, you can still hang vinyl if you read the preceding section.

Prepare the walls as for wallpaper. Always remove old wallpaper and old vinyl coverings. If you want to cover concrete, concrete blocks, or cinder blocks, paint them with acrylic latex block filler to seal in alkalies and to level and smooth the surface.

Use the type of adhesive specified by the vinyl manufacturer. And check whether you are required to size the wall first.

Also, check whether all strips are to be hung top up or whether they are to alternate top up, bottom up, top up, etc.

Raise the heat in the room to 60° or higher.

Cut and match the strips like wallpaper. Apply the adhesive with a paste brush or medium-napped paint roller. The latter is easier to use because the patterned vinyl surface is very slippery, and it is hard to hold a strip on the paste table while brushing out the thick adhesive.

When folding the strips, don't crease them too hard because the creases will be difficult to obliterate. Roll the strips into loose rolls and set them aside for a little while to soak up the adhesive. A good procedure is to paste, fold, and roll about three strips at a time.

To trim vinyl on the wall, use a razor blade and wide wall scraper. The blade cuts more cleanly than shears, though you can't do without the latter.

Take extreme pains to work out blisters because they don't disappear by themselves. Go over each strip repeatedly. If necessary, pull it loose and paste it down again. An ordinary smoothing brush is satisfactory on thin wall coverings, but for heavy coverings, trim the bristles of your smoothing brush to 1-in. length. Or use a piece of 1/8-in. tempered hardboard with a smooth edge.

After a strip has been on the wall about 15 minutes, check again for blisters by holding a strong light close to both edges. If you discover a blister after the adhesive has dried, pierce it with a large needle and press down. You should also pierce blisters that may show up several days after the wall is completed; then squirt a little water into them with a tiny oil can before smoothing them down.

PANELING
WALLS WITH WOOD...

If you are thinking of the magnificent paneling you see in old traditional houses, hire a cabinetmaker. I can't think of anyone else who can make this kind of installation. But you shouldn't be afraid to install paneling yourself if you are content with simple board paneling. (And why shouldn't you be? It's beautiful, too.)

Most board paneling is made of pine and is kept in stock in good lumberyards. The boards have a smooth surface with tongue-and-groove edges that are also usually beveled. But for a price you can order just about anything you want in the way of woods, textures, and edge treatments. Just don't get too fancy. The loveliest paneled walls have dignified restraint.

Let the lumberyard figure out how much paneling you need because it's a tricky business. Just tell them how high and how long your walls are, and what the total square footage of all doors and windows, including trim around them is.

Watch over the yard hand as he picks out your paneling. Inspect each board yourself, and if you see it is warped or has numerous flaws, reject it.

If you plan to use moldings with the paneling and the entire wall is to be stained, try to get moldings of the same wood as the paneling; otherwise, you won't be able to match the color exactly. If the wall is to be painted, however, any moldings will do.

When the paneling is delivered, lay it on the floor in the room in which you will use it, and leave it for about 48 hours. This is to let it become acclimated to its new surroundings.

If you are going to paint the wall, sand the boards and prime the knots with stain-killer. Then cover the face and edges of the boards with alkyd primer and sand lightly when dry.

If you're going to stain the wall, apply oil stain to the edges of the board, but try not to get it on the face. When dry, sand the boards all over. (It is necessary to paint or stain the edges of the boards before installation so you won't see raw wood when the boards later expand and contract.)

If you're paneling a basement wall, it's advisable to cover the backs of the boards with aluminum paint to keep out moisture.

INSTALLING BOARD PANELING   The following directions apply when you install boards vertically—the way they are almost always placed.

Remove baseboards, door and window trim, and other moldings; then tear out the old wall surface. Cut 2 x 4s into short lengths to fit tightly between the studs. The pieces are called blocks or blocking (Fig. 4-15). Nail two horizontal rows across the wall approximately 32 in. up from the sole plate on which the studs rest and 32 in. down from the top plate above the studs. To simplify nailing of the blocks and to increase their strength, stagger those in each row so that those in the first row are 2 in. higher (or lower) than those in the second; those in the second will be 2 in. lower (or higher) than those in the third; those in the third will be 2 in. higher (or lower) than those in the fourth; etc. Then instead of toenailing the blocks to the studs, drive spikes through the studs into the ends of each block.

If you are paneling a basement wall, fasten 1 x 2- or 1 x 3-in. wood furring strips to the wall to serve as a nailing base for the paneling (see in Chapter 3, "Fastening Things to Walls"). Four strips are needed: one at the base of the wall,

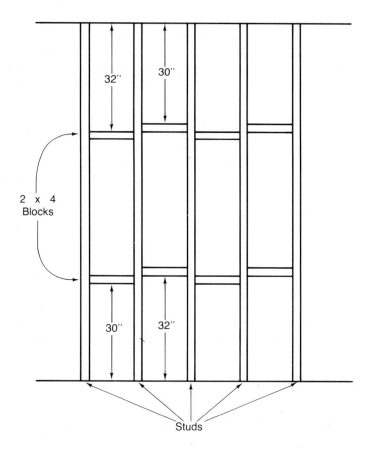

Fig. 4-15   Nailing blocks across a wall between studs.

one at the top, and two more equally spaced between. If the wall tends to feel a little damp now and then, protect the paneling further against moisture by stapling large sheets of heavy polyethylene film to the face of the furring strips.

Note that furring strips can be used over a stud wall, too. But they add to the thickness of the wall.

Board paneling with beveled or otherwise milled edges is best put in without baseboards or ceiling moldings that complicate the installation if they are used properly and detract from the appearance of the wall if they are used improperly. This means that the panels must be measured and sawed to fit neatly between floor and ceiling. Cut one board at a time as you build the wall. If you happen to cut a board a little short, let the gap be at the floor line.

Panel a wall from one end to the other. To avoid having the last board turn out to be an unattractive toothpick width, measure the length of the wall and divide by the face width (not including the tongue) of the paneling boards. You can then adjust the width of the first board—if necessary—so the last board is approximately the same width.

After cutting the first board, set it groove first into the starting corner and, using a plumb line or carpenter's level, adjust it until it is plumb. If it doesn't fit snugly into the corner at all points, secure it temporarily at top and bottom with a couple of nails. You must now scribe it to the corner.

Open a compass or pair of dividers just a shade wider than the widest part of the gap between the corner and board. Hold one leg against the corner, the other on the board; and draw them from ceiling to floor (Fig. 4-16). The line left on the board is exactly parallel to the corner. Remove the board from the wall, and with a saw and/or plane, trim the edge back to the line.

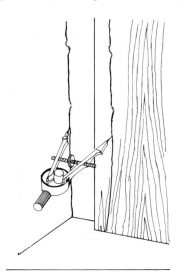

Fig. 4-16   Scribing paneling.

Nail the board up permanently and continue paneling across the wall. Snug each board tight to the other. If you can't always do this with your hands, lay a scrap board against the edge and rap it with a hammer. Check every fourth or fifth board with a plumb line or level before you nail it up, and if you find it isn't vertical, make it so.

Nail the boards to the plates and blocking with 2-in. finishing nails. If the wall is to be painted, drive the nails through the face of the boards about an inch from the tongue edge; countersink them and cover with spackle.

If the wall is to have a transparent finish, drive the nails diagonally through the tongue edge of each board so they will be concealed. The only boards that should be face-nailed are those in corners and those over 6 in. wide. In these cases, drive the nails only into the plates, countersink them, and cover them with beeswax or plastic wood that matches the color of the final finish.

There are only a few problems you may run into:

1 • If you are paneling around an inside corner, the first board need not be tight in the corner since the adjoining board will cover the gap. But if the paneling ends in a corner, the last board must be scribed to fit, and this will make it a little difficult to wedge into place. There are several ways around the problem:

    a • If the last board is narrow, remove the tongue from the preceding board.

    b • If the last board is wide, don't nail the preceding board when you come to it. Bevel the scribed edge on the back of the last board. Pull the tongue edge of the preceding board away from the wall a little and fit the groove of the last board over it. Then push the two boards against the wall and face-nail them.

2 • At an outside corner, let one board project the thickness of the paneling beyond the corner, and butt the second board to it. You may then have to plane or sand the projecting edge slightly. This is not as attractive as a miter joint, but it is much, much easier to make and resists splintering better.

3 • Around doors and windows, the paneling runs to within about 1 in. of the jambs, and the gaps are then covered with the trim boards (casings). You will have no problems if the paneling is the same thickness as the wall surface it replaces [Fig. 4-17(a)]. But if the paneling is thicker than the old surface, there will be gaps between the edges of the jambs and trim, and these must be filled with wood strips [Fig. 4-17(b)].

4 • Because of the flanges on it, an outlet box should be disconnected from the cables when you come to it. Cut a hole for it in the paneling with a drill and keyhole saw. (See Chapter 11.) Set the board in place, but don't nail it. Insert the box through the hole and reach behind the board; feed the cables into the box and connect them. Screw the flanges to the board.

Switch boxes are handled in the same way. Boxes for light fixtures can be left in place since they don't have flanges. But if the paneling is thicker than the old wall surface, pull the boxes forward so the rims are almost flush with the paneled surface.

5 • If for some reason you run out of wall-high boards, don't try to substitute a pair of short boards butted end to end. That ruins the effect of the wall. Go back to the lumberyard and buy some more boards.

When the wall is completed, sand it once more with fine sandpaper or steel wool. Then apply one or two coats of alkyd enamel if you want an opaque

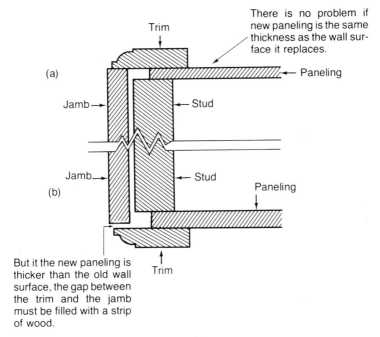

Trim

There is no problem if
new paneling is the same
thickness as the wall surface it replaces.

(a)

Paneling

Jamb →

← Stud

Jamb →

← Stud

Paneling

(b)

But it the new paneling is
thicker than the old wall
surface, the gap between
the trim and the jamb
must be filled with a strip
of wood.

Trim

Fig. 4-17 Installing paneling that is (a) the same thickness as the wall it
replaces and (b) thicker than the wall it replaces.

finish. For a transparent finish, apply oil stain to change the color of the wood.
Then apply interior varnish for a tough, soil-resistant, cleanable finish. For a
softer but less durable finish, simply go over the paneling with furniture polish
or floor wax. To retain the natural color of wood and at the same time give the
wood some protection against soil, apply a clear penetrating sealer.

INSTALLING
HORIZONTAL
BOARD PANELING

Board paneling need not be vertical. There are several
other ways you can install it, but of these only
horizontal paneling is attractive. And I much prefer it
when it is used only in a wainscot about 3 ft. high.

On a stud wall all you have to do is nail the boards to the studs. No
blocking is needed. In a basement, however, you must install vertical wood
furring strips 2 ft. apart.

Since the wall may well be longer than the paneling you buy, you will
probably have to butt boards end to end. Don't use very short pieces, however.

At outside corners the boards must be mitered to hide the coarse end
grain.

If you build a wainscot, you can top it off with a narrow board projecting
from the wall like a window sill. A common alternative is to top off with a

narrow board 1-1/4 in. thick (such boards are often known as 5/4-in. boards). This is nailed flat to the wall.

No matter how the wall above a wainscot is finished—with vertical boards, gypsum board, etc.—a row of blocking must be installed between the studs just above the top of the wainscot to serve as a nailing base for the material above.

PANELING
WALLS WITH PLYWOOD...

When should you use plywood paneling rather than wood? That's a tougher question than the plywood makers would have you think. Here are the pros and cons.

Most of the plywood paneling on the market is a rank imitation of board paneling, and while much of it is attractive, it still doesn't hold a candle to solid wood.

Plywood paneling is cheaper than wood. Some of it is a great deal cheaper—but watch out for that stuff. It looks second-rate and it's only 5/32 in. thick, which means that unless you install it on a firm, level base, it acquires the contours of the Sahara Desert. Never buy plywood paneling less than 1/4 in. thick.

Plywood paneling is somewhat easier to install than wood on an unbroken wall—but wood is somewhat easier on a wall broken up with doors and windows.

You can complete a plywood installation faster because the panels are prefinished at the factory. However, you must handle them with more care to protect the finish.

Because it's thin, plywood paneling does not stop the transmission of sound between rooms anywhere nearly as well as board paneling. This means that if you build a new frame wall between rooms or if you have to resurface an old wall completely, you should cover the studs with 1/2-in. or 5/8-in. gypsum backer board before installing the plywood. That not only doubles your work but also knocks out plywood's cost advantage.

On the other hand, if you are simply trying to improve the appearance of an existing wall, you can apply plywood paneling directly to it—as long as it is level. This is easier than tearing out the old wall surface in order to put up board paneling. And you increase the sound resistance of the wall.

GETTING READY TO   Most plywood panels measure 4 x 8 ft., but 7-, 9-,
INSTALL PLYWOOD   and 10-ft. lengths are available. You should order
                           these if your ceilings are not the normal 8 ft.

To estimate how many panels you require, measure the length of the walls to be covered and divide by four. Then subtract a half panel for each door and fireplace and a quarter panel for each window (unless, of course, the doors, fireplace, and windows are unusually large, in which case determine their total square footage and subtract from the square footage of the walls).

Have the panels delivered to your home two days before you need them and put them in a stack on the floor. Separate each panel from the other with a couple of boards so that air can circulate around them. But don't remove the protective paper on the surface of each panel.

INSTALLING THE PLYWOOD
Some time before starting your installation, tilt the panels against the wall and arrange them in the most attractive sequence. This is necessary because no two panels are exactly alike in color and texture.

Installing plywood directly over an existing wall
The wall must be level. Check it by sliding a long, straight board across it. Fill low spots with gypsum board joint compound. Chip down high spots.

Take off baseboards, moldings, and trim around doors and windows. Boxes for light fixtures, outlets, and switches must be pulled 1/4 in. further into the room so the rims will be flush with the plywood surface. If the boxes are rectangular (as most are), remove the nails or screws attaching them to studs, pull forward, and renail. Unscrew or break off the rectangular mounting flanges (if any) at the top and bottom of a box—but don't tamper with the small rounded flanges to which the light, switch, or outlet is attached.

If the box behind a light fixture is a small, round, solid "pancake" box, unscrew it or pull it from the stud on which it is mounted, insert a scrap of plywood underneath, and renail it.

Locate the center of one of the studs with an electric drill. Then measure across the wall and mark it every 16 in. (Studs are normally on 16-in. centers—that is, the center of one stud is 16 in. from the center of the next stud.) Then drill through the wall at each pencil mark to make sure the studs are really 16 in. apart. If not, you'll have to do some more drilling to locate them.

Once you've found all the studs, strike a chalk line over each one. Also make marks on the ceiling above them.

The panels are installed from one end of the wall to the other. Measure the wall height. If you're planning to install a cornice molding and a baseboard or shoe molding, cut the panel 1/2 to 1 in. less than the wall height. If you omit the cornice molding, cut the panel just a fraction of an inch less than the wall height. You must then scribe the panel to the ceiling—which is a nuisance and therefore a good reason for using a cornice molding.

To saw plywood, place it on a pair of 2 x 4s laid across two sawhorses. It should be face up if you're using a hand saw, face down if you're using an electric hand saw. The saw blade must have sharp, fine teeth.

After cutting the first panel to the right height, set it into the starting corner, plumb it with a plumb line or level, and secure it with a couple of nails. Then scribe and cut the edge to fit the corner.

Set the panel into the corner again and note whether the other edge is centered over a stud. If it isn't you must trim it until it is because the edges of all plywood panels must fall over supports to which they can be nailed. The trimming should be done at the scribed corner edge.

If paneling over plaster, use 1-3/4-in. finishing nails. Over any other material, use 1-1/2-in. nails. The nails should be spaced 6 in. apart around the sides of the panel, 1 ft. apart through the center. Drive them diagonally through the beveled edges and through the grooves that divide the panel into "boards". The latter are spaced so that they will fall directly over studs spaced 16 in. on center. Countersink the nailheads and cover them with the colored filler stick sold by the plywood maker.

An important point to remember is that you should always nail panels from edge to edge and top to bottom. If you nail the corners first and work in from there, you may buckle the panels.

After putting up the first panel, cut and install the second in the same way, then the third, and so on. Butt the edges close together.

When you come to a door or window, hold the panel alongside, and measure and mark on it the cuts to be made. Then before taking saw in hand, check the measurements again. This is the safest way to avoid cutting panels in the wrong way.

After the panel is installed, if you use your old trim, you must close the gap between it and the jamb with 1/4-in.-thick lattice strips. You can, however, buy new trim that compensates for the gap.

The final step in paneling a wall is to install the cornice molding, baseboard, or base shoe. Use those sold by the plywood manufacturer because they are made to match the color of the paneling.

Installing plywood paneling over a masonry wall or a wall that isn't level   In this type of installation you must fur out the wall with 1 x 2- or 1 x 3-in. wood strips. In the case of a masonry wall, the furring provides a nailing base for the plywood. In the case of a wall that isn't level, the furring provides a level base for the plywood.

Nail one furring strip to the wall at the floor line, another at the ceiling; nail additional horizontal strips in between on 16-in. centers. Vertical rows of short furring strips are needed in the corners and every 4 ft. across the wall to give support to the vertical panel edges (Fig. 4-18).

When applying furring to an unlevel wall, insert wood shingles under the strips where the wall has hollows. Chisel grooves through high spots or shave down the backs of the furring strips. In other words, you must not simply nail the furring strips to the wall because they won't be any more level than the wall.

The actual installation of panels follows the procedure described above. The only difference is that you should use 1-in. brads to fasten the panels.

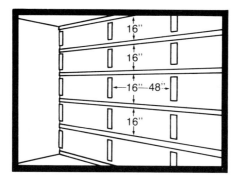

Fig. 4-18 Furring out a wall.

Installing plywood paneling on a stud framework As noted earlier, you should not apply plywood directly to studs if the wall separates one room from another or a room from a noisy street. But there's no reason why you shouldn't nail it to studs if there is nothing but a closet on the other side. Use 1-in. brads.

PANELING WALLS
WITH HARDBOARD...

Hardboard is a dense, heavy, durable, strong, stable sheet material made of wood fibers bonded together under heat and pressure. It has become a popular interior paneling material because it is only moderately expensive and is available in innumerable patterns, colors, and textures. No further finishing is called for.

Because hardboard comes in the same sizes as plywood, order it like plywood. Let it become acclimated to your house. Then install it much like plywood.

You can panel directly over any existing wall that is level. Use 1/8- or 3/16-in.-thick sheets.

First, remove baseboards, moldings, and trim. Wash the wall if greasy. Remove wallpaper and loose paint. Sand glossy paint. If the wall is covered with unfinished gypsum board, prime it with latex paint.

Scribe the first panel to the starting corner. Cut all panels 1/2-in. less than the wall height. Before installing a panel, dry-fit it to the wall and draw a pencil line down the free vertical edge.

Then remove the panel and, with a caulking gun, apply to the wall an adhesive recommended by the manufacturer. Run a continuous, slightly wavy bead all the way around the perimeter of the panel about 1/2-in. from the edges [Fig. 4-19(a)]. Then apply horizontal rows of adhesive, consisting of 3-in. strips 6-in. apart, at 16-in. intervals down the wall [Fig. 4-19(b)].

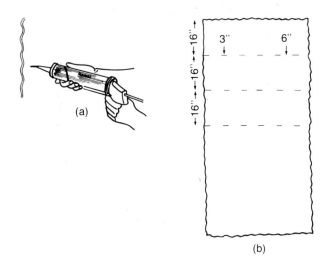

Fig. 4-19   Applying adhesive for installing hardboard panels.

Place a strip of wood 1/4-in. thick at the base of the wall, and set the panel on this. Press the panel to the wall, and put in several small finishing nails at the top to hold it. Then go over the entire panel, pressing it down firmly; after 15 minutes, press it down again.

If you're paneling a masonry wall or wall that isn't level, install furring strips as for plywood.   Use 3/16-in.-or, better, 1/4-in.-thick panels. Apply adhesive to the strips around the perimeter of each panel and in 3-in. dashes across the intermediate horizontal strips.

Install hardboard directly to studs only on the outside of a closet wall—and even then use nothing less than 1/4-in.-thick panels. The material has better sound resistance than plywood—but not too much. You can install the panels with adhesive applied to all studs and plates or with special annular-ring hardboard nails colored to match the panels. Space the nails 4-in. apart around the perimeter and 8-in. apart over the intermediate studs.

When hardboard is finished to resemble wood paneling, use the special moldings made to match the panels. With other patterns, however, you can use ordinary wood moldings and paint or stain them as you please.

INSTALLING
CERAMIC TILE ON WALLS...

See Chapter 10 for a complete description of how to install ceramic tile.

COVERING
WALLS AND CEILINGS
WITH GYPSUM BOARD...

Gypsum board is today's standard wall-building material. Use it—when you don't want paneling—to surface a new wall or to resurface an old one. It's low in cost and easy to work with, and it produces a smooth, fairly durable wall that is easy to decorate.

The standard gypsum board size is 4 x 8 ft., and it's the one do-it-yourselfers most often install because it is small enough and light enough to be handled with relative ease. But if your walls are much less or much more than 8 ft. high, ask for another length.

If the gypsum board is going directly over studs or over joists in a ceiling beneath an occupied space, don't use anything less than 1/2-in. thick board. As a sound-stopper, 5/8-in. board is a little better. But if you really want to stop sound, two layers of 1/2-in. board are by far the best. Three-eighths-inch board should be used only on ceilings on the top story. Quarter-inch board is restricted to resurfacing existing walls.

ESTIMATING GYPSUM BOARD REQUIREMENTS Figure the total square footage of the walls to be covered; subtract the square footage of doors and windows, and divide by the size of the panels you need.

For a ceiling, just divide the square footage by 32. Don't try to use panels larger than 4 x 8—even though larger panels may mean making a few less joints—because they are too heavy and awkward to handle.

For every 200 sq. ft. of wall you should buy 75 ft. of tape for making joints and 1 gal. of ready-mixed joint compound. Do not bother with powdered joint compound that must be mixed with water.

INSTALLING GYPSUM BOARD Use annular-ring nails only. The proper lengths for different panel thicknesses are 1-1/4-in. for 3/8-in., 1-3/8-in. for 1/2-in. and 5/8-in., 2-in. for 1/4-in. (because 1/4-in. panels are installed only over an existing wall).

Installing gypsum board directly over studs or furring strips Install furring strips vertically on 16-in. centers, and install horizontal rows of short strips at the floor line and ceiling line. Mark on the ceiling the centers of all strips and studs.

The panels should be cut (as you need them) a little short of the wall height. They are then jacked up to the ceiling by setting them on a piece of 1/4-in. plywood that is, in turn, placed atop a narrow wood strip serving as a fulcrum. Stepping on the back of the plywood lever raises the gypsum board.

After cutting the first panel to the proper height, set it into the corner where you are starting the installation, plumb it, and scribe it to the corner. Because the corner joint will later be filled with joint compound, you need not scribe the board as carefully as wood or plywood paneling—but it's a mistake to leave very much of a gap.

To cut gypsum board, slice through the white paper on the front with a sharp knife and bend the board backward. This breaks the core. Then cut the back paper and smooth the edge. To make a hole in a panel for an electrical box or heating register, push the knife point through the panel at the corners of the hole; then insert a keyhole saw, and saw out the opening.

When you come to a door or window opening in an existing wall, make the necessary cutouts in the panels before installing them. Leave a little space between the jambs and panel edges. In a new wall, however, if a door frame has not been installed, you can nail a complete panel over the opening and then cut it out. (But this is impossible at window openings because windows are installed in a house long before the interior walls are finished.)

After panels are set against the wall, nail the top from the center toward the two sides. Nail the bottom in the same way. Then strike plumb lines through the center of the panels below the marks made on the ceiling, and go down these, driving nails. Finally nail the vertical edges.

The best nailing method is called double-nailing. Space the nails around the perimeter 6 to 8 in. apart and 3/8 in. in from the edges. Over the center studs, drive the nails in in pairs 2 in. apart. The space from the center of one pair to the center of the next is 12 in.

All nails should be set 1/32 in. below the surface. To ensure that the panel is fastened tightly, put pressure against it as you drive each nail.

The edges of adjacent panels should butt, but only slightly. If you are installing panels with tapered edges, don't butt a tapered edge to a cut edge because you'll have trouble concealing the joint.

Installing gypsum board   Remove baseboards, moldings, and trim around doors
over an existing wall surface   and windows. Pull electric boxes forward 1/4 in. so
the rims will be flush with the wall surface.

The old wall need not be sound, but it must be level; otherwise, the gypsum board will have the same contours. Leveling means that high spots must be cut down or cut out; low spots must be built up by gluing pieces of shingle, laths, or several thicknesses of cardboard into them.

Find the studs and mark their centers on the ceiling. Strike plumb lines over those studs that will be under the edges of the panels. The panel edges must bear upon studs so they can be nailed securely.

The actual installation procedure is similar to that described above.

Installing gypsum board   If you're doing over an entire room, the ceiling
on ceilings   should be covered with gypsum board before the
walls.

If the joists are exposed, the panels are nailed directly to them. On an existing level ceiling, the panels are nailed right over it into the joists. In both cases, the panels are installed with the long edges at right angles to the joists.

To facilitate nailing, mark on the walls the locations of the joists and strike chalk lines over them on the panels.

The panels are then put up in the manner described. Unless the room is out of square, it will probably be unnecessary to scribe the panels to the walls because slight gaps around the edges will be hidden by the wall panels.

You will, however, need someone to help hold the panels while you are nailing them. In addition, you should use a T-shaped brace. Make this out of a 2 x 2 or a 2 x 4 cut about 1 in. longer than the ceiling height so it can be wedged between ceiling and floor. Use a narrow, 2-ft.-long board as the crosspiece on which the panel rests.

Taping joints   If you do this job slowly, you will save yourself work
in the long run and end up with a better looking wall
and ceiling. In fact, if the joints in a gypsum board surface are properly finished, you won't be able to tell it from a plaster surface, even when decorated with paint.

The first step in taping a room is to apply corner beads to all outside corners with nails or adhesive (Fig. 4-20). Corner beads are long, thin steel strips folded lengthwise into a right angle to produce a sharp, wear-resistant corner. Install them with annular-ring nails.

Finish the joints in any sequence that suits your fancy—but make sure to finish one joint before going on to the next.

With a 4-in. flexible wall scraper, spread a thin ribbon of gypsum board joint compound over the joint for its entire length. Center over the joint the 2-in.-wide paper tape used to reinforce it; and as you roll it out, press it into the compound with the scraper (Fig. 4-21). If the tape swerves from the joint, either pull it up and smooth it down again, or tear it in two, press down the end, and keep on going with a new strip. When you reach the end of the joint, hold the tape down with the edge of the scraper and tear off the tape against it.

Then spread another thin ribbon of compound over the tape for its entire length. Try not to leave any ridges or hollows. Smooth the edges to feather thickness.

Allow the compound to dry overnight. The room should be above 55° and should have some ventilation to allow moisture from the compound to escape. Then sand the joint fairly smooth, and apply a second thin layer of compound.

Use a 6- or 8-in. scraper and spread the compound about 2 in. to either side of the first ribbon. Feather the edges.

Let the compound dry overnight, sand it again, and apply a third thin layer. This should be 10 to 12 in. wide. Take pains to make it as smooth as possible and very thin at the edges. When dry, sand it carefully, remove the dust, and check it with both eye and hand to make sure it is perfect. If it has a few hollows or rough spots, spread more compound into them.

Fig. 4-20   Outside corner bead.

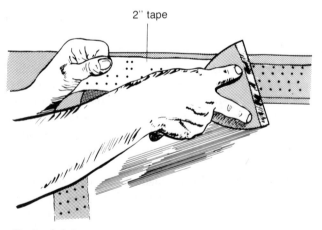

2" tape

Fig. 4-21   Taping joints.

Inside corners are finished in the same way. After spreading the first layer of joint compound into them, cut a piece of tape to the proper length and fold it in half lengthwise to form a right angle. Press this into the compound and build up compound from there.

On outside corners, the compound is spread directly over the corner beads. Use the above technique.

Nailheads are covered at the same time you finish the joints. Simply spread joint compound over them, let it dry, and apply another coat. Finish by sanding.

TEARING OUT WALLS...

Don't rush into this work until you have checked the following:

Is the wall a bearing partition?

If it is, you must employ a carpenter to tear it out and replace it with a large wood or steel beam to bear the load resting on it.

All exterior walls are bearing walls, but relatively few interior walls fall into the same category. However, you can't tell a nonbearing wall from a bearing wall just by looking at it. Bore a fairly large hole through the ceiling close to the wall and poke a long, stiff wire through it parallel with the wall.

If the wire goes straight ahead without striking an obstruction, it indicates that the joists are parallel with the wall and the wall is not bearing a load. You can take it out without fear.

On the other hand, if you hit an obstruction, poke the wire in the opposite direction. If you hit another obstruction, it means the joists are at right angles to the wall, and that the wall may be bearing a load. To make sure, open the hole so you can see into the joist space. If the ends of the joists are above the wall, it's a bearing partition. If the joists continue beyond the wall, however, it's a nonbearing partition.

Are there plumbing or heating pipes or heating ducts in the wall?

If there are pipes or ducts, it may be difficult—even impossible—to move them. The best way to find out about pipes and ducts is to look down into the wall from the attic or look up from the basement or crawl space. The only other thing you can do is make sure there are no plumbing or heating outlets on the upper floor in the vicinity of the wall. This is a pretty good indicator—but it is not 100 per cent reliable. We have a second-floor bathroom that is well removed from the wall in which the pipes are installed.

I also recall the time when we remodeled our first kitchen. The old kitchen had a crude corner cupboard with several heating pipes running through it. They interfered badly with plans for the kitchen because there didn't seem to be any way to get rid of them. Then for some reason I crawled down under the house to have a look at them. Much to my delighted surprise, I found they were not connected to anything—which goes to show that when you find pipes in the walls of an old house, don't just take it for granted that they are doing anything.

Are there electric cables in the wall?

The answer is yes if there are outlets, switches, or lights; and it is *probably* yes if there are any of these things in a wall directly above. But don't let this stop you from tearing out the wall.

Cables are not always easy to dispose of, but because of their flexibility, they are less troublesome than pipes. If there's enough slack, you can reroute them through walls, floors, or ceilings. If there isn't enough slack, you can run them into a junction box and add a new length of cable.

When you remove the wall, what will you do to fill in the gap left in the flooring?

You won't have any trouble filling it: Just nail in a board of the proper width and thickness. The real question is: Can you fill it so that it looks good? That's not easy unless there are floor boards paralleling the wall on both sides. In that event, you can put in new boards to match. Even if they are not quite the right width, you won't be offended by them.

If the floors are made in any other way, however, the only way to avoid creating an eyesore is to relay more or less the entire floor or to put down wall-to-wall carpet or a resilient floor.

Once these questions are answered satisfactorily, roll up your sleeves and go to work. Try to save the baseboards, trim, and moldings because they are made of good lumber and are valuable. Whatever other lumber you can save is all to the good, but there's a limit to the work the salvage is worth. Old studs, for instance, are sometimes so full of spikes and nails that by the time you wrestle them free they are splintered to shreds.

One rule I make for myself is to pull all nails immediately from each piece I take out. That's a safeguard against stepping on one. It makes the lumber, etc., easier to stack. And it protects the rest of the house when I carry the scrap down to the basement or outdoors.

When the wall is torn out, fill in the gaps that remain. Those in the ceiling and adjoining walls are easily filled with strips of gypsum board covered with joint compound. Those in the floor—hopefully you have an answer.

BUILDING A NEW
STUD WALL IN AN EXISTING ROOM...

If the wall is to run at right angles to the joists in the ceiling, it can be located anywhere you like since the top plate is nailed to each of the joists it crosses. If the wall is to parallel the joists, try to center it under one of them. But if this is impossible, you must knock out the ceiling between the joists on either side of the new wall. Nail 2 x 4 blocks between the joists about every 16 in. The bottoms of the blocks should be 25/32 in. above the bottoms of the joists. Nail a 6-in.-wide board to the blocks (Fig. 4-22). The top plate is then nailed to the center of the board, and gypsum board that replaces the torn-out ceiling is nailed to either side.

Having established the location of the wall, pencil the outline of the top plate on the ceiling, and drop a plumb line to fix the location of the sole plate on the floor.

Remove baseboards and moldings from the walls at the ends of the new wall.

Cut the sole plate and top plate out of 2 x 4s, and nail them into place with 4-in. nails. Then starting at one end of the wall, mark the center line of each stud on the sole plate. Allow 16 in. from center line to center line. If in an unbroken wall, you wind up at the other end of the wall with less than a 16-in. space between the last two studs, both studs still should be installed. On the other hand, if you are going to have a door in the wall, measure from both ends of the wall toward the door. If the stud spaces on either side of the door are less than 16 in., you may be able to change the location of the door so that there is

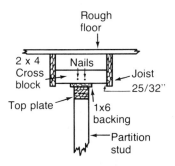

Fig. 4-22   Fastening a partition between joists.

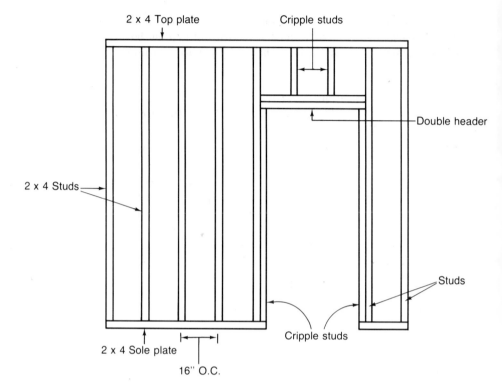

Fig. 4-23   Completed stud wall.

only one narrow space. But do not omit a stud if it means creating a stud space greater than 16 in.

Cut studs out of 2 x 4s to fit tight between the two plates, and toenail them to the plates with 3-1/2-in. nails. The wall is then ready to be covered with gypsum board or other paneling (Fig. 4-23).

If you build a wall that turns a corner, install three studs at the corner, as shown in Fig. 4-24. This is necessary so you can nail gypsum board or other paneling to the front and back of the wall.

If there's a masonry floor in the room in which you build a new wall, set lead shields in it and drive screws through the sole plate into them.

COVERING A CEILING
WITH ACOUSTICAL TILE...

Acoustical tile is used to reduce the noise level within the room in which it's installed. It cannot reduce the transmission of noise from one room to another.

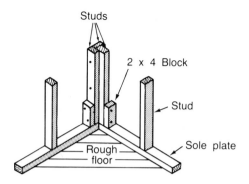

Fig. 4-24 Assembling three studs for an outside corner.

In very noisy rooms, use tiles with a noise reduction coefficient (abbreviated NRC) of 0.60 to 0.70. In less noisy rooms you need an NRC of only 0.40 to 0.50.

Because of their attractive surface finishes, acoustical tiles may also be used to improve the appearance of badly cracked or otherwise unattractive ceilings. But if this is your only reason for considering them, install ceiling tiles without acoustical properties and save money.

If the old ceiling is sound and level, the tiles are glued to it with adhesive recommended by the manufacturer. First, lay out the installation as you do for a resilient floor. (See Chapter 5.) Snap chalk lines lengthwise and across the ceiling to divide it into four equal quarters. Measure from the center point to one of the end walls in inches, and divide by 12 if using 12-in. tiles or by 16 if using 16-in. tiles. Now measure from the center point to one of the side walls and divide by 12 or 16. In each case, this exercise tells you how many full tiles will fill the space; the remainder tells you the width of the border tiles next to the walls.

The border tiles on parallel walls should be of the same width; and ideally, those on the end walls should be more or less equal in width to those on the side walls. In other words, if the border tiles on the end walls are 10 in. wide while those on the side walls are only 2 in. wide, the layout will not look right. To improve matters, measure half the width of a tile to any side of the center point and then measure to the wall and divide by 12 or 16. This will either reduce or increase the width of the border tiles along the wall to which you measured, and make them more equal in width to the border tiles along the adjacent walls. For example, if you move 12-in. tiles 6 in. toward either one of the end walls just mentioned, the border tiles along the walls will be 4 in. wide instead of 10 in. These would look better with the 2-in.-wide border tiles on the side walls. However, such narrow tiles are not very attractive, so it would be better to move the tiles 6 in. toward either of the side walls. This would make the border tiles along the side walls 8 in. wide rather than 2 in.; and they would look good with the 10-in. end tiles.

To install the tiles, start at the center point or adjusted center point, and fill in one quarter of the ceiling after another. Put five daubs of adhesive (one at each corner and in the center) about 1-1/2 in. across and 1/16 in. thick on the backs of 12-in. tiles; nine daubs (one at each corner, in the middle of each side, and in the center) on 16-in. tiles. Press the tiles firmly on the ceiling, and interlock them with the adjacent tiles.

Scribe each corner tile to the wall individually just as you scribe resilient floor tiles. (See Chapter 5.) Then, holding the tile face up, trim it with a fine-toothed saw or very sharp knife.

On a ceiling that is weak, broken, or unlevel and on a basement ceiling, install the tiles on 1 x 2- or 1 x 3-in. wood furring strips nailed across the joists at right angles. Snap chalk lines lengthwise and across the ceiling or, if covering a basement ceiling, stretch strings across the ceiling. Figure the width of the border tiles in the way described and adjust the lines or strings as necessary. Then center a furring strip over the chalk line or under the string that crosses the joists, and nail it up.

Nail up the other furring strips parallel to the first. Space them 12 in. on centers for 12-in. tiles, 16 in. on center for 16-in. tiles. The last two strips on opposite sides of the room are nailed alongside the walls. As you install the strips, check them with a carpenter's level and/or a long, straight board. If they bow downward at any point, remove them and notch the joists or cut channels through the ceiling for them. If they bow upward, drive wedges behind them.

Rent a staple gun to attach the tiles to the furring strips with 9/16-in. staples driven through the flanges of the tiles. At the borders and in corners, cut off the flanges as necessary, and face-nail the tiles with finishing nails. Countersink the heads.

The completed ceiling may need to be sponged off with detergent solution to remove fingermarks, but it doesn't need immediate painting. It can, however, be painted repeatedly without losing its sound-absorbing characteristics. Use either alkyd or latex paint.

INSTALLING
A SUSPENDED CEILING...

Suspended ceilings are made with acoustical or nonacoustical panels placed in a metal framework that is hung below an existing ceiling or open joists. The ceilings are used to lower objectionably high ceilings and/or to serve as oversized light fixtures. (See Chapter 12.)

The ceilings are sold in assemblies consisting of the framework, panels, and, if you want them, fluorescent light fixtures. Since each system is slightly different, follow the manufacturer's installation directions. The general procedure, however, is to determine the height of the ceiling and draw a horizontal line around the room on the walls. (The height should not be less than 7 ft. 6 in.) Framing members are nailed to the line. Then a grid of framing members is connected to the wall units and supported at the cross joints in the center of the room with wires attached to screw-eyes driven into the old ceiling or joists (Fig. 4-25).

Depending on the system, the light fixtures are mounted on the ceiling or attached above the framework, and large diffusing panels are set into the grid below them. Finally, the ceiling panels are pushed up through the grid and dropped back onto the support flanges.

Fig. 4-25   Installing a suspended ceiling.

5

Floors

Next to the interior walls, the floors are the most obvious part of the house; and as luck would have it, they get far and away the most wear. In an old house, they also run up and down hill, have warped boards, and are badly burned in front of fireplaces.

The quick-and-easy solution to most problems is to carpet the floors wall to wall. But, unfortunately, this costs at least $10 a square yard and has a life expectancy of only about 10 years in any room that gets much traffic.

Other solutions are less expensive and longer lived—and you can effect them with your own hands.

BASIC REPAIRS...

SAGGING FLOORS Floors that are lower along one wall than another are not repairable because if you try to jack them up, you simultaneously jack up the wall, and all manner of fearful things will happen. But a floor that sags in the center can usually be leveled to a certain extent—perhaps perfectly—if it is above a basement or crawl space. All you need is one or two (if the sagging area is large) jack posts or jack screws (Fig. 5-1). Short jack posts will extend to 3 ft., long jack posts to 8 ft. Jack screws extend to 1 or 2 ft. Whatever you use, set it on top of a couple of 2 x 4s or 2 x 6s (which help to spread the load). Set another pair of timbers on top of the post under the sagging area and at right angles to the joists. Then screw the post up tight, but don't try to level the floor all at once. Do it gradually—perhaps 1/4 to 1/2 in. every week.

When the floor is reasonably level, you can replace the jack post with an 8 x 8 timber or a lally column—a large steel pipe filled with concrete.

WEAK FLOORS Strengthen these with several 8 x 8 timbers or lally columns.

119

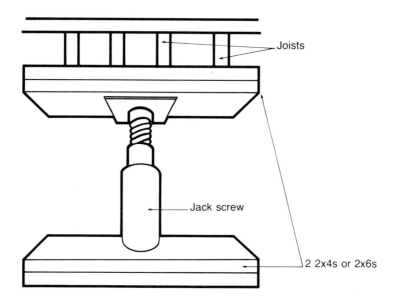

Fig. 5-1   Raising sagging floors.

VIBRATING FLOORS   A vibrating floor appears weak, even though it may not be. The cure is relatively easy, provided the joists under the floor are exposed. If the joists are spaced more than 16 in. on centers or if they are made of 2 x 6s, nail another timber of the same dimensions and length to each one. However, widely spaced or undersized joists are a less common problem than lack of bridging.

Bridging consists of the braces between each pair of joists (Fig. 5-2). Some bridging is cut out of the same type of timbers used for the joists. But most bridging is made of two 3-in. or 4-in.-wide boards nailed between the joists in an X. If you find there is less than one row of bridging per 10 ft. of joist, install one or two additional rows.

SQUEAKY FLOORS   If you can get at the underside of the floor, check for gaps between the joists and floor, and drive wood shingles into them. If you can't get under a floor or if the shingles don't stop the squeaks, drill small holes diagonally through the faces of the squeaky boards and drive in long screw nails. Countersink the heads and cover with plastic wood.

CUPPED FLOOR
BOARDS   Most cupped boards are unnoticeable when covered with a rug cushion and carpet. But if they are badly cupped, they should be either cut out with a rotary power saw and replaced, or flattened with a large floor sander and then fastened to the subfloor with the screw nails.

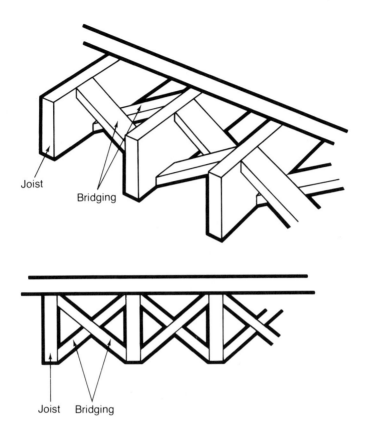

Joist

Bridging

Joist   Bridging

Fig. 5-2   Bridging.

REFINISHING A WOOD FLOOR...

You should attempt this only on floors made with boards running in one direction. For herringbone or parquet floors, hire a floor finisher.

To do the job you must rent a large drum-type floor sander to sand the center of the floor and a disk-type edger to do around the edges. For each machine buy three or four sheets each of coarse, medium, and fine sandpaper. Any you don't use will be repurchased by the rental agency. You will also need a hand scraper.

Strip the floor of all furnishings because sanding stirs up a lot of dust. Open the windows and close the door. Before starting up the sander, go over the floor, setting all nailheads below the surface with a nailset. Nail down loose or squeaky boards. Remove the shoe moldings next to the baseboards.

Use the drum sander first. Start with coarse paper, progress to medium, and always finish with fine. If the floor boards are very badly cupped, it may be necessary to run the sander across them at a 45° angle when using coarse sandpaper. Otherwise, always operate the sander with the grain, especially on the final pass with the fine sandpaper.

The proper way to use a drum sander is to start at one end of the room and sand in a straight line to the other; then back up over the same strip before moving to the next strip. Keep the sander moving at all times that the drum is in contact with the floor; if you stand still even for a second, the drum will cut a furrow.

The edger must be operated across the floor boards as well as with them, but since it has a rotary action, it does not make hard-to-get-out scars. Here again, you should progress from the coarse to the fine sandpaper. Keep the machine moving, with the disk flat on the floor.

Although sanders are equipped with dust bags, they don't suck up all the dust; consequently, you must stop sanding occasionally and sweep the floor so you can see how you are getting along. Dump the dust in the garden to improve the soil.

After you have finished sanding, use your scraper to clean up the corners and other spots the sanders cannot reach. To be of any value, the scraper must be sharpened frequently with a medium-coarse file. When working with the scraper, bear down on the blade with one hand while pulling with the other.

If stained areas remain after sanding, brush on a solution of 1/2 cup oxalic acid crystals and 1 gal. water. Let this dry and make additional applications until the color of the wood returns. Then neutralize the areas with 1 cup borax in 1 qt. hot water. When dry, sand the wood by hand until the grain raised by the moisture is smooth.

Whether you should stain the floor is up to you. All floor finishes deepen the color of wood slightly; and most homeowners are satisfied with the result—especially on oak and fir. Pine and maple, however, usually look better when stained.

Use an oil stain if you use any at all. Brush it on fairly evenly over an area that is no deeper than you can reach across; let it stand a few minutes, and wipe it with clean, dry rags to remove excess stain and even out the color as much as possible. (See Chapter 4.) Then go on to the next area. Do the closets first. Then work across the room to the exit door. Be careful not to trap yourself in a corner.

Let the floor dry 48 hours before applying the final finish—either gym seal or urethane varnish. The latter has slightly greater resistance to scratching; but at a later date, if you try to touch up worn areas, new varnish will stand out. New gym seal, however, blends in with old.

Whichever you use, apply two coats and follow with a coat of paste wax.

INSTALLING
A NEW BOARD FLOOR...

I've never known anyone who tore out an old floor and put in a new one, but that doesn't mean it hasn't happened. However, there are other more likely reasons for installing a new floor: because a room never had anything except a subfloor; because you want to replace a worn-out wall-to-wall carpet laid directly on a subfloor with a wood floor; or because you are making a new room in the garage, basement, or attic.

If the floor is to be laid over an existing subfloor made of boards, the new boards must be put down perpendicular to the subfloor boards. If the subfloor is made of plywood, however, the new boards can be laid in any direction—but usually parallel with the floor boards in nearby rooms.

If you're building a room in an attic or any other unfinished space with exposed floor joists, build a subfloor of 1/2-in. plywood and lay the finish floor on this.

To build a floor over a concrete slab, clean the slab and coat it with unfibered asphalt roofing cement. When this is dry, cover the floor with 1 x 2- or 1 x 3-in. wood furring strips laid in parallel rows 16 in. on centers. The strips should first be impregnated with wood preservative. Stick them down in ribbons of asphalt.

Over the furring strips, stretch a continuous piece of heavy polyethylene film to serve as a moisture barrier. The strip should be extended up the wall on all sides a couple of inches. Then nail a second layer of furring strips over the first. Ideally, you should then install a plywood subfloor; but this is often omitted—in which case the finish floor boards are laid directly on the furring strips, perpendicular to them.

Board flooring—also called strip flooring—is available in several widths, but the most commonly used is 2-1/4 in. wide. Standard thickness is 25/32 in. The flooring is sold in bundles of assorted long and short pieces, all of which are tongued and grooved along the edges and at the ends. To order 2-1/4-in. flooring, find the square footage of the area to be covered and multiply by 38 per cent. The answer tells you the number of board feet required. Add another 5 per cent for waste.

Flooring is available unfinished and finished. As with other building materials that are finished at the factory, the latter costs more but saves work. On the other hand, you must handle it with great care.

Before installing flooring, lay out several rows on the subfloor and shuffle the boards around until you get a desirable arrangement of end joints, colors, and grains. The end joints in adjacent rows should always be staggered at least 6 in. Take pains not to bunch up a lot of short pieces or a lot of long pieces—especially at the ends of the room (Fig. 5-3).

Fig. 5-3   Laying strip flooring.

Allow 1/4-in. expansion space between the grooved edge of the first board and the adjacent wall. The same space is also provided between the last board and the wall and at both ends of the floor.

All side and end joints between boards must be snug. To make them so, lay a scrap of flooring against the edge or end of the board you are installing and rap it with your hammer. Never hit the board itself. If a board is warped, throw it out. You can't make a good joint with it, no matter how hard you try.

Use 2-1/4-in. screw nails or 2-1/2-in. cut nails. Drive the nails at a 45° angle through the tongue, and hammer them level with the tongue with a nailset. They should be spaced about 2 ft. apart. The boards next to the side walls must be face-nailed, however.

If you use unfinished boards, go over them with electric drum and disk floor sanders to level and smooth them, as described above; then apply the finish. The final step is to nail baseboards and shoe moldings to the walls. Prime the shoes with paint before installing them: It reduces your chances of getting paint on the floor. Nail the shoes with finishing nails driven at a 45° angle into the subfloor. Countersink and spackle the heads before applying the final coat of paint.

LAYING A NEW PLANK FLOOR...

Plank floors are usually made of wide boards in random widths. The boards come from the mill in assorted lengths, usually between 10 and 18 ft., and are tongued and grooved along the edges but not at the ends. They are unfinished and secured to the subfloor with screws driven through the faces of the boards.

Planks are installed much like boards, but there are several points of difference.

For one thing, a plank floor has many fewer end joints. You may use some planks that run the full length of the room alongside a row of two or even three short lengths. Make any arrangement that looks attractive. Just vary it enough so that you don't get several adjacent rows of uncut boards or several adjacent rows of short boards.

The boards are installed with flat-head screws about 1-1/4 in. long. The screw heads are countersunk and covered with wood plugs 3/4 in. across and 1/4 in. thick. The easiest way to bore the holes for the screws and plugs is with a special electric drill bit called a countersink-counterbore (Fig. 5-4). This simultaneously drills a hole of the proper length and diameter for the screw shank, another hole for the screw head, and a third hole for the wood plug.

Install the screws at random. Usually there are two at the ends of each board and singles or pairs up and down the boards at about 30- to 48-in. intervals. After all the planks are screwed down, set in the plugs. Generally they fit tightly enough so they don't have to be glued: The floor finish serves as glue.

If the planks have as smooth a finish as those I have put down, they don't require sanding. If any plugs project above the surface, shave them down carefully with a sharp block plane. But if the planks have any roughness or are slightly cupped, sanding with machines is called for. This will also level the plugs.

LAYING A WOOD
BLOCK OR PARQUET FLOOR...

Wood blocks are made either of solid wood or of laminations glued together like plywood. Parquet blocks are made with strips of wood glued side by side. The

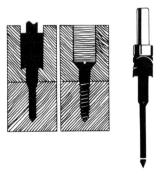

Fig. 5-4   Combination countersink-counterbore.

blocks in both cases are made in squares of several sizes. Never install anything except prefinished blocks.

The blocks can be laid over a plywood or smooth board subfloor; a smooth, sound-finish wood floor; or a smooth concrete slab that is on or above grade—never below grade. Today the main use for blocks is for surfacing slabs.

Test whether the slab is dry by placing several rubber mats on it in various places for 24 hours. Then if you find moisture under the mats, delay putting down the floor or give up the idea entirely.

To make an installation, coat the slab with unfibered asphalt roofing cement and let it dry. Then apply the adhesive recommended by the flooring manufacturer with a notched spreader and set the blocks in this.

Arrange the blocks according to the following directions for resilient tiles. Alternate the direction of the grain in adjacent blocks. Leave a 1/4-in. space between the border blocks and the walls.

COVERING A FLOOR
WITH RESILIENT TILES...

This is the easiest of all floor-laying jobs and the most popular. But in their efforts to interest more people in do-it-yourself projects, manufacturers have oversimplified some things. Self-stick tiles, for instance, frequently don't stay stuck down. Tiles you can cut with shears are, in many cases, so thin that they crumble at sight of shears.

Old-style, nonstick, top-grade vinyl tiles are the best. They cost more than vinyl-asbestos and asphalt tiles and lesser grades of vinyl tiles, but when you get them down, you have a floor that is going to last and stay attractive for years. I used to be partial to vinyl-asbestos tiles, but my last experience with the best available was disastrous. On the other hand, I still like asphalt tiles when I want a tough, inexpensive floor for a basement playroom.

To order 9 x 9-in. tiles, measure the length and width of the room in inches, divide each answer by nine, and then multiply the two numbers. To order foot-square tiles, measure the length and width of the room in feet and multiply the numbers.

If a room has an offset, figure the requirements for each area and add the answers.

To allow for waste, buy about 5 per cent more tiles than are required. Also order 1 qt. of brush-on adhesive for each 50 sq. ft. of floor area (trowel-on adhesive doesn't go as far).

When the tiles are delivered, store them in a warm room for at least 24 hours before putting them down.

PREPARING THE   Remove the shoe moldings or, if there are not any,
SUBFLOOR   the baseboards. Old resilient flooring must be taken
up. You will very often hear that this is unnecessary.
That is true if the old flooring is sound and if sheet material is installed over
it by professionals. But tiles are another matter, so don't ruin a new floor by
trying a short-cut. The old flooring is easy to rip up with a square-edged garden
spade. Then scrub off all the old adhesive with water.

Paint, varnish, grease, oil, and floor wax must also be removed completely
so that the adhesive can penetrate the subfloor.

Reset popped nails and nail down loose boards. Take down high spots in
the floor; fill holes and low spots with latex cement.

If you're tiling a floor that has never been covered with resilient flooring,
additional preparatory steps must be taken:

1 • If a wood floor is a single thickness of tongue-and-groove boards that
are more than 3 in. wide or of square-edged boards of any width,
cover it with 1/4-in. plywood. Use annular-ring nails and space them
6 in. apart throughout the panels. On a single-thickness floor made
with tongue-and-groove boards less than 3 in. wide, nail down 1/4-in.
hardboard underlayment.

2 • Quarter-inch underlayment should also be installed over double-
thickness floors with face boards more than 3 in. wide. But if the
boards are narrower than this, you can lay the tiles directly on them
after filling holes, sanding down cupped boards, etc. Lining felt is
needed only if the joints between boards are not tight. First, cover
the floor with linoleum paste applied with a notched spreader. Roll
the felt into this and smooth it down well.

3 • A dusty, porous concrete floor must be coated with a special primer
sold by the flooring dealer. The same primer is used to test whether
a concrete floor is damp. In this case, brush it on 3 x 3-ft. areas here
and there, and let it dry for 24 hours. If it then scrapes off easily,
the floor must be allowed to dry further or you should not tile it.

LAYING OUT   Find the middle of the two end walls, stretch a
THE FLOOR   chalked cord from one to the other, and strike a line
on the floor. (In finding the midpoints, ignore
alcoves, bays, pilasters, etc.) Then find the exact center of the line and draw a
line at right angles with a carpenter's framing square. Align the chalked cord over
this line and strike a line from side wall to side wall.

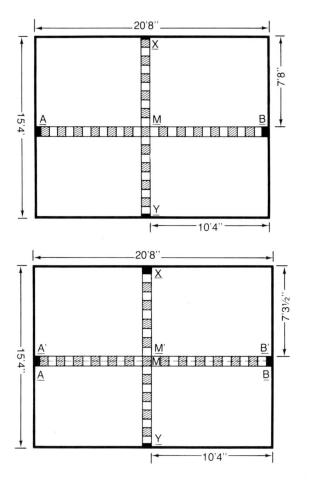

(a) Border tiles at walls <u>A</u> and <u>B</u> should be of equal size. Border tiles at <u>X</u> and <u>Y</u> should also be equal to each other and as nearly equal as possible to those at <u>A</u> and <u>B</u>.

(b) If end tiles at walls <u>X</u> and <u>Y</u> are not nearly equal to end tiles at walls <u>A</u> and <u>B</u>, move center tile up half a tile. Establish new center line <u>A'B'</u> and new midpoint <u>M'</u>.

Fig. 5-5   Laying out a tile floor.

Starting at the cross-point, lay tiles along the lengthwise line to the end walls and along the crosswise line to the side walls, as shown in Fig. 5-5. The end tiles of each row will be of equal width, and hopefully those at the end walls will be more or less equal in width to those at the side walls. But suppose those at the end walls are, say, 7 in. while those at the side walls are only 2 in. In that case, you should take up the tiles, move the center tile half of its width to any side of the cross-point, and relay the rows of tile.

For example, if you are using 9 x 9-in. tiles, move the center tile 4-1/2 in. toward either one of the end walls. This will make the end tiles in that row 2-1/2 in. wide. Since the width of the side tiles remains 2 in., you have achieved your aim of making all the border tiles almost equal in width. However, such a narrow border is not overly good looking; so it would be better to move the center tile

4-1/2 in. toward one of the side walls. The end tiles at the side walls then become 6-1/2 in. wide, while those at the end walls remain 7 in. The result is an attractive arrangement of border tiles, and you should therefore rub out the lengthwise line and strike a new one alongside.

LAYING THE FLOOR   Use the adhesive recommended by the flooring dealer. Most are applied with a paint brush. But some are applied with a notched spreader. In either case, don't cover any more floor at one time than the directions stipulate.

To set a tile, tip one edge to the floor, drop the other edge, and smooth the tile into the adhesive. You can walk on it at once if you're careful not to slide it out of place.

Start at the center point and tile a quarter of the room at a time. If you butt each tile to the next, the rows should be perfectly straight—but don't take this for granted. Check them frequently. If using marbelized tiles, the direction of the pattern in adjacent tiles should be alternated.

When you reach a wall, cut the border tiles to fit neatly between it and the last row of whole tiles. To do this, lay a tile (labeled A in Fig. 5-6) squarely on top of the whole tile; and lay a second tile (B in the sketch) on top and push it against the wall. Draw a line on A along the edge of B. Cut A on this line and paste the tile to the subfloor with the cut edge toward the wall.

Cutting is best done with a sharp linoleum knife [Fig. 5-7(a)]. This has a semi-hooked end with a sharp point. Place the tile on a scrap of plywood, hold it firm, and zip the knife across it [Fig. 5-7(b)]. Asphalt tiles must be scored repeatedly and then broken in two. This is no problem when making straight cuts but complicates irregular cuts. For these, soften the tile a little in a warm oven. You can then cut it easily.

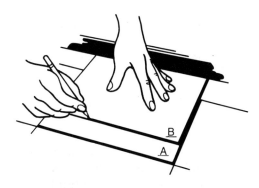

Fig. 5-6   Cutting border tiles.

(a)   (b)

Fig. 5-7   (a) Linoleum knife; (b) Cutting resilient flooring.

Fit tiles carefully around pipes, radiator legs, bathtubs, and other irregular obstacles (but it's better to take up a toilet and let the tiles extend under it an inch or so). To do this, make a paper pattern of the space to be filled and transfer this to the title. If a tile fits completely around an object such as a pipe, cut out the appropriate hole and then make a slit from the nearest edge to the hole (Fig. 5-8). When bending the slit edges around the object, be careful not to break or tear the tile.

If, despite all efforts, there is a slight gap between a tile and something it butts against, you can fill it with a plastic filler available from the flooring dealer.

After covering a large area, go back over it and press the tiles down once more. On all except asphalt tiles it is advisable to use a roller rented from the flooring dealer. If an asphalt tile is only partially stuck down, heat it slightly with a propane torch and mold it to the subfloor while it's soft.

When the entire floor is completed, replace the shoe moldings or baseboards. Wait a day or two before applying wax.

COVERING A FLOOR WITH
RESILIENT SHEET MATERIAL...

This is a job for a professional. If the floor is already covered with sound, level resilient sheets or tiles, he will probably lay the new flooring over it. But don't let him try this on unsound flooring or on a floor that has dents, holes, and high spots.

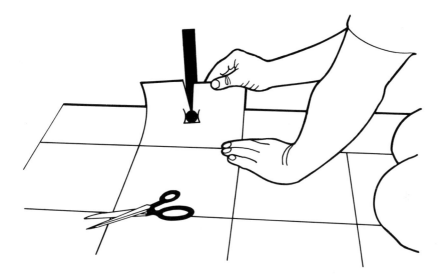

Fig. 5-8   Laying tiles around pipes or other obstructions.

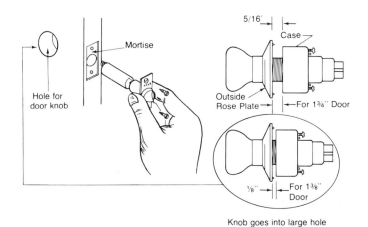

Hole for door knob

Mortise

5/16"

Case

Outside Rose Plate

For 1¾" Door

⅛"

For 1⅜" Door

Knob goes into large hole

Windows
and Doors

There was a story in *Yankee* magazine a while ago about an experience a family on Nantucket had when they applied to the town fathers for permission to initiate a program of replacing the single-pane windows in their old Colonial home with multi-pane windows. Two pictures illustrating the piece were convincing evidence of the desirability of the change. One showed the family's house; the other, an almost identical neighboring house with authentic 12-over-12 windows. Simply because of the small panes, the neighboring house was by far the better looking.

Single-pane windows are appropriate to contemporary, Victorian, and late Federal houses, but other styles of architecture usually look best with multi-pane windows. So here is a change that might improve your home.

From a labor standpoint, it's easy to make. But the cost of the sash can run high if stock units are not available and you must go to a millwork shop to have the sash made. In fact, this is the reason why the Nantucket family asked to be allowed to change the windows a few at a time: The special size sash for a single window cost $90.

Most old windows are counterbalanced with weights concealed behind pockets in the side jambs. You can buy new windows of the same type—but you will be better off to put in sash with spring balances in an aluminum track. When ordering these, give the height of each sash and the total width of the window opening between the jambs.

To remove the present windows, pry off the stops that keep the bottom sash from falling into the room. Work from the back edge so that any damage you do with a chisel will not be visible. Lift out the sash, cut the cords, and let them fall back behind the jambs. Pull out the parting strip behind the bottom sash. It is only wedged in, not nailed. Then remove the top sash and cut the cords. Unscrew the pulleys from the jambs.

Set the new sash in their aluminum tracks and place the assembly in the window opening. Nail the tracks to the jambs and renail the stops.

MAKING A NARROW
WINDOW APPEAR WIDER
INSIDE THE HOUSE...

This is easily done by hanging draperies a foot or more to each side of the window. Test several widths by having someone hold drapery material beside the window. It should lap over the side jambs enough so you're unable to tell exactly how wide the window is.

When you settle on the total width of the installation, build a cornice to hang over the top of the window and the draperies. Make it of 6-in. pine boards. Cut the face board to the proper length; the returns at the ends should be 6 in. long. Miter the ends of the face board and the front edges of the returns if you intend to paint or stain the cornice; but if you cover the cornice with fabric, you can simply butt the returns to the face board. Fasten the three pieces together with glue and finishing nails.

Cut a board to fit inside the cornice, and nail it in to form a top. To hang the cornice, drive two nails into the top edge of the trim above the window (Fig. 6-1). They should protrude 1 in. Center the cornice over the window, against the wall, and mark the location of the nails on the underside of the top. Then drill holes through the top, and drop the cornice down over the nails.

Install the drapery hardware as close as possible up under the top of the cornice. You will probably need toggle bolts or hollow wall screw anchors to hang it on the wall.

Cornices can also be made without tops. If so, hang them by screwing 4-in. angle irons inside the returns. The irons should parallel the face of the cornice. Then fasten them to the wall with toggle bolts or screw anchors.

For how to build a lighted cornice, see Chapter 12.

INSTALLING SHUTTERS...

Shutters are made of wood, aluminum with a baked-on factory finish, and vinyl which is colored integrally. The aluminum and vinyl types are much easier to maintain than wood, which needs frequent repainting and may in time rot. But they look phoney—especially since they are screwed tight to the window trim and adjacent wall.

Order shutters that are half the width of the window opening and the same height as the opening. One of the worst things you can do to a house is to install shutters that are so narrow that they obviously would not fill the window openings if they were closed. (After all, the original purpose of shutters was to allow the homeowner to close his windows against the sun, weather, and enemy attack.)

Hang each shutter with two screw hooks and strap hinges so that they can

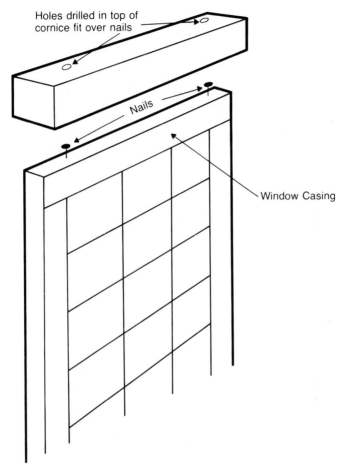

Holes drilled in top of
cornice fit over nails

Nails

Window Casing

Fig. 6-1   Building a cornice over a window.

be closed whenever you wish and taken down for painting. Screw the hinges to
the back of the shutter about 1 in. from the top and bottom edges. The circular
end should project 1/2 in. beyond the side of the shutter.

Set the shutter in the window opening, and mark the location of the
hinges on the window trim. Then drill holes, and screw in the hooks. They
should be 1/2 in. from the edge of the window opening.

To hold the shutters open, install hooks and eyes behind them or center
S-shaped hold-backs just below the bottom of the shutters.

Before painting shutters, it's a good idea to treat them with a paintable
wood preservative. Then prime them with an alkyd exterior primer, and apply
one or two coats of alkyd exterior trim paint.

HANGING DOORS...

One of my current projects, which I am pursuing slowly, is to replace several of the interior doors in our house. Most of the doors are traditional types with six raised panels. But for some reason the previous owner put in a half dozen doors with five horizontal recessed panels. I wouldn't go so far as to say they are hideous, but they certainly detract from the house.

That is true of many doors in many homes—not just interior doors, but also front doors and other exterior doors.

Order new doors to fit the existing opening. But if you want to change the size of the openings, there's no reason why you shouldn't. (See following sections.) In this case, fit the openings to the doors. Standard widths of hinged doors are 18, 24, 28, 30, 32, 36, and 40 in. The most common height is 6 ft. 8 in. Interior doors are 1-3/8 in. thick and are hung with two butt hinges. Exterior doors are 1-3/4 in. thick and should be hung with three butt hinges.

Start fitting a door by setting it on a pair of sawhorses and cutting off the lugs at the top. Measure the door opening carefully. The door should be 1/8 in. narrower than the opening and 1/8 in. shorter if there is a threshold across the opening. If there isn't a threshold, the bottom of the door should be cut so that it just clears the rug in the room into which it will swing.

Saw off the bottom of the door as necessary. Then plane down the edge in which the latch will be installed. In order to get an absolutely square edge, you must set the door on the other edge on the floor and hold it in a perpendicular position by clamping it to something such as your workbench.

Before you plane the latch edge all the way down to the measured line, set the door in the opening, hold it tight against the hinge jamb, and draw another pencil line down the door alongside the latch jamb. This will help you to fit the door perfectly to the opening. Then finish planing the edge and round the sharp corners a little.

Use 3-1/2-in. hinges on interior doors up to 32 in. wide, 4-in. hinges on wider doors. Exterior doors require 4-1/2- and 5-in. hinges. All the hinges should have loose pins.

Set the door in the opening and push it against the hinge jamb by inserting a wedge on the latch side. Lay a 1-1/2-in. finishing nail on the top of the door, and wedge the door up to the top jamb (Fig. 6-2). Mark the position of the hinges on the door and jamb. They should be at the same height as the hinges on other doors in the house.

Again, clamp the door upright on the floor, with the hinge edge at the top. Using a square and a very sharp pencil, outline the hinges on the edge. The hinge leaves should extend over the edge only 1-1/8 in. Mark the position of the hinges on the jamb in the same way.

With a sharp chisel and hammer, make vertical cuts along the pencil lines on the door edge. Then make a series of slanting cuts across each mortise from

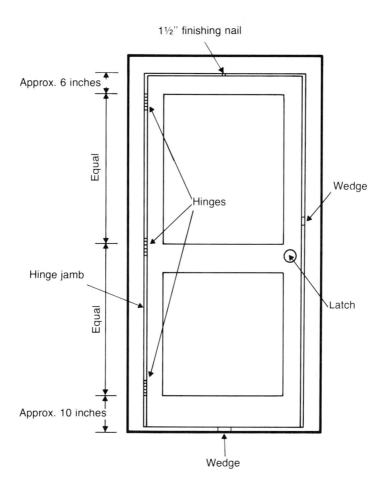

Fig. 6-2 Installing a door.

top to bottom [Fig. 6-3(a)]. They should be only about 3/16 in. apart and no deeper than the thickness of the hinge leaves. Scrape out the chips; then smooth the bottom of the mortises with the chisel [Fig. 6-3(b)] and set in the hinges. The leaves should be flush with the surrounding wood.

Complete the hinge mortises in the jamb in the same way.

Screw the hinge leaves to the door and jamb so that the pin will be facing up. Use only one screw in each jamb leaf to start with, and don't drill the holes for the other screws. This makes it a little easier to fit the door leaves into the jamb leaves. If they don't quite fit, loosening the screws in the jamb a little usually solves the problem. Then while the door is hanging, install the remaining screws.

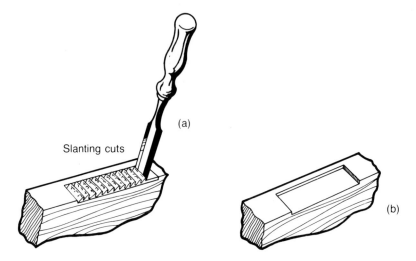

Fig. 6-3   (a) Scoring wood for a hinge mortise; (b) Completed hinge mortise.

The lock and latch sets most widely used today are of cylindrical design. The knob is installed 38 in. above the floor. Follow the very explicit directions that come with the set. In general, all you have to do is bore a large hole with an expansive bit through the face of the door, and intersect this with a smaller hole through the door edge (Fig. 6-4). Mortise out around the small hole to receive the latch front. Assemble the lock in the door and secure it with two bolts. Then cut a mortise in the latch jamb for the strike plate, dig or bore a deep hole for the latch tongue, and install the plate with screws.

The best lockset for exterior doors is a mortise design. To install this, unhang the door and set it on the floor with the latch edge up. Then follow the manufacturer's directions. The first step is to make a long, shallow, rectangular mortise in the edge of the door for the lock front. Drill a row of large holes several inches into the door edge in the center of the mortise [Fig. 6-5(a)]. With a chisel, square these up to form a rectangular slot for the lock body [Fig. 6-5(b)]. Holes are then drilled through the face of the door for the door knob or latch and for the lock. Finally, the lock body is installed and the other elements are fastened to it.

CLOSING A DOOR OR
WINDOW OPENING IN A WALL...

Remove the door or sash first. Then remove the trim and jambs. If the front and back edges of the studs are not exposed when the trim is removed, cut the wall surfaces back 1 in. from the sides and top of the opening.

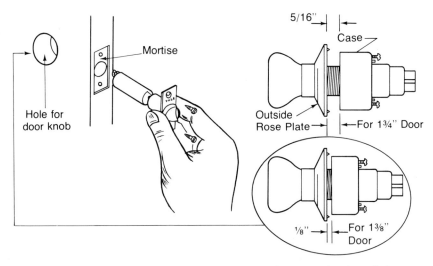

Knob goes into large hole

Fig. 6-4 Installing a cylindrical lock.

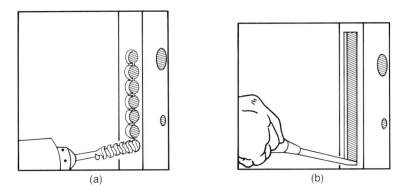

(a)   (b)

Fig. 6-5 Installing mortise locks: (a) Drilling rough opening; (b) Chiseling out opening.

If you're closing a door opening, cut a 2 x 4 to fit between the studs at the sides of the opening and nail it to the floor across the opening. Then cut a 2 x 4 the height of the opening, center it in the opening, and nail it at top and bottom (Fig. 6-6). Cut gypsum board panels to cover the opening on both sides of the wall and nail them in with annular-ring nails. The panels should be the same thickness as the old walls; if not, fur them out from the studs with lattice strips. Finish the joints around the panels with gypsum board joint compound and tape.

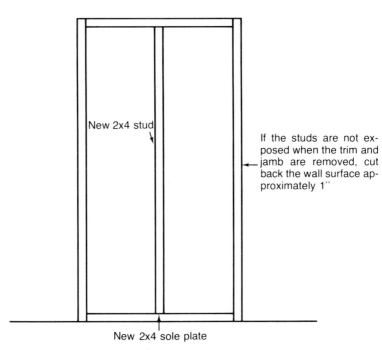

Fig. 6-6   Closing a door opening.

If you're closing a window opening, nail a 2 x 4 up and down the center of the opening. Install insulating batts. And close the opening on the inside with gypsum board. Closing it on the outside is more difficult because if you just fill in with the appropriate siding, the result will be an obvious, unsightly patch.

Fill the hole first with plywood sheathing. If the wall is surfaced in shingles or clapboards, you should then remove some of them on either side of the opening in an irregular pattern so that the joints in one course do not line up with those in another course. (See Chapter 16.) Then cover the opening with building paper and nail up the siding.

Masonry siding should be handled in the same way. But since this is a very difficult job even for a professional, it's a good reason not to close a window in a masonry wall.

OPENING A NEW DOOR IN A WALL...

To save work, make the door opening next to an existing stud. To put in a 24-in. door, measure from the side of the stud 30-3/8 in. to the side of the second stud

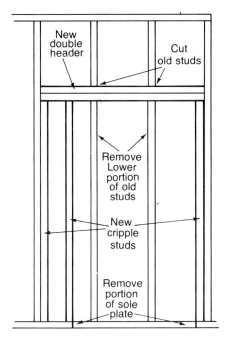

Fig. 6-7   Making a door opening.

removed. For a larger door, measure 46-3/8 in. to the side of the third stud removed. Cut out the wall surfaces on both sides of the partition between the studs and from the floor to the ceiling. Remove the studs within the opening (Fig. 6-7).

The rough door opening should equal the width of the door plus 2-1/2 in. to allow for the jambs and adjustments. The height of the rough opening should be the height of the door plus 1-3/4 in.

Out of 2 x 4s, cut three cripple studs equal to the height of the door plus 1/8 in. (A cripple stud is a stud of less than normal height.) Nail one to the stud on the right side of the opening, another to the stud on the left side of the opening.

Cut two lengths of 2 x 4 to the width of the opening above the cripple studs and nail them together flat side to flat side to form a double header. Set this on top of the cripple studs and nail it in.

Mark the width of the rough door opening on the header; drop a plumb line from that point to the sole plate, and mark the sole plate. Then nail the third cripple stud to the header and sole plate, and saw out the sole plate in the new door opening.

Cut one or two cripple studs to fit between the header and the top plate. The number required depends on the number of studs you removed when you opened the wall. Nail them above the header in the locations of the studs you removed. The rough opening is now completed.

Buy door jambs precut to accommodate the door you are hanging. They should be 1/16 in. wider than the total wall thickness. Fit the short head jamb into the notches in the side jambs and nail it.

Center the frame in the rough opening and make sure the head jamb is level. As shown in Fig. 6-8, cut a board—the spreader board—to fit snugly between the side jambs just below the head jamb. The ends must be perfectly square. Place this on the floor between the side jambs.

Determine how the door will swing. One side jamb then becomes the hinge jamb; the other, the latch jamb.

Split wood shingles into about 2-in. widths and push two of them between the hinge jamb and the adjacent cripple stud at the height of the head jamb. Insert one shingle from the front of the door opening, the other from the back, so that they form a flat wedge.

Insert shingles in the same way between the latch jamb and cripple stud. Then repeat the procedure on both sides of the frame just above the floor.

Check whether the hinge jamb is plumb, and adjust the bottom wedges until it is. This should automatically plumb the latch jamb, but check it anyway. Then drive finishing nails through the jambs and wedges into the cripple studs, but let the nailheads protrude.

Now install additional wedges behind the jambs, but be careful not to drive them in so hard that they warp the jambs. On the hinge jamb, install wedges 11 in. and 40 in. above the floor and 7 in. below the top jamb. On the latch jamb, install wedges 18, 36, and 58 in. above the floor. Drive two finishing nails through all the wedges, and after checking once more to see that the jambs are straight, countersink the heads. Saw off the shingles protruding from the front and back of the jambs.

Fit gypsum board panels around the side and top of the door and nail them to the studs. Then install the trim boards on both sides of the doorway. The edges should be set 5/16 in. back from the faces of the side and head jambs. The trim boards across the top are usually butted to the ends of the side pieces [Fig. 6-9(a)], but you can miter the joints if you prefer [Fig. 6-9(b)]. Nail the trim boards to the edges of the jambs and also to the cripple studs with finishing nails.

MAKING A DOORWAY
WIDER OR NARROWER...

Widen a doorway in the same way you install a new one.

To narrow a doorway, remove the trim, head jamb, and one of the side jambs—say, the latch jamb. Measure from the hinge jamb the width of the door

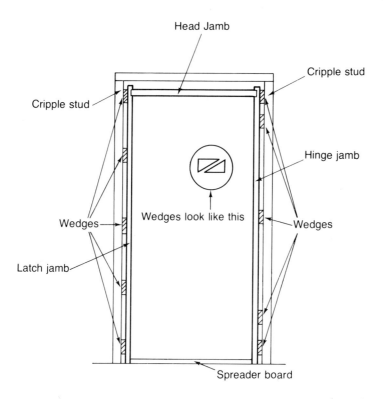

Fig. 6-8   Installing door jambs.

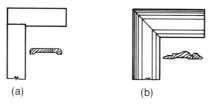

Fig. 6-9   Trimming around a door.

plus 1-3/4 in. Make the measurement just below the header, drop a plumb line to the floor, and mark the floor. Out of a 2 x 4 cut a piece to fit between the mark on the floor and the stud that had been next to the latch jamb. Nail it to the floor to become a sole plate.

Cut a cripple stud to fit between the top of the new sole plate and the header, and nail it into place. Then shorten the head jamb, reassemble it with the latch jamb, and rebuild the door frame.

OPENING A NEW
WINDOW OR CHANGING THE SIZE
OF A WINDOW...

The work is very similar to that just described but more complicated and demanding. Hire a carpenter.

7

A

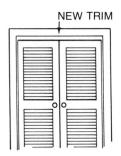

NEW TRIM

Closets

One of the newest money-making schemes now sweeping the country is to build huge warehouses and divide them into cubicles that are then rented to homeowners to store the things they can't wedge into their houses. The idea is a sad commentary on the lack of storage space available in contemporary homes. But whereas old houses have attics and basements in which you can store all manner of things, they generally have inadequate closets.

BUILDING A CLOSET...

Building a closet into a corner of a room doesn't usually enhance the appearance of the room, so you may prefer—at least in a large room—to build an enormous closet across an entire wall. But one is constructed like the other.

The first step is to build a stud wall according to the directions in Chapter 4. If space is at a premium, turn the studs so they parallel the wall. Thus, wall thickness is reduced to 2 in. Ideal depth for the closet if it's to be used for clothes is 24 in.

Cover the wall on the outside with 1/2-in. gypsum board or 1/4-in. plywood or hardboard paneling. Inside you can use 3/8-in. gypsum board since noise transmission is not a problem. The alternative, if the closet is to be used for mothproof storage, is to line it with cedar boards. These are tongue and grooved along the edges and at the ends. They are 3/8 in. thick, 2 to 4 in. wide, and 2 to 8 ft. long; and are sold in bundles covering about 30 sq. ft.

Install the cedar boards horizontally, one wall at a time from the floor up. Scribe the first boards carefully to the floor and secure them with two 1-1/2-in. finishing nails in each stud. Succeeding boards need only one nail per stud. Interlock the edges and ends carefully. The end joints need not be made over a stud.

For the neatest job, scribe the boards to fit corners. But if you want to save work, simply make the joints as tight as possible without scribing and cover them with quarter rounds.

To make the closet doubly effective in repelling moths, cover the floor and ceiling and back of the door with cedar boards and make the shelf of 1-in.-thick cedar.

The door in a cedar closet must be of the conventional hinged type to keep moths from getting through the cracks around the edges. Even so, weatherstripping is advisable.

HINGED DOORS   In ordinary closets, you have a wider choice of doors. The hinged door, in fact, should be used only if the closet is narrow enough so that you can reach the side walls without stepping part way into the closet. In wider closets, accessibility is greatly improved by making the door opening almost as wide as the closet and installing sliding, folding, or bi-fold doors.

SLIDING DOORS   The best sliding doors are designed to push back into pockets in the walls on either side of the door opening, but because they're expensive and rather difficult to install, bypass sliding doors are used instead. Hung in parallel tracks, these slide back and forth between the jambs in the opening. Because of this, you cannot get into more than half of the closet at one time—an obvious disadvantage. Another problem with sliding doors is that dust and moths can get around the edges into the closet. A third problem is that, because the doors are attached only along the top edges, there is nothing to prevent them from warping. But on the other side of the coin, the doors do not take up any space within the room.

Sliding doors are usually 1-3/8 in. thick, although 3/4-in. thicknesses are available. Standard widths are 24, 30, 36, and 48 in. If you're installing two doors, the width of the finished door opening between the jambs should be twice the width of a single door minus 1 in. The height of the opening should be the height of the door plus 1-1/2 in.

Make certain that the top jamb is level, and screw the track for the doors to it 7/8 in. back from the front edge (Fig. 7-1). Attach two hangers to the upper edge of each door near the corners. Drop the hanger wheels into the track by holding the doors upright and tilting them outward at the bottom. Then align the doors with the side jambs by adjusting the height of the hangers. (On the best hangers this is done by turning a cam.)

Screw the door guide to the floor at the center of the door opening. Then nail a trim board across the top of the opening to conceal the track.

FOLDING DOORS   Folding doors are made of narrow vertical strips hinged together at the sides. The doors are hung from a track at the top of the door opening. When closed, they have a corrugated look. When they are pushed open toward a side jamb, the strips fold together into a neat bundle.

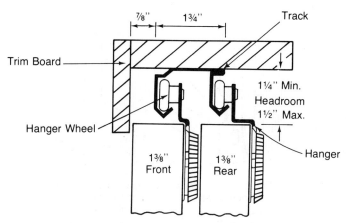

Fig. 7-1 Installing sliding doors.

Folding doors have gained popularity at the expense of sliding doors because they permit access to a much larger closet area, and they don't warp or jump the track. They do, however, take up a little more floor space—though nowhere nearly as much as hinged or bi-fold doors.

Standard folding doors close openings 28, 32, 36, or 48 in. wide and up to 80 in. high. If hung in pairs, you can double the width of the door opening.

To install the doors, screw the track to the center of the top jamb. Cut the door at the bottom so it clears the floor or rug by 1/2 in. Then insert the glides at the top of the door in the track, and screw the door to the jamb that you push it open against. Install a latch in the latch jamb. To conceal the track, nail a molding in front of it and paint it to match the trim.

BI-FOLD DOORS   Bi-fold doors are made of two wide, equal panels that are hinged together so that they fold like a hinge. If you haven't seen them in buildings, you've certainly run across them in telephone booths. The only difference is that in a phone booth the door folds inward whereas in a closet it folds outward. Thus, you must allow a certain amount of space in the room when they are open; but the space is equal to only half that required for a conventional hinged door.

A single bi-fold door (two panels) can be used in an opening 2 to 4 ft. wide. A pair of doors (four panels) can be used in openings 3 to 8 ft. wide. The doors' main advantage over sliding and folding doors is that they are much more attractive. You can buy them in styles to match almost all hinged interior doors.

Buy doors that have been equipped with hinges and pivots at the factory, and follow the manufacturer's installation directions. The procedure varies somewhat from brand to brand, but in general all you have to do is screw a track to the top jamb (Fig. 7-2). It should be positioned so that when the door is

(a) Pry off door stops. Fill hinge gains.

(b) Install top track and bottom pivot. Use plumb line.

NEW TRIM

(c) Insert pivot A in track. Lift door, insert bottom pivot.

(d) Trim may be added to hide top track if desired.

Fig. 7-2   Installing bi-fold doors.

closed, the front is aligned with the front edge of the jamb. Then drop a plumb line, and screw a bracket to the floor against the hinge jamb. Insert the pivots in the top and bottom edges of the door into the track and floor bracket. The door swings open and shut on these. Insert the roller guide on the latch side of the door into the track. Finally, install the door knob (there is no latch). The track can be concealed by the trim.

SHELVES AND RODS   In a clothes closet, the shelf is usually installed 68 in. above the floor of the room but may be installed as high as 74 in. If the closet floor is higher than the room floor, the space between it and the shelf should not be less than 62 in.

Shelves made of wood are usually 1 ft. deep. They must be supported not only at the ends but also along the back edge on 4-in. boards. The boards under the ends should be the full depth of the closet. Coat hooks are screwed to the boards just above the bottom edge.

The closet rod is installed 2 in. below the shelf and a fraction of an inch back from its front edge. Hang the rod, if made of wood, in plastic holders that are screwed to the shelf supports.

Prefabricated, prefinished steel shelves and rods are available. They can be adjusted to the width of the closet and are supported on special brackets.

BUILDING A LINEN CLOSET...

The perfect closet is difficult to design because you use it to store things of many different sizes. My best plan is for a closet no less than 26 in. wide and no more than 20 in. deep (both are inside dimensions). It has an 8-ft.-high hinged or bi-fold door that should be only a few inches narrower than the closet. Thus you can make maximum use of the space for storage and also have ready access to all parts of it.

Either at the top or bottom of the closet install two or three shelves 20 in. deep for pillows, blankets, quilts, and mattress pads. Space them 1 ft. apart. The rest of the shelves, to be used for sheets, pillowcases, and towels, should be 16 in. deep. They can be spaced 8 to 12 in. apart. The purpose of the shallow shelves is to make it easier to find and reach small articles stored at the back.

Hang 4-in.-deep shelves on the back of a hinged door, opposite the 16-inchers, and use them for washcloths, hand towels, toilet paper, and other very small articles. (Nothing can be hung on the back of a bi-fold door.)

BUILDING SHALLOW CABINETS OF PLYWOOD...

Deep closets of the type just discussed usually look best when their walls and doors match the others in the house. But for some reason, cabinets and closets no more than about 15 in. deep do not require this treatment. Even though they are clearly an addition to the house, they look very attractive when built of plywood; and because their walls are only 3/4 in. thick, they take up much less space than a conventional closet.

The uses for shallow cabinets are legion. They are ideal for supplementing bathroom storage, which is almost always grossly inadequate. They are ideal also for storing cleaning equipment, excess dishes, utensils, canned goods, jams and jellies, folding tables and chairs, toys, etc.

Cut the sides 1 in. shorter than the ceiling height and scribe the back edges to the wall at the points where they will touch. (This should be directly over studs.) Cut the top and bottom to fit between the sides, and assemble the four pieces on the floor with finishing nails. Install shelves as needed. Then nail 1 x 2-in. pine boards flat to the side and top edges, thus concealing the edges of the plywood and reducing the size of the door opening slightly (Fig. 7-3).

Tilt the cabinet into place and drive finishing nails through the sides diagonally into the studs. If this is impossible, install angle irons inside the cabinet, and secure them to the wall with screws, toggle bolts, or hollow-wall screw anchors. Then nail a cornice molding around the top of the cabinet to close the gap above it.

The closet door can be made of plywood, but 3/4-in. particleboard is better because it is more resistant to warping. If the opening is less than 2 ft. wide, a single door is all you need. Use two narrow doors for a wider opening: They will be less likely to warp, will not swing so far out into the room, and do not put such a load on the hinges.

Because screws do not hold well in the edge grain of particleboard or plywood, use wrap-around cabinet hinges that are screwed not only to the edge of the door but also to the back (Fig. 7-4). Install three hinges on a door more than 6 ft. high.

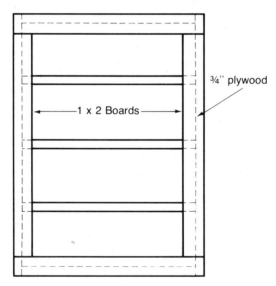

Fig. 7-3   Building storage cabinets.

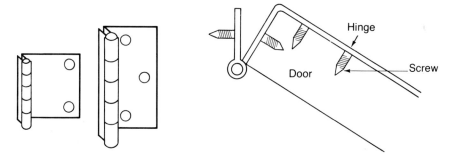

Fig. 7-4   Wrap-around hinges.

Fireplaces

It's one thing to remodel a fireplace—quite another to build a new one. Home improvement stores to the contrary, I don't think installation of fireplaces and chimneys is a proper occupation for most do-it-yourselfers.

This isn't to say, however, that you shouldn't put in a new fireplace if you think it will improve your house. Just make life easier for yourself by recognizing the facts of life.

INSTALLING A FIREPLACE...

If you want an honest-to-goodness fireplace and chimney, place them against an exterior wall so that the chimney will be entirely outside the house. Then get a mason who has a reputation for building fireplaces that work. Even for an expert it's difficult to build a fireplace and chimney inside an existing house because extensive reconstruction of the framework is required.

It's entirely possible, however, to build an attractive fireplace against an interior wall if you buy a packaged metal fireplace and chimney. These are so well insulated that they can be placed against wood flooring and framing with safety. You don't need sturdy footings. No masonry is used. The fireplace is simply set on the floor against the wall or in a corner. The chimney is then dropped down through holes in the roof and ceiling and connected to the fireplace. Finally, the whole thing is built in with gypsum board, plywood, or what have you so that only the fireplace breast, opening, and hearth are exposed.

Another type of inside fireplace you can put in is a free-standing Franklin stove or one of its modern relatives. It must be placed on a fireproof base at least 3 ft. out from a combustible wall, and connected by a metal flue pipe into an insulated chimney like that used for a packaged fireplace.

Packaged and free-standing fireplaces are the types you're supposed to be able to put in yourself—and there's no doubt that they are a lot easier to install than a masonry fireplace. But as I said in the beginning, don't try. Hire a carpenter to make at least the basic installation.

159

REMODELING A FIREPLACE...

Remodeling a fireplace either to change its appearance or to improve its operation is well within the average homeowner's competence, however.

MAKING A MANTEL   This is a very simple thing to do but it calls for a little
SHELF DEEPER   experimentation to determine the best thickness of
the new shelf and how it should be joined to the old shelf.

Basically all you have to do is cut a knot-free white pine board 1 to 2 in. wider and 2 to 4 in. longer than the existing shelf, and nail it on top. If you want a heavy-looking shelf, use a 1-1/4-in.-thick board instead of a 1-in. board. Or for an even thicker shelf, nail 1 x 1- or 1 x 2-in. boards to the bottom of the new shelf around the front and ends. Miter the joints at the corners, and fill the cracks between the shelf and the strips with spackle.

If the present shelf has square edges, the installation usually looks better if the edges are covered with small cove moldings bearing against the bottom of the new shelf.

REPLACING A MANTEL   Mantels are appliqués without structural value. They
are simply applied around the edges of the fireplace breast and over the adjacent walls after the walls are completed. For this reason, they are easy to rip out and replace. Take a hammer and have at it.

Unless you feel competent to design a new mantel, use one of the numerous stock units on the market. Order the size that fits your fireplace. In doing this, bear in mind that all woodwork must be at least 3-1/2 in. from the edges of the fireplace opening; and for appearance's sake, most mantels are set 6 in. or more from the edges of the opening. The mantel shelf must be 1 ft. above the top of the opening. This much space is also required for any woodwork that projects more than 1-1/2 in. out over the opening.

Stock mantels come knocked down but are easily assembled with finishing nails according to the accompanying plans or picture.

RESURFACING A   An old fireplace breast faced with ugly bricks can
FIREPLACE   often be greatly improved if it is resurfaced in some
other way. To do this, remove the mantel first.

If the bricks are unfinished, wash them thoroughly to remove dirt and stains; if they're painted, take off as much of the paint as possible with an electric or paste-type paint remover. Then to provide a smooth surface, trowel a thin layer of latex cement over the bricks.

The easiest new finish is epoxy paint. This produces a glossy, almost tile-like surface which is colorful, durable, washable, and easy to redo if it wears out.

Ceramic tiles are an excellent choice. Use mosaics or individual tiles. The latter are available in an amazing range of colors, patterns, textures, and shapes; however, if the width of the fireplace opening is not exactly divisible by the width of an individual tile, some of the tiles will have to be trimmed, and this will flaw the layout. Cutting of mosaics is less noticeable because the tiles are so small.

Stick the tiles to the fireplace breast with adhesive recommended by the tile dealer. For how to install tiles, see Chapter 10. Start the installation at the top of the fireplace opening and work up to where the mantel should be. Then work down to the floor along the sides of the opening. When replacing the mantel, lap the inner edges over the tiles. The outer edges must be furred out with wood strips the thickness of the tiles.

Slate and marble are favorite materials for surfacing traditional fireplaces. They are available in the form of rather big tiles. They are also available in three large pieces that go around the sides and top of the opening. Both types are installed with silicone rubber adhesive that is applied with a notched spreader. Press the stones firmly into this. It's a good idea to brace large pieces until the adhesive sets. Joints between all pieces should be very snug, and are not grouted.

IMPROVING
FIREPLACE DRAW

This starts out as a cleaning and repair job. Clean the damper with a wire brush and make sure it opens and closes easily. If it's broken, have it replaced. Clean the smoke shelf above the damper with a wire brush. Have a chimney sweep clean the chimney. If these efforts don't correct conditions, there are two things which can be done.

First, if the top of the chimney extends less than 2 ft. above the peak of a pitched roof or less then 3 ft. above a flat roof, or if it is surrounded by trees or buildings, it should be capped. This doesn't require skill, but it does require strength, so you should attempt it only if the roof is flat enough to work on safely. Lay up four columns of bricks on top of the chimney at the four corners. Stick the bricks together with a mortar made of 1 part portland cement, 1 part hydrated lime, and 6 parts sand. Over the bricks lay a thin flagstone slab (Fig. 8-1). This should be high enough above the chimney top so that the four openings under it have a total area equal to or greater than the area of the flue opening. If a chimney has more than one flue, a solid wall of brick, called a withe, should separate each from the other.

The second way to make a fireplace draw better and smoke less—regardless of whether the chimney is capped—is to reduce the size of the opening. Get a good fire going. Then lay a long, wide board across the fireplace breast and gradually lower it down over the opening until smoke stops escaping into the room. Measure the distance from the bottom edge of the board to the top of the opening. Then raise the bottom of the firebox with bricks equal to this measurement.

For a trial, lay in any bricks without mortar. If this works, make a permanent installation with firebricks laid in a mortar called fire clay. (Both materials are available from a masonry supplies outlet.)

Other ways to reduce the size of a fireplace opening are to lay bricks up one or both sides or to have a metal hood made to fit across the top of the opening.

If you have a smoky fireplace that is open on two or three sides—not just one—call in an expert and cross your fingers.

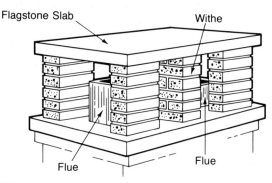

Fig. 8-1   Building a chimney cap.

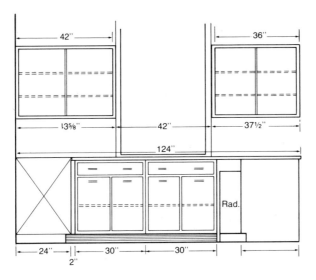

Kitchens

When George and Alma Tatum renovated the Victorian house they bought five years ago, they tore out what had been the kitchen and made it into a dining room, and built a brand new kitchen in the old maid's room. Thus, in one fell swoop they enlarged their living area and converted an anachronistic 1890 floor plan into a functional 1970 plan. And they got an attractive, workable kitchen to boot.

Although it falls under the heading of "unusual", moving a kitchen is sometimes a very good idea; and you should not overlook it simply because it seems like a major undertaking. The fact is that, if you are going to redo a kitchen completely anyway, moving it to another location doesn't complicate matters very much. You have to cap the piping to the sink and run in new piping. And you may have to disconnect some of the old appliance wiring and run in new wiring. But that's about it.

However, there is no point in laying too much stress on kitchen relocation because relatively few houses require it or are adapted to it. But remodeling the kitchen in its present location—despite the hundreds of magazine articles on the subject in the last 30 years, I venture to say that most existing houses (and those who live in them) would still benefit enormously by such work.

What has held things back?

Money is one thing, of course. To remodel a whole kitchen costs several thousands of dollars; and while it's possible to ease the pain by doing a step-by-step remodeling over a period of years, it's not as simple as it sounds because the first improvement immediately whets the appetite for the improvements to come. Furthermore, in this period of soaring prices, the cost of the kitchen will turn out to be more than if you redid it all at once.

The other reason why many kitchens have not been remodeled is that their owners believe themselves incapable of visualizing what changes should and can be made. This attitude, however, is ridiculous.

For one thing, if you don't trust yourself, you can always ask a kitchen dealer or other kitchen planner to give you his ideas. And I mean "give": You don't have to pay a cent until you hire the man to go to work.

165

But even more to the point: Kitchen planning simply is not all that difficult. Most of the people who claim to be experts don't know any more about it than you do. And in one sense, they don't know anywhere nearly as much because they don't know how you use a kitchen, what you need and don't need in it, etc.

THE FIRST STEP IN
PLANNING YOUR KITCHEN...

A few basic questions must be answered before anything else is done:

How do you use a kitchen?

Is it used strictly for preparing family meals and occasional parties? Or do you also put up lots of food? Do you do considerable large-scale entertaining? Do you sit around in the kitchen and talk or watch TV? All such things have an effect on the size, layout, and decoration of the room.

Do you have physical characteristics, limitations, or habits that affect kitchen design?

If you're very tall, for instance, you ought to raise the counters, range, and sink a few inches higher than they are normally installed. If you're physically handicapped, you might reduce the size of the work area. If you like to buy unusual foods in anticipation of use, you need extra storage space. And so on.

Who uses the kitchen and when?

This can also influence the size and arrangement. In some families, two or even three people cook and wash up at the same time. In other families, different people cook in shifts.

What is to be stored in the kitchen?

This requires making a pretty complete list. And don't forget the nonkitchen things that often get stored there—vases, liquor, dog food, etc.

Which appliances do you want and in which types and sizes?

Even if you know this already, you should take a look in a store to see what new appliances are on the market. But try not to commit yourself too definitely to a particular design because it may interfere with the development of the kitchen plan. In most appliances there are several good alternative designs to choose from.

BASIC
PLANNING PRECEPTS...

The work area of a kitchen is the area in which you cook and wash up afterwards. It incorporates the range, refrigerator, and sink plus counter space and cabinets for storage. In many houses the kitchen is so small that the whole thing is work area. In large kitchens, however, the work area is frequently separated in some way from the rest of the room.

Whatever the size or arrangement of a kitchen, the work area is, of course, the critical area from the planning standpoint. This doesn't mean that you should plan it without reference to whatever else the room is used for, because they are interdependent. But the work area should get priority.

When you sit down to plan it, don't let yourself be influenced by whatever you have read or heard about U-shaped kitchens, L-shaped kitchens, two-wall kitchens, one-wall kitchens, island kitchens, etc. Years ago, kitchen planners used to feel that if a kitchen was to be any good, it had to fall into one of these molds. But that isn't necessarily true, and it's a mistake to go at kitchen planning with a preconceived idea of the shape your kitchen area should take. On the contrary, your plan should be dictated by the following facts:

1 • The work area should be small enough for efficient, relatively effortless work; but at the same time it must be large enough to provide ample counter space and storage and to permit the occupants of the kitchen to move around easily, without bumping into things and one another. A healthy man or woman will be happier in a kitchen work area that is too large than in one that's too small.

2 • Kitchen work is easier and less messy if the counter is continuous from the range to the sink to the refrigerator.

3 • Maximum efficiency is gained when the range, sink, and refrigerator are arranged in a triangle with 4 to 6 ft. between each appliance.

4 • Because the sink is the hub of most kitchen activities, it is best placed between the range and refrigerator in the continuous run of

counter. The range, however, may occupy center position—but not the refrigerator, because it breaks the counter space and stops the flow of work.

5 • Of the three main appliances, the range should be closest to the dining room or wherever most meals are eaten; the refrigerator should be closest to the door through which you carry in groceries.

6 • When appliances are installed on parallel walls, the floor space between them has to be at least 42 in. wide to permit you to open appliance and cabinet doors and look inside. A 48- to 60-in. space is better.

7 • Traffic through the work area is a nuisance as well as a possible hazard. It should be rerouted around the work area by relocating both the back door into the kitchen and the door from the kitchen to other parts of the house. If this is impossible, the work area should be laid out or located so that the traffic does not pass right through the center of it.

PLANNING DETAILS
FOR THE WORK AREA...

SINKS AND APPLIANCES   The following items are generally considered essential in an up-to-date kitchen, and their size and location should be considered carefully in your new kitchen plan.

Sinks   The average single-bowl sink occupies a cabinet 24 to 30 in. wide. For a double-bowl sink, figure 30 to 36 in. No matter how large the sink or how many bowls it has, provide 30 in. of counter space on both sides.

There is no rule that a sink must be placed under a window. You can use it just as easily on an inside wall, and in that location it may make the kitchen more functional. Hang a wall cabinet 24 in. above it.

If you install a sink in the corner of an L-shaped counter, use a double-bowl corner model that "wraps around" the corner.

The value of a double-bowl sink is negated when there's a dishwasher next to it. But in a large kitchen, a second single-bowl sink outside the work area will prove to be a great convenience because it allows you to divide the dishwashing job between the two sinks (and possibly between two people). You also have a separate sink for flower arranging, drink mixing, preparing meals for pets, etc.

In the immediate vicinity of the sink, make provision for storing a garbage can, dishwashing supplies, towels and paper towels, everyday china and glasses, and other utensils and supplies normally used at the sink.

Ranges   The average width of a range is 20 to 40 in.; a built-in
                                      oven, 24 to 30 in.; a built-in cooktop, 22 to 33 in.

When locating a range, consider how you can best carry off the smoke, water vapor, and grease arising from it. In an old house, this is most easily done by placing the range against an outside wall—but there are other possibilities. See "Ventilating the Kitchen" below.

Remember:

1 • Never place a range or built-in cooktop at the open end of a wall counter, peninsula, or island where people passing by may brush hot pots on to the floor.

2 • Never place a range or cooktop under a window with curtains that may catch fire.

3 • Never place the burners of a range or cooktop close to a side wall: Working space is confined and there is danger of fire.

If you have a built-in cooktop or range with burners centered in the top, provide 18 in. of counter space on each side of the unit. But if you have a range with burners on one side, provide 24 in. of counter space on that side and 12 in. on the other side. Ideally, one section of the counter surface should be heat-proof.

Provide 18 in. of counter space on either side of a built-in oven.

A built-in oven must be installed at one end of the work area or the other—never in the middle where it would interrupt the flow of work.

Don't sacrifice counter space for a built-in oven in a small kitchen. A built-in's principal advantage—the fact that you don't have to stoop to see what's cooking in it—can also be had by installing a free-standing range with eye-level oven—and you don't lose counter space.

Hang wall cabinets no less than 30 in. above a counter-height range or built-in cooktop.

Provide cabinet space near the range for skillets, roasting pans, griddle, large spoons and forks, paper towels, pot holders, seasonings, etc.

Refrigerators   The average refrigerator is 27 to 36 in. wide, but you
                                      must allow an additional 3 in. of space so that it can
                                      be serviced.

Place the refrigerator so that the door opens away from the work area; otherwise, you must walk around the door to get into the refrigerator. If this is impossible, buy a refrigerator with a door that swings the other way. Both right- and left-hand-door models are on the market.

If a counter extends into a corner, a refrigerator must not be placed next to it at right angles because this creates a completely useless pocket. Extend the counter around the corner at least 1 ft. (Fig. 9-1).

Install a counter 18 to 24 in. wide on the latch side of the refrigerator.

A wall cabinet can be installed within 1/2 in. of the top of a refrigerator if the heat is exhausted from the front of the box; but if the heat is exhausted from the back of the refrigerator, allow at least 2 in. between the box and a cabinet.

Unless the refrigerator is in an isolated location, most people prepare most foods close to it. In that situation, you should provide nearby storage for canned and packaged foods, mixing bowls, casseroles, cake pans, can opener, mixer, cooking knives, forks and spoons, etc.

Dishwashers   All dishwashers are 24 in. wide. This means that if you don't plan to install one immediately, you can still make provision for it by putting in a 24-in. base cabinet for the time being.

Install a dishwasher next to the sink so they can share the same piping and drain. If you normally hold dishes in your left hand and scrub with your right, put the dishwasher on the left side of the sink. Reverse the arrangement if you work in the opposite way.

Never place a dishwasher less than 18 in. from a side wall or a corner in a counter. You need at least this much space if two people are to use the dishwasher at one time. You also need this space to permit drawers or cabinets in an adjacent counter to be opened while the dishwasher is open.

If you have two single-bowl sinks, consider placing the dishwasher next to the sink outside the kitchen work area. Thus, you can devote the work area entirely to basic cooking operations. Except for washing of utensils, all dishwashing and dish storage can be outside the work area.

Satisfactory operation of a dishwasher depends on having an adequate supply of unusually hot water. Your water heater should be set at not less than 140°—and ideally it whould be set at 160°. If this is too hot for someone's tender skin, you must take steps to temper the water in the bathrooms.

Garbage disposers   Garbage disposers add relatively little to the cost of a kitchen but do a great deal to save time and work when you're preparing meals and washing dishes. They also eliminate waste before it turns into garbage.

With a few exceptions, disposers are permitted in all American communities with sewer systems. They can also be used in homes with septic systems but not cesspools; however, your community may require you to increase the size of your septic tank.

A disposer can be installed in the drain of any modern sink. If you have two separate sinks, you must decide which will be used more for disposal of wastes. It's possible that you should have a disposer in both.

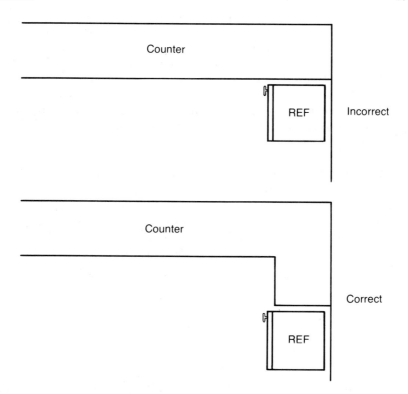

Fig. 9-1   Positioning the refrigerator.

Compactors   A compactor is a new electrical appliance that compresses household wastes into a dense, plastic-wrapped block that is then carried off to the town dump. It eliminates handling and storage of disagreeable garbage, reduces the number of garbage collections, and makes for much neater collections. In contrast to a garbage disposer, it is a shade more troublesome to use and does not remove waste so swiftly from the house. On the other hand, it can be used for all kinds of waste, including fabrics, metals, and glass—not just food.

Compactors are 15 in. wide and fit under the kitchen counter. They are usually placed next to the sink, though this is not essential.

KITCHEN STORAGE   The standard depth of base cabinets—as well as sinks, dishwashers, ranges, and compactors—is 24 in. They are topped with counters 25 in. deep and 36 in. above the floor. Cabinet widths range upward from 12 in. by increments of 3 in. to a maximum of 60 in.

Wall cabinets are made in the same widths but are only 12 in. deep. Those used over counters are 30 to 36 in. high. The recommended space between the bottom of a wall cabinet and the counter is 18 in.; but if necessary, this can be decreased to as little as 12 in. Wall cabinets used over ranges and sinks are usually 24 in. high, and those over refrigerators and freezers are 15 or 18 in. high. The tops of such short cabinets should, of course, be aligned with the tops of full-length cabinets.

The minimum storage space in a kitchen work area should be 6 running feet of base cabinets and 12 running feet of wall cabinets at least 30 in. high. Cabinets less than 30 in. high, cabinets under sinks, and open shelves do not count.

When possible, use one large wall cabinet rather than two or three small ones totaling the same width because they cost less and provide less chopped-up shelf space. Adjustable shelves, in effect, increase the capacity of the cabinets.

Base cabinets with drawers cost more than those with shelves but are much easier to see and reach into. As a practical matter, however, you need both.

When cabinets extend around an inside corner, there are three things you can do to avoid loss of valuable storage space right in the corner:

1 • Install cabinets with revolving shelves. But the cost is high.

2 • Set a shelf cabinet all the way into the corner against one wall, and butt a shelf or drawer cabinet up against it on the adjacent wall [Fig. 9-2(a)]. This creates a hard-to-get-into pocket, but it's useful for storing items you don't use often.

3 • Set a drawer or shelf cabinet in the corner, but turn it around so that is opens into an adjoining room or area outside the kitchen work area [Fig. 9-2(b)].

Many special cabinets are on the market. For instance, there are tray cabinets, linen cabinets with closely spaced sliding shelves, little spacemaker cabinets that fit under wall cabinets, base and wall cabinets with doors on both sides for use in a peninsula between the kitchen work area and an eating area. But if your primary need is for lots and lots of storage space, there is nothing better than a simple floor-to-ceiling cabinet 12 in. deep. Use several side by side to create a storage wall close to but not right in the work area.

FILLER STRIPS   These belong in the foregoing discussion of cabinets, but I cover them separately because I want to focus attention on them.

Filler strips—or simply fillers—are strips of wood or metal finished to match the cabinets. Some are made for use with base cabinets, others for use with wall cabinets. They range from 1 to 3 in. in width. If the cabinets are metal, the strips are separate from the cabinets. But in the case of wood or plastic-surfaced cabinets, the strips are sometimes separate and sometimes made a part of the cabinet. In the latter case, they are known as extended stiles.

The strips have three purposes:

1 • To piece out a row of cabinets to fill a wall space. For example, if a wall is 97 in. long, a 1-in. filler is inserted in the row of cabinets somewhere.

2 • To permit fitting a cabinet tight to a crooked or slanting wall. In this case, the filler is placed between the cabinet and wall and is scribed to the wall.

3 • To permit opening drawers and doors of cabinets installed in an inside corner. This kind of strip is rarely needed if drawer and door fronts are narrower than the cabinet frames. But if drawer and door fronts are the same width as the cabinets, they cannot be opened unless they are set an inch or two out from the corner. Hence the need for a corner filler strip, which is shaped like a corner.

COUNTERS   The counter space called for next to appliances may
                                       be reduced a little if one space serves two appliances.
For example, if there is a continuous counter between the sink and the latch side

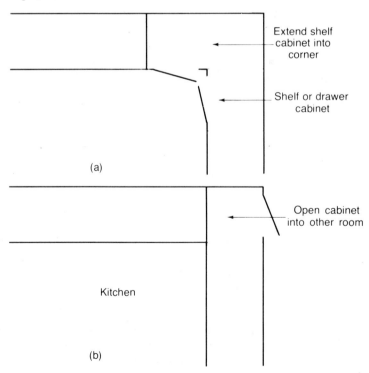

Extend shelf
cabinet into
corner

Shelf or drawer
cabinet

(a)

Open cabinet
into other room

Kitchen

(b)

Fig. 9-2   Providing maximum utilization of storage areas.

of a refrigerator, it need not be a full 54 in. long. But since one can almost always make good use of more counter space, this should not be cut down more than about 6 in.

Backsplashes that protect the walls and keep crumbs and liquids from falling down behind counters and cabinets are advisable on all counters in the work area and in any other part of the kitchen where work is done. They are not necessary, however, in storage areas. Normal backsplash height is 4 in., but in many kitchens the entire wall from the counter to the bottom of the wall cabinets is covered.

The best all-purpose countertop material is laminated plastic. Use a patterned material rather than a solid to hide scratches. Ceramic tile is more durable and heatproof—but noisier. It also chips glassware and is extremely difficult to keep clean. Small sections of hard maple can be set into any counter as cutting blocks, but the scratches in the surface harbor dangerous bacteria.

VENTILATION   The only type of fan you should use in a kitchen is one that is ducted to the outdoors so that it can carry away smoke, grease, odors, and water vapor. Since nonducted fans do not remove water vapor and have small effect on odors, you should use them only if ducting is absolutely impossible.

Ducted hood fans that hang directly over a range or built-in cooktop are a little more efficient than nonhooded fans—but only if the bottom of the hood is no more than 30 in. above the burners and covers almost the entire cooking surface. If you can hang a hood lower than 30 in., so much the better; but don't hang it so low that you can't see into a tall pot on the back burner. And never install a hood with sharp or toothed edges.

If you use a ducted fan without a hood, the best location for it is in the wall behind the range and 18 to 24 in. above the cooking surface. Second choice is in the ceiling centered over the range.

Whichever type of ventilating fan you put in, be sure to buy the largest size available. Size is rated in cubic feet per minute (CFM).

Remember also that a fan must not have a duct that is more than 10 ft. long or has more than one bend. If the duct does not meet these requirements, try to relocate the range. Or if you live in a one-story house, try running the duct through the roof rather than an outside wall. Or if worse comes to worst, install a nonducted hood fan over the range and build a ducted fan into an outside wall.

HEATING AND COOLING   Radiators and registers often interfere with kitchen planning—but don't give up hope. After you work out a tentative plan, ask a heating expert whether they can be moved. If not, the easiest solution is to install electric heating or—if you also need cooling—a heat-pump room conditioner. (See Chapter 13.)

WIRING   You probably will need at least one or two new
                    wiring circuits in a new kitchen, but you cannot
determine the full extent of the work that must be done without consulting an
electrical contractor. To give you some idea of what you'll need, however, here
are the types of circuits required for kitchen appliances and lighting:

1 • One 15-amp., 120-volt circuit for the lights, ventilating fan, and
    clock. (The same circuit may also be capable of supplying power to
    lights in other rooms.)

2 • Two 20-amp., 120-volt appliance circuits for the convenience outlets
    into which you plug the toaster, mixer, and other small appliances.
    The circuits will also serve a small refrigerator, gas range, and
    free-standing ice-maker. In addition, they can be used to serve a gas
    dryer in the laundry and small appliance outlets in the laundry
    and/or dining room.

3 • One 20-amp., 120-volt circuit for a combination refrigerator-freezer.

4 • One 20-amp., 120-volt circuit for a dishwasher and garbage disposer
    or compactor.

5 • One 50-amp., 240-volt circuit for an electric range.

6 • One 20-amp., 120-volt circuit for a food freezer.

7 • One 20-amp., 120-volt circuit for a washing machine.

8 • One 30-amp., 240-volt circuit for an electric clothes dryer.

Appliance outlets should be installed at 4-ft. intervals above all counters in
the work area.

LIGHTING   For instructions on installing lighting fixtures of
                    various types, see Chapter 12.
    Large windows also help to light the kitchen, but if they face south or
west, the room will get unbearably hot on sunny days. And if the view is poor or
if the glass takes up space that might better be used for wall cabinets, what have
you gained?
    If you do put in new windows, select them with care. Sliding windows or
casements are better over counters than double-hung windows because they are
much easier to open. In a cold climate, put in windows with double-pane
insulating glass so they won't fog up when you are cooking or doing dishes.

DOORS   Don't hesitate to move doors if they make it
                    impossible to develop a perfect kitchen plan by
routing traffic through the work area or preventing best utilization of available
space. A fairly common problem is a door that is placed so deep in a corner that

you cannot extend a counter into the corner. To correct this, try to move the door out of the corner at least 25 in.

FLOORING The carpet industry to the contrary, the only flooring to use in a kitchen is one on which you can see spills and dirt and which is easy to clean. Vinyl and linoleum are the best. Vinyl-asbestos and asphalt tile are several notches below because they don't wear as well and are less resilient. Other possibilities are ceramic tile, brick, flagstones, and slate (provided the last three are treated with a penetrating masonry sealer). They last forever but are much harder underfoot.

WALL COVERINGS Above all else, these must be washable. Semi-gloss alkyd enamel and vinyl wall coverings are top choices because they meet all requirements and are low in cost. But you should also look into hardboard paneling.

If you want the rich, warm beauty of real wood paneling, go ahead and put it in. But be sure to protect the wood and make it washable by applying a coat of water-white shellac followed by a coat or two of varnish that is rubbed down with steel wool to reduce the gloss.

PLANNING THE KITCHEN
OUTSIDE THE WORK AREA...

To repeat: For efficient, easy kitchen work, the work area must be separate from the rest of the kitchen—assuming that the kitchen is large enough to have a "rest". This doesn't mean there must be a physical barrier between the two. But there has to be an obvious separation of some kind.

Our former kitchen exemplified both kinds of separation. It was a big L-shaped room divided into three areas. The work area in the corner of the L was physically divided from the eating area by a peninsula that bisected the L's horizontal line and incorporated the range. The refrigerator positioned about half way up the vertical line separated the work area from a big storage area which contained the dishwasher, a second sink, and a built-in oven. There was no real separation between the work area and the storage area, but it was implied by the bulk of the refrigerator, which divided an otherwise continuous counter into two parts.

How you use the kitchen outside the work area depends on the size and shape of the room, the layout of the work area, and, of course, what you want to do.

OVERFLOW STORAGE Work-area storage should be limited to the items you use frequently. Extra china and glassware, vases, little-used utensils and small appliances, jams, jellies, and pickles, pet food, cleaning supplies, etc., should be stored outside the work area. Foods such as cookies and soft drinks that are consumed between meals should also be stored here.

Although many of these items can be stored in a floor-to-ceiling storage wall like that mentioned before, counter space in the storage area is essential. It needn't be 25 in. deep, however. An arrangement I have found extremely good is this: For base cabinets use 30-in.-high wall cabinets set on top of a board framework to create a toespace. If you use stock wall cabinets, turn them upside down so that the handles are at the top. Build a 13-in.-deep counter on top of the cabinets. It does not require a backsplash. Then hang more wall cabinets 15 to 18 in. above the counter.

A SECOND SINK
OR SECOND RANGE
I cannot overemphasize the value of a second sink installed with or without a dishwasher and/or disposer outside the work area. In our house we couldn't live without it.

I feel the same way about a second range. In our previous house this was only a built-in oven; but in our present house we have gone all out. Both Elizabeth and I like to cook, and when our daughters come for a visit, everyone gets into the act. So to keep everyone happy and out of everyone else's hair, we have a four-burner range with a single large oven in the work area and a three-burner apartment-house range with a small oven outside the work area close to our second sink.

If you put in either a second sink or a second range or both, be sure to provide counter space alongside. But it need not be as wide as that provided in the work area.

FREEZER
A freezer can be located anywhere outside the work area—but the closer, the better. This is particularly true if you are in and out of it frequently. If you open it only occasionally, there's no reason why it should be in the kitchen at all.

Upright freezers average 32 in. in width; chests run 46 to 60 in. In both cases, you should allow an additional 3 in. for servicing. Hang 15- or 18-in.-high wall cabinets over both.

Since most uprights have right-hand-hinged doors, they should be installed in a corner where the door can swing back against the wall to the right. Left-hand-door models are available, however.

A minor problem with many chest freezers is that they are a little over 37 in. high, which means they project above the kitchen counters slightly and interfere with the work flow.

Whichever type of freezer you install, be sure there is a counter close by or, better still, immediately adjacent. Make it as wide as possible, because when you start hunting around in a freezer for something or when you defrost the freezer, you need a great deal of space to stack the contents.

LAUNDRY   Many women dislike doing the wash in the kitchen. But if you don't share this feeling and if you don't use the kitchen for eating and television viewing, the area outside the work area is a good place to install the washer and dryer. For one thing, it's on the first floor, so there's no trudging to the basement. For another thing, a washer needs the same kind of hot water as a dishwasher; and it's easier to assure that both are well supplied if they are close together and share the same run of insulated pipe from the water heater.

But a laundry requires quite a lot of space. Both automatic washers and dryers are 30 in. wide, and you must allow a little extra for servicing. A deep laundry tub or simply an ordinary sink is essential. This adds another 24 in., unless you use the second sink I have talked so much about for laundering operations, too. Finally, you really should have a 24-in.-wide counter for sorting and folding laundry. (Put a 24-in. base cabinet underneath for laundry supplies.)

In other words, the minimum total space required for a clothes-washing-drying area is 9 ft. long by about 7 ft. deep (measuring from the back of the appliances) to allow for ironing.

Hang standard-height wall cabinets over the appliances. The dryer must be placed so that it is within 20 ft. of an exterior wall or roof so it can be vented to the outdoors by a 4-in. metal or plastic vent pipe.

BARBECUES   Prefabricated barbecues that are built into a 36-in.-high, 25-in.-deep counter require 21 to 33 in. of space along the wall. In addition, you should provide 24 in. of heatproof counter space on at least one side.

The entire cooking surface must be covered with a hood incorporating a *commercial* exhaust fan. (Ordinary residential fans do *not* have the capacity to carry off the dense smoke, heat, grease, and carbon monoxide fumes given off in barbecuing operations.) The duct must be as short and straight as possible.

EATING AREA   Good locations for an eating area in the kitchen include—but are not limited to—the following: on the back side of a peninsula in which the range is installed; at the open end of a U-shaped work area; diagonally opposite the corner of an L-shaped work area.

The minimum space required is as follows:

- *Bar*: 18 in. deep. Width per person: 24 in.
- *Rectangular table for three or four persons*: 30 x 36 in.
- *Rectangular table for six*: 42 x 60 in.

- *Square table for six to eight*: 48 x 48 in.
- *Round table for four*: 31-37 in. diameter. For each additional person, increase the maximum diameter 6 in. Thus, for five people you need a table 38-45 in. in diameter; for eight people, 61-68 in. in diameter.
- *Chairs, whether at a table or a bar*: Provide 24 in. from the table edge to the back of the chair. (This allows you to push back the chair to get out of it.)
- *Bar stools*: Allow 20 in. from edge of bar to the back of the stool.

PLANNING DESK   This can be located anywhere outside the kitchen work area; and it is the one and only "extra" that can be installed in the work area. The reason for this is that it is used only by one person, who obviously can't get in his own way. But you should put it in the work area only if the desk is completely usable as counter space; if the space beneath it is not needed for base storage; and if the chair or stool can be pushed all the way under the desk when not in use.

AND SO FORTH   The descriptive listing above obviously does not exhaust all the possible ways of using the space outside the kitchen work area. In fact, one of the favorite uses today requires more space than anything discussed. Call it the "family living area" for lack of a better name. It's just a big area where the entire family sits around and talks and watches television and toasts marshmallows in the fireplace and so on. Since it's all very much an individual family matter, I have no suggestions for how it should be laid out, just as long as it is well separated—physically separated—from the work area.

PLANNING A NEW KITCHEN...

The first step is to measure the kitchen you already have. This must be done very accurately and thoroughly. I repeat: *accurately* and *thoroughly*. Follow these directions to the letter. If you don't, you cannot possibly develop a new kitchen plan.

Use a 6-ft. folding rule. You're less likely to make mistakes with it than with a steel tape rule. Draw the plan with a hard, sharp pencil on graph paper with four squares to the inch. Each square represents 3 in. Use a ruler so your lines will be stright.

1 • Check whether the corners of the room are 90°. You can use a carpenter's framing square, but the most accurate method is to

measure 3 ft. from the corner along one wall and make a mark; measure 4 ft. along the adjacent wall and make a mark; then measure the distance between marks. If it's 5 ft., the corner is square. If it's more than 5 ft., the angle is more then 90°—but this probably won't cause any trouble. But if the distance is less than 5 ft., you may have problems.

2 • Measure the overall length of each wall—corner to corner—and outline a plan of the room on graph paper. For greatest accuracy, make the measurements above the baseboards.

If any of the corners is less than 90°, make a second measurement 25 in. out from the wall, and use the shorter of the two measurements in making your plan.

3 • Measure the length of each section of each wall: from a corner to the edge of the trim around a door, the width of the door including the trim on both sides, from the door trim to the edge of the trim around the window, etc. Indicate all measurements on your plan. They should add up to the same figure as the overall wall measurement. If they don't, remeasure the wall.

4 • Measure the width of the trim around doors and windows and indicate it on the plan.

5 • Go around the room again and determine the location of all radiators and registers, thermostats, pipes, drains, lights, switches, outlets, etc., and mark them on the plan. Also find and mark the location of any built-in objects that hang from the ceiling or stick up from the floor in the middle of the room: for example, a ceiling fixture, floor register, or pipe that isn't concealed in the walls.

6 • Measure the ceiling height and note it on the plan somewhere.

7 • From the floor upward measure the heights of the door and window openings, lights, switches, outlets, registers, ventilating fans, etc. Note the figures in the margins of the plan.

8 • If your plan is pretty messy, draw a new one.

You're now ready to get on with the actual planning of a new kitchen.

9 • Lay a sheet of tracing paper over the plan and rough in a new kitchen plan. You don't have to use a ruler or draw perfectly straight lines, but try to be reasonably accurate about the size of all kitchen components.

Start with the kitchen work area and locate the sink, dishwasher, range, and refrigerator. Then draw in the counters. Then draw in the wall cabinets with dotted lines. Then go on to whatever you want outside the work area.

10 • Study the completed plan. Try to put yourself right into it to see whether it will work.

11 • Draw another plan. And another. And another. Study them in the same way. For the first kitchen we remodeled we drew a dozen plans before we were satisfied with the arrangement.

12 • When you hit on a good plan, redraw it accurately, using a ruler (Fig. 9-3). You'll undoubtedly find that the positions of some cabinets, appliances, etc., must be altered slightly; but remember that there are three things to help you make minor adjustments:

a • Cabinets increase in size by 3-in. increments.

b • Filler strips are made in 1- to 3-in. widths and can be trimmed to any width.

c • The trim around doors and windows can be made narrower to accommodate a cabinet or counter.

When positioning appliances and cabinets, try to line up the wall cabinets with the base cabinets.

13 • Draw the elevation of each wall (Fig. 9-4). This isn't absolutely necessary, but it gives a much better picture of how the kitchen will look. If you bypass this step, you must note on the floor plan which base cabinets are to have drawers and which are to have shelves.

TEARING OUT THE
OLD KITCHEN AND PUTTING
IN THE NEW...

You can farm out the entire job or do *some* of the work yourself. Here's the rundown. The work is listed in its normal sequence.

- *Measuring and building counter tops.* If they are to be made of laminated plastic, a counter top builder must do the work.
- *Ordering cabinets.* If you are sure of your plan, do this yourself. If you want the plan double-checked, go to a cabinet dealer or kitchen installer, and let him draw a finished plan and order the cabinets for you.
- *Tearing out the old kitchen.* You can do almost all of this.
- *Roughing in plumbing.* A plumber's job.
- *Laying a new subfloor.* You can do this easily. (See Chapter 5.)
- *Building a new stud wall.* You do this. (See Chapter 4.)
- *Installing wiring and lighting.* Leave it to an electrical contractor.

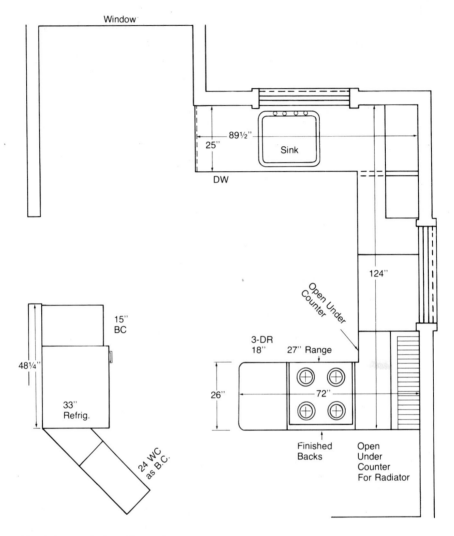

Fig. 9-3   Kitchen floor plan.

- *Surfacing the new wall, and resurfacing old walls and ceiling.* Your job. (See Chapter 4.)
- *Installing cabinets.* You can do this.
- *Installing counter tops.* If they are laminated plastic, you can install the straight sections—but let the top builder fiddle with the others. If you're going to cover the counters with ceramic tile, you can build them yourself in the same way you tile a wall or floor. (See Chapter 10.)

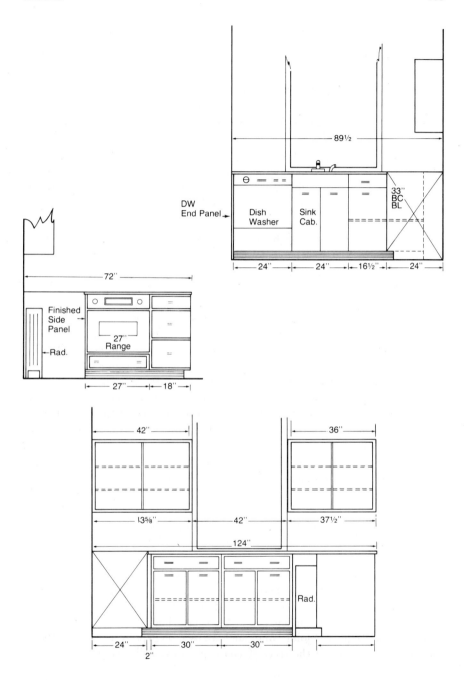

Fig. 9-4   Kitchen elevations.

- *Installing sink, dishwasher, and disposer.* The plumber comes back again.
- *Putting down finish floor.* You.
- *Installing range and refrigerator.* Leave it to the dealer who sold them.
- *Decorating room.* You finish up in a blaze of glory.

INSTALLING WALL CABINETS

This is heavy work, so get a helper to assist you in positioning the cabinets properly. Draw a horizontal line across the wall to mark the bottoms of the cabinets. Then mark the position of each cabinet, making sure you have them in the order planned.

Find the studs and mark their location below the horizontal line. Then lift a cabinet against the wall parallel with the horizontal line and drill four holes through the back into the studs. Hang the cabinets with 4-in. round-head screws.

Fasten each cabinet to the one alongside with a bolt near the bottom and another near the top.

If a filler strip is needed between a wall and the cabinet next to it, draw a vertical line on the wall marking the edge of the cabinet. If the gap is equal in width from top to bottom, cut the filler strip to this measurement and attach it to the cabinet, flush with the surface, before hanging the cabinet. Use nails in wood or plastic-surfaced cabinets, machine bolts in metal cabinets.

If the gap is irregular, temporarily screw the cabinet into its proper position on the wall. Hold the filler strip against the face of the cabinet, flush with the side edge, and scribe a line on it. Then cut it to this line, take down the cabinet, and attach the strip.

If the next-to-the-wall cabinet has an extended stile instead of a separate filler strip, measure for it and cut it before hanging the cabinet.

The space above a row of wall cabinets can be left open—but it looks infinitely better if closed. More important, this seals it against dust and grease. Use 1/8-in. tempered hardboard, 1/4-in. plywood, or whatever thickness of gypsum board you happen to have around the house. Cut it into a strip to fit the space.

Attach 1 x 2-in. furring strips to the tops of the cabinets, back from the fronts the thickness of the covering material. Nail furring strips to the ceiling directly above. Then nail the covering material to the two rows of strips.

If there's an objectionable gap at the ceiling line, cover it with a molding. Gypsum board tape and joint compound are used on gypsum board. But there's no need to worry about the crack if you apply vinyl wall covering to the entire board.

A crack between the covering board and the cabinets is usually concealed with a small molding.

INSTALLING   Baseboards and shoe moldings must be removed.
BASE CABINETS   Then look the wall over carefully for holes that mice
                        can come through, and tack aluminum flashing over
them. Close holes around pipes in the floor, too. Contractors never do this—but it's the surest way to keep rodents out of the kitchen.

With a carpenter's level, find the highest spot in the floor along the wall.

Place the cabinets against the wall in their exact positions. If a filler strip is required at one end of the row, handle it in the way previously described.

Install the cabinet at the high spot first. Level it side to side and front to back, and attach it to the wall with a pair of screws driven into the studs.

Succeeding cabinets must be made level and flush with one another at the front and top. Use wood shingles or thicker wood strips to shim them up. Then screw them to the wall, and fasten one to the other with two bolts.

After the new flooring is laid, if there's a crack between the cabinets and the floor, cover it with a quarter round. Another idea is to fit and paste floor tiles to the toeboard.

INSTALLING   This gets troublesome if the tops don't fit perfectly.
COUNTER TOPS   That's why you should let the top maker install a top
                        that turns a corner or is an irregular shape.
But a straight top is a simple matter. Just position it on the base cabinets, and drive screws up through the frame of the cabinet into it.

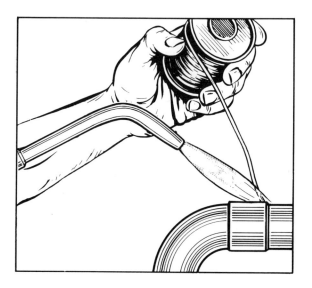

Bathrooms

Throughout this book I have tried not to compare the value of one renovation with another because what does most for a Cape Cod on Cherry Street may do little if anything for a contemporary on Red Coat Lane. But I must say that, since few things date a house as much as the bathrooms, there are few better ways to rejuvenate a house than by adding another bathroom or by modernizing those you already have.

Sadly, I must point out that there are few more expensive ways to rejuvenate a house. True, it's possible to hold down costs by installing medium-grade fixtures and by finishing the room with some of the many moderate- to low-cost wall coverings, flooring materials, etc. But no matter how much you skimp, you are bound to wind up paying a good many hundreds of dollars for a new bathroom or a completely remodeled oldster.

ADDING A
NEW BATHROOM...

This is the most costly plumbing job you can do because it involves installation of water pipes, drains, and vents—and this is work you should leave to a plumber.

The water pipes (supply lines) are usually made of copper tubing with soldered joints. The horizontal runs are made with rigid, "hard" tube to keep them from sagging. The vertical runs, called risers, may be made of hard tube or semiflexible, "soft" tube. The latter is much used in remodeling because it comes in long coils that can be unwound and pushed up inside walls.

The main house drain, generally made of large cast-iron pipes, collects and carries all the wastes from the house to the sewer. Smaller drains feed into it from the bathroom, kitchen, and laundry fixtures. These used to be made with cast-iron pipes with an inside diameter of 4 in. The outside diameter was almost 6 in.; consequently, the walls through which the pipes ran—called plumbing walls—had to be 50 per cent thicker than the average interior stud wall. But all

189

this has changed. Fixture drains are now usually made with rigid copper tube with an inside diameter of 3 in. and an outside diameter small enough to permit running through a normal stud wall.

All drain lines, including the main drain, must be sloped toward the sewer and must incorporate U-shaped traps just below each fixture. (Toilets have built-in traps.) The traps are full of water at all times to prevent sewer gases from escaping into the house.

Vent pipes are usually made of the same material as the drains. They are connected into the drains just below each trap; and all lead into a larger vent pipe that extends up through the roof. The purpose of the vents is to exhaust sewer gases to the atmosphere and to maintain atmospheric pressure in the drains.

I recommend that you hire a plumber to put in a new bathroom—not because the pipes are difficult to fit together, but because the supply lines, drains, and vents must be sized and laid out exactly to ensure good, safe operation. This requires long training and experience. And when the work is done, it must be inspected and approved by the local building department.

Developing plans for a new bathroom is another matter, however. This you can do, and should do, because you know your house and your family's habits far better than any outsider. But final approval must come from the plumber because only he knows whether it's feasible to install the pipes in the way your plan requires.

Determine who is going to use the bathroom and how!

Will two or more persons use it at the same time? Do you need a full bathroom or a half bath with only a toilet and lavatory? Do you want a tub, shower stall, or both? Must the bathroom incorporate special features to serve someone who is ailing or elderly? Will the bathroom be used also as a laundry or dressing room?

Look for space!

In a big house, this usually isn't hard to find unless you have filled the house with a large family. You might be able to turn a whole bedroom into a bathroom. Or you can at least take a chunk out of a bedroom or hall.

But in a small house, space is limited and you must think in terms of minimum bathrooms.

The smallest I know of measures a little less than 5 ft. square. It is a prefabricated unit with walls, floor, ceiling, tub, lavatory, medicine cabinet, towel bars, and paperholder molded out of two pieces of fiberglass that are bolted together to form a cube. The toilet is installed separately but fits into the unit.

Conventional bathrooms with a tub start at about 5 x 6 ft. Substituting a shower stall for a tub saves a little space, but not much.

The smallest powder room, or half bath, measures 2-1/2 x 4 ft. It has a corner lavatory.

To simplify installation of the new bathroom, try to locate it close to other plumbing facilities!

This reduces the cost of the piping and the labor to put it in, because the new bathroom is connected into the old piping.

One thing you should do, if possible, is to put the new bathroom next to an old one or to the sink in the kitchen or to tubs in a laundry. If possible, the new fixtures should be located so they are back-to-back with those on the other side of the wall. Then you can tie into the old piping with very short lengths of pipe.

A possible alternative is to install the new bathroom directly over or under an old one, or over or under the kitchen sink or laundry tubs.

In a one-story house built on a slab, back-to-back or side-by-side installation of the new bathroom is almost imperative because the existing piping is buried in the slab, and you don't want to knock any larger hole in the slab than necessary. Placing the new bathroom at a distance from an old one causes problems because you can't pitch the new drain enough to produce adequate flow into the old drain. In this situation, you might have to install a pump to get rid of the wastes.

Check the location of walls!

Also to simplify installation, if you put the bathroom on the second floor, make sure there is a wall under it that runs through to the basement. You need this to conceal the pipes. If you put the bathroom on the first floor of a two-story house, you need a wall running through to the attic to conceal the vent pipes. Keep in mind, particularly when selecting a wall to conceal the supply pipes, that an interior wall is better than an exterior wall because there is little danger of the supply lines freezing in winter.

If there isn't a wall below the bathroom, it may still be possible to get the pipes down to the basement through a more distant wall. But here you can run into trouble if the joist space under the bathroom is not deep enough to permit the drains to be pitched properly. The solution is either to raise the floor under which the pipes run or to lower the ceiling beneath them.

Don't rule out an inside bathroom!

Windows are not essential if you put in a ventilating fan that turns on automatically with the bathroom light.

Provide drainage for a basement bathroom!

If the new bathroom is to go in the basement, its location depends mainly on how the house drain to the sewer is installed. If the drain is under the basement floor, put the bathroom close to it so you don't have to break open too much of the floor. If the drain is just above the floor, the bathroom should be raised above it to provide for natural flow of wastes into it. This requires ample headroom in the basement. If the drain runs across the basement ceiling or a little below it, you must put in an ejector pump to lift the wastes into it.

Provide adequate space!

The dimensions and arrangement of a new bathroom depend not only on the size of the fixtures you install but also on how much space you provide for the occupant. To determine what fixtures are available, visit the showrooms of plumbing dealers and wholesalers who handle different lines. While almost all bathroom fixture manufacturers produce some more or less standard fixtures, a number also have special sizes and designs.

(Note that it is difficult to convince plumbers of this because each man usually has a favorite wholesaler from whom he buys all supplies. Consequently, when you ask for an unusual fixture, your plumber may tell you that such a thing doesn't exist because his wholesaler doesn't carry it. But stick to your guns and make him shop elsewhere.)

Floor space required by the bathroom occupant is easily determined if you observe the following minimum standards:

- Provide 2 ft. of space between the front rim of a lavatory and a facing wall or fixture.
- Provide 18 in. from the front of a toilet to a facing wall or fixture.
- Provide 15 in. from the center line of a toilet to a wall on either side. That is, if the toilet is recessed in a niche, the niche should be at least 30 in. wide. A 30-in. space is also required if the toilet is set between a wall and lavatory; but if it is set between a wall and a tub, the distance to the tub can be reduced somewhat.
- Provide 2 ft. of space from the side of a tub to a facing wall or fixture. Ideally, this much space should be provided for the entire length of the tub, but this may be reduced to only two-thirds of the tub length.

Decide which way doors will swing to maximize space!

Normally, bathroom doors are installed so that they swing into the bathroom; but if this is impossible because of the small size or layout of the room, the door may be swung out. The alternative is to install a door that slides into a pocket in the wall.

To assure privacy in the bathroom, use a raised-panel door or a solid-core flush door. Hollow-core doors have about as much sound-stopping ability as a sieve.

Determine the most efficient way to heat the bathroom!

The easiest way to heat a new bathroom is to recess an electric heater in a wall or ceiling. In a very small bathroom, you might use a ceiling fixture that incorporates a heater and a light. Some models also incorporate a ventilating fan.

REARRANGING AN EXISTING BATHROOM...

Many old bathrooms can be greatly improved by putting in new fixtures in new locations. But it's foolish to rush into such a project without making very certain that you can't accomplish just as much simply by putting in new fixtures in the old locations. This is much simpler and less expensive.

Rearrangement of a bathroom requires a plumber to take apart and put together the piping. And this means tearing up the floor and opening up some of the walls. Even then, you may not be able to do what you want to do because of the difficulties of relocating and concealing the piping—particularly the drains and vents.

COMPARTMENTING
A BATHROOM...

Although dividing a bathroom into two or sometimes three separate compartments does not actually increase bathroom facilities, it makes it easier for two persons to use the bathroom at the same time—and this has much of the effect of increasing facilities. Not all bathrooms can be compartmented, however—only those of better-than-average size are suitable.

In one of the commonest arrangements, the tub and toilet are grouped in one compartment, the lavatory in another. Or the toilet may be isolated from the lavatory and tub. Or the tub may be isolated from the lavatory and toilet. Another possibility, but less common, is to build a separate compartment for each fixture.

Whatever the arrangement, there should be a door between compartments. And ideally each compartment should have its own door to the hall. To save space, use doors that slide into the wall. Bi-fold doors also save space, though not so much.

Compartmenting a bathroom may require relocation of some of the fixtures, in which case you need a plumber. Otherwise, the only work involved is to build a partition or two. For how to do this, see Chapter 4.

REPLACING
BATHROOM FIXTURES...

TUBS   Few people replace a built-in tub, even though it's an
                                   old model: There simply isn't enough to be gained.
Furthermore, to take the tub out and put in a new one involves chopping open the walls around it. And then you may find that when you try to maneuver the tub out of the bathroom and down the stairs, you can't do it because it was moved into the house in the early stages of construction.

Tubs on legs are different. Even though one bathroom fixture manufacturer is trying to revive interest in them, I feel they look archaic and ugly—and the floor underneath is almost always a mess. Taking out a tub of this type is easy if you have the strength to move it. All you have to do is loosen the hot and cold supply lines and the drain. But installing its modern, built-in replacement generally calls for a plumber because the drain has to be moved and the supply lines probably have to be changed, too.

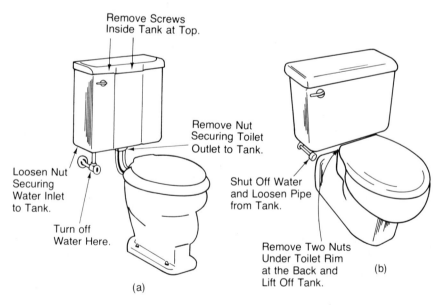

Fig. 10-1   (a) Wash-down toilet; (b) Two-piece toilet.

Some carpentry work is also involved, but this is not difficult. For one thing, the wall at the back of the tub must be cut open so that the flange on the tub rim can be pushed against the studs. This must also be done if the tub fits against a wall at the rounded end. A wall must also be built at the foot of the tub to hide the piping. (To prevent back siphonage, the faucet and handles for a modern tub are always installed about 8 in. above the tub rim.) The wall usually extends from the floor to the ceiling and contains a shower head; but if you don't want a shower in the tub recess, the wall may be topped off 4 or 5 in. above the faucet.

TOILETS   This is an easy job with one possible complication: Old toilets with tanks mounted on the wall projected farther from the wall than most modern toilets. As a result, when you install a new toilet over the mouth of the drain, you may find that there is a sizable gap between the tank and the wall. The best way to avoid this problem is to take out the old toilet and measure from the wall to the center of the drain opening. Then order the toilet with the closest corresponding measurement.

To remove the old toilet, turn off the water at the valve on the wall behind it, and flush the toilet. Hold the stopper until the water drains down to the outlet; then bail out what remains with a cup and sponge. With a wrench, loosen the nuts securing the water inlet to the tank.

If the toilet is of the wash-down type, with the tank completely separated from the bowl except by an L-shaped pipe [Fig. 10-1(a)], loosen the nut that secures the pipe to the bottom of the tank. Then remove the two screws inside the tank that attach it to the wall. You can now lift off the tank. Be sure to wash and paint the wall behind it before installing the new toilet.

If the toilet is a more modern two-piece unit with the tank resting on the back of the bowl [Fig. 10-1(b)], remove the two nuts at the back under the toilet rim, and lift off the tank.

Now pry off the four ceramic caps at the base of the bowl. Use a slender knife and go easy because the caps are easily broken. This will expose four screws that should be removed. Then lift the toilet from the floor. A little of the water in the trap will probably spill out but not enough to worry about. After cleaning off the putty-like material from around the drain opening, you are ready to install a new toilet. This may be a one-piece unit, but the chances are that it's a two-piecer because it costs less, though it works just as well.

First, install the flush mechanism in the tank (Fig. 10-2). You can use the old one if in good repair, but it's usually better to buy new.

Place a thick wax ring available from the plumbing supply store over the drain outlet in the floor. Position the bowl outlet over this, and press the bowl to the floor. Make sure it's level. Then replace the four large screws that fasten it down.

Push the thick rubber gasket that comes with the toilet onto the outlet pipe under the tank, and set the tank in place on top of the bowl. The inlet pipe in the tank should simultaneously be slipped down over the riser above the valve in the wall. It may be necessary to bend the riser somewhat to make this connection. Then secure the tank to the bowl with the bolts and gasket provided. Finally, wrap graphite wicking or simply cotton thread around the riser just below the tank inlet, and secure the riser by tightening the nut around it on the inlet pipe.

Fill the tank with water and flush the toilet. Do this several times, checking for leaks, before setting the ceramic caps over the screws in the base of the toilet with plaster of Paris or caulking compound.

CONVENTIONAL   Turn off the water at the valves below the lavatory,
LAVATORIES   and loosen the nuts that connect the risers to the hot
                        and cold water faucets. Loosen the large nut just
above the U-shaped trap. If the lavatory is set tight against the wall, lifting straight up will now free it. If there's a gap behind the lavatory, however, you must unbolt it from the brackets on which it rests.

Conventional lavatories of modern design are installed almost exactly like those of yesteryear. All are wall-hung, although they may not seem to be at first glance. The cheapest lavatories with a high backsplash simply hook over metal brackets screwed to the wall. Except for the pipes underneath, they have no other means of support. Better lavatories stand out from the wall about an inch. At the back, they rest on brackets screwed to the wall. At the front, they usually rest on two stainless steel legs which are adjustable in height. In a few cases, however, the legs are eliminated and the lavatories rest on a central pedestal.

Lavatories are normally installed with the rim 31 in. above the floor, but they may be hung lower or higher. The fact that the lavatory you are replacing was hung at a certain height does not affect the installation of the new lavatory

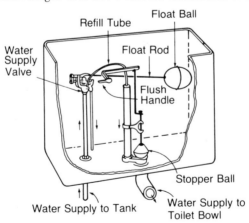

Fig. 10-2   Installing the flush mechanism in a toilet tank.

because you may not be able to use the old wall brackets and because changes made in the design of the faucets and other fittings may necessitate replacement of the supply pipes and drain.

In other words, when installing the new lavatory, decide on the height you want it to be and install the wall brackets accordingly. The screws used to support them must be driven into wood; they will not hold in plaster or gypsum board.

Before hanging the lavatory, mount the faucets and pop-up drain on it. Then place the lavatory in the brackets and support it well while you measure the distance from the faucets to the valves and from the tailpiece on the lavatory drain to the top of the trap. (As I just pointed out, it is unlikely that the new fittings can be connected directly to the old risers or trap.)

Risers for lavatories [Fig. 10-3(a)] are made of 3/8-in. chrome-plated, flexible copper tube. After you cut them to the proper length, secure them to the faucet and valve with nuts that fit over the tube.

The drain pipe [Fig. 10-3(b)] is a chrome-plated, rigid copper tube that is slightly larger at the upper end than at the bottom. Simply slide the upper end over the tailpiece on the lavatory and slip the bottom end down into the trap. The bottom end must be cut to extend into the trap about 2 in. A large nut at the top of the trap holds it tight and prevents leaks.

BUILT-IN LAVATORIES   The vanity—a built-in storage cabinet with one or two lavatories recessed in a large counter top—has become

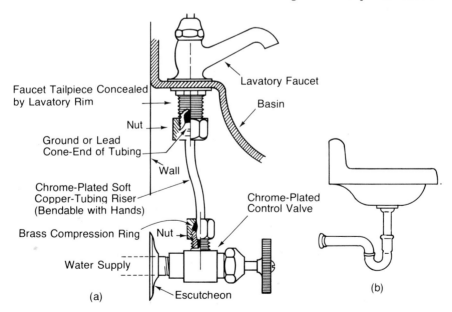

Fig. 10-3   (a) Riser and (b) drain pipe for lavatory.

the hallmark of the modern bathroom in the eyes of most Americans. So if you're rejuvenating your home with the thought of selling it at a profit, it is a good thing to install.

Vanities have a threefold appeal: They are supposed to give you more counter space than you get with a conventional lavatory. There is storage space underneath. And because they are built tight to the walls and floors, cleaning of the bathroom is made a bit easier. I must point out, however, that many vanities are so small that the storage space is virtually useless and the counter is no larger than that on a number of conventional lavatories. Yet, they cost more than a conventional lavatory.

In other words, you gain little if anything by installing a vanity unless it is at least twice as wide as the lavatory set into it.

You can build your own vanity base out of 1-in. lumber and 3/4-in. plywood, but you will get a more finished piece if you buy a stock cabinet. The alternative, if you can't find what you want in stock, is to have a local cabinet shop build the base for you.

Stock counter tops are also available. But most people have tops of laminated plastic made by a local cabinet shop or counter top maker. A marble top must be made and installed by a marble contractor. If you want a top of ceramic tile, however, there is no reason why you can't make it yourself. The base for the tile should be either 3/4-in. exterior-grade plywood or particleboard. Cut the opening for the lavatory with a saber saw or keyhole saw. Set the tile according to the directions given below for tiling a wall.

Built-in lavatories are installed in several ways. The easiest to handle is a self-rimming unit with a rim that rests directly on the counter top. Leakage under the edges of the rim is prevented by bedding the rim in plumber's putty. Another easy-to-handle lavatory is hung in a flat stainless steel rim that is placed in the hole in the counter top. The lavatory is held secure with clamps under the top.

The faucets for both types of lavatories are mounted on the lavatory.

If you install a built-in lavatory in the exact location of the unit you are discarding, plumb it like a conventional lavatory. But if you move the lavatory far to one side or the other of the old unit's position, you must use soft copper tube to connect the faucets to the valves. The trap is moved directly under the lavatory by inserting a horizontal pipe between it and the waste pipe in the wall.

LAVATORY AND SINK FAUCETS   Replacing these is complicated by the fact that you must work in an extremely awkward position, often in a very cramped space. In addition, some of the nuts that must be turned are so placed that you need an open-end wrench to grip them, and in many cases, you need a basin wrench.

If each of the old faucets you are taking out has its own spout, replace them with the same type of faucet. But if the faucets have a central spout, measure as carefully as possible the space between the centers of the holes through which the faucets fit into the lavatory or sink. There are two holes if the faucets and spout are assembled in a single unit, three holes if the faucets and spout are separate from one another. Before removing the faucets from the lavatory or sink, check with local plumbing suppliers to make sure that modern faucet units are available with the same spacing. They may not be—and in that event, it's better to replace the entire lavatory or sink than to attempt make-shift remodeling of the controls.

To remove old faucets, shut off the hot and cold water supply and detach the risers from the faucets. Also detach the lower section of the rod that raises the pop-up stopper (if any).

Then, if the faucets are a one-piece unit, unscrewing the large nuts that clamp the unit to the underside of the lavatory permits you to lift off the unit. The replacement unit is installed by the same steps in reverse.

A three-piece faucet unit (Fig. 10-4) is more difficult. First, remove the faucet handles and escutcheons and the large nuts securing the faucets to the lavatory. Then remove the spout by twisting it round and round. This frees the linkage under the lavatory so you can remove it.

To install the new unit, push the underside linkage up through the holes in the lavatory, and insert the risers for the hot and cold water supplies in the base of the faucets. Connect the spout and faucets to the underside linkage. Then draw them down to the top of the lavatory by tightening the large nuts under the lavatory.

COPPER TUBING   When iron pipe rusts or becomes clogged with scale, it must be replaced. Similarly, when yellow brass pipe corrodes, it must be replaced. Use rigid copper tubing for horizontal runs, soft copper tubing for vertical runs.

Fig. 10-4   Three-piece faucet unit.

How much of the old piping you replace is up to you. In a former house, I started by replacing one section at time as it became defective. But as the years went by and more and more sections gave up the ghost, I got fed up with piece-meal, emergency-type operations and did everything that was left at once.

I assume here, however, that you will start out as I did.

The first step is to measure the length of pipe that has gone sour. For simplicity, let's say it is a straight, unbroken run; so measure from the fitting at one end to the fitting at the other.

Determine the diameter of the pipe. Tie a knot in a short length of string, wrap the string around the pipe once, and then measure from the point that touches the knot to the knot. If the string is 2-5/8 in. long, the pipe is 1/2 in. in diameter. If the string is 3-1/4 in. long, the pipe is 3/4 in. in diameter. Replace either 1/2-in. or 3/4-in. steel or brass pipe with 1/2-in. copper tube.

Copper tube is best installed by soldering; so when you buy the tube you must also buy several solder, or sweat, fittings (Fig. 10-5). For the job described, you need a 1/4-in. union plus two "reducing male" adapters with 3/4-in. outside threads at one end and a smooth 1/2-in. inside joint at the other. You should also buy a spool of tape dope (used instead of the old-fashioned paste to make tight threaded joints), a coil of solder, a bottle of acid flux, and a propane torch.

When you're ready to make the change, shut off the water. Remove the defective length of pipe with a hacksaw. Place a bucket underneath to catch the water that will come gushing out. Then, with a pipe wrench, unscrew the two pieces of pipe from the fittings.

Wrap a short strip of tape dope around the threaded ends of the adapters, and screw them into the old fittings with a wrench. Then measure carefully from the open end of one adapter to the open end of the other adapter; add 1 in. to allow for inserting the copper tubing into the adapters; then subtract 1 in. to allow for installation of the union. Cut the copper tube to this length. If you use a fine-toothed hacksaw, hold the tube in a vise, and take pains to cut straight across it. Smooth the cut edges inside and out with a file.

A better way to cut copper tube is with a special, wheeled tube cutter (Fig. 10-6). This clamps on the tube and cuts as you turn it round and round while simultaneously tightening the handle. Ream out the end of the tube with a file.

Now cut the tube once more to accommodate the union. This is a three-piece fitting. The two end pieces are soldered to the tube, and are then clamped tightly together with a large central nut. The purpose of a union is to permit easy installation and removal of a pipe that is connected between fittings that cannot be spread apart. (The reason you had to saw through the old steel pipe was because you couldn't unscrew it from the fitting at one end without tightening it in the fitting at the other end. If there had been a union in the run, however, you could have opened it and then unscrewed the two pieces of pipe from the fittings independent of each other.)

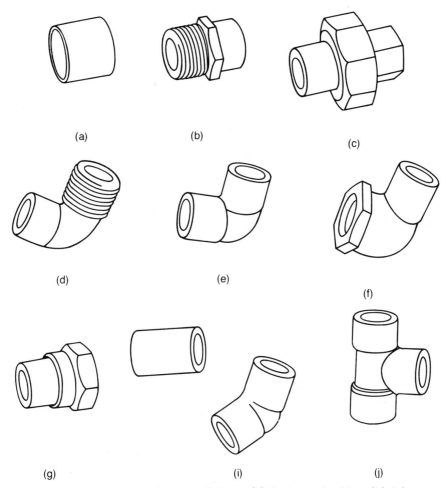

(a)   (b)

(c)

(d)   (e)

(f)

(g)   (i)   (j)

Fig. 10-5   Several types of copper fittings: (a) Reducing bushing; (b) Adapter; (c) Union; (d–f) 90° elbow; (g) Adapter; (h) Coupling; (i) 45° elbow; (j) Tee.

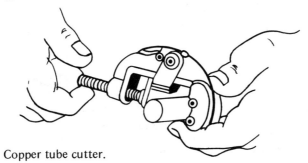

Fig. 10-6   Copper tube cutter.

With steel wool, polish the ends of the copper tubes and the inside surfaces of the fittings as far back as the shoulders. This is an extremely important operation—don't neglect it even though the tubes and fittings look clean.

Apply acid flux with a small paint brush to all the polished surfaces.

Put one of the tubes into a vise, slip one end of the union over it, and push the union on as far as it will go. (Take the union apart before doing this.) Light your propane torch and play the flame over the fitting and adjacent tube for 20 seconds or so (Fig. 10-7). Then touch the tip of the solder ribbon to the edge of the fitting. Continue to apply heat—but not directly on the solder. When the tube and fitting reach the proper temperature, the solder will melt and flow by capillary action into the joint. Feed in solder until the joint is full and will take no more. This takes only a few seconds. Then withdraw the flame and quickly wipe off excess solder with a cloth. Allow the joint to cool for about a minute. You may then cool it off completely with a wet rag.

Apply the other end of the union to the other tube in the same way. Then slip the big nut onto the tube with the unthreaded union joint.

If the acid on the other ends of the tubes has dried, brush on a little more. Then insert one tube into one of the adapters, the other tube into the other adapter. If you have measured correctly, the faces of the union should just about touch.

Solder the tubes into the adapters. If there's a combustible surface such as a ceiling joist close behind the adapters, be careful not to play the flame on it. If you're working in very close quarters, slip a piece of asbestos or asbestos-cement board behind the adapters.

When the joints at the adapters have cooled, pull the end pieces of the union together by tightening the large nut around them. Then turn on the water and check for leaks. If one of the soldered joints drips, you must turn off the

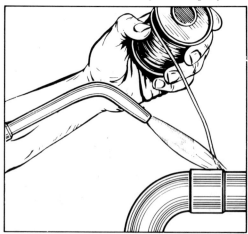

Fig. 10-7   Soldering a copper tube and fitting.

water aga   drain the line, reheat the joint, and feed more
solder int   der pipe that is full of water—it just doesn't work.
   Altl   s of piping that fail may be of somewhat more
intricate (ced in essentially the same way. But the following
points sho

1 •   t copper tube in a vertical run (but never in a
                             a union is unnecessary because you can bend the
                             to slip it into the fittings at the ends.

2 •   tubes into two or three ends of fittings such as
                         gs, and tees, the heat you apply at one end may melt
                         soldered joint at the other end. To help prevent this,
                      play the flame on the completed end, or wrap the
                      d with a wet rag.

3 • (advantages of copper tube is that it can be bent around
corners. Thus, many fittings can be eliminated. Unless you invest in
a special bending machine, you should not try to bend rigid tubes.
However, soft tube can be given a slight bend with your hands. If
you want to make a sharp bend of, say, $45°$ or more, place the tube
on the floor and put a knee on it. Gradually pull up the end of the
tube around your knee. Shift your knee a little from time to time to
assure a smooth bend without kinks.

4 • You have undoubtedly heard it said that two dissimilar metals
should never be joined together in the presence of moisture because
this sets up a galvanic action that hastens corrosion at the joint. This
is true—and when you join copper tubing to steel pipe, you're asking
for potential problems. Remember, however, that you are already
having trouble with the steel pipe and that, once this has started in
one section of the plumbing system, it will undoubtedly progress to
other sections within a reasonably short time. Consequently, it
doesn't make much sense to replace the defective steel with new
steel just to avoid a copper-to-steel joint. The sooner you can replace
all the steel pipe with copper, the better. So take a chance and get
started.

RENOVATING
EXISTING FIXTURES...

CHANGING THE COLOR   This is quite feasible as long as you don't expect
OF BATHROOM   perfection. Wash the fixtures thoroughly and take
FIXTURES   pains to scrub off copper and rust stains. Roughen
                            the surface with powdered pumice and a damp rag;

then rinse and dry thoroughly. Take off whatever metal fittings are easily removable (faucet escutcheons, for example). Cover the others with masking tape.

Apply a two-part epoxy enamel according to the directions on the can. For the smoothest, evenest finish, use a spray gun. Brushing is possible, however.

CAULKING CRACKS   This is a minor but important step in the renovation
AROUND A TUB RIM   of the bathroom. First, scrape the crack open with a
                             knife or screwdriver, blow out the crumbs, and let it
dry for several days. Then fill it with white silicone caulking compound. This comes in a tube with a detachable nozzle. Cut off the end of the nozzle to make an opening approximately the width of the crack. Force the caulking well into the crack by moving the tube along it with the nozzle pointed forward. Smooth at once with a knife. Remove caulking from adjacent surfaces with paper towels; and when it is dry, scrape off any that remains with a razor blade.

If the crack is too wide to be caulked satisfactorily with silicone, install quarter-round ceramic tiles sold in a kit for the purpose (Fig. 10-8). First, caulk the crack with silicone. Then cover the joint between wall and tub with the tiles. These are glued down by buttering the edges with silicone caulking. The joints between the ends of the tiles are also sealed with caulking. Inside corner joints are made by mitering two tiles with a fine-toothed saw—preferably a hacksaw. Tiles with rounded ends are used at the open ends of the line of tiles.

INSTALLING
BATHROOM ACCESSORIES...

MEDICINE CABINETS   Two types of medicine cabinet are on the market:
                             surface-mounted and recessed. The former is the less

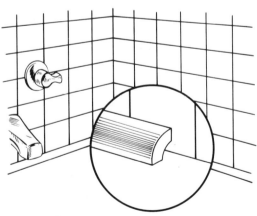

Fig. 10-8   Quarter-round ceramic tiles.

popular because it projects into the room. This makes for a somewhat unattractive installation, even though the cabinets themselves are as well designed as recessed models. However, they are useful when you cannot, for some reason, cut a hole in a wall for a recessed model or when a wall is not thick enough for a recessed model. To install one, simply screw it to the wall with four round-head screws that are long enough to penetrate at least 1 in. into the studs. Or use toggle bolts or hollow-wall screw anchors.

Recessed cabinets are made 3-1/2 in. deep so they will fit into a standard stud wall, and the smaller units are made only 14 in. wide so they will fit between studs spaced 16 in. on centers. Large units require two stud spaces.

The first thing to worry about when installing a 14-in. recessed cabinet is whether there are any pipes in the wall where the cabinet is to be installed. If the cabinet is to go over a lavatory, the chances are that the wall space is empty unless there's a bathroom or radiator directly overhead—but the odds are against you if you prefer a location over the toilet. You'd probably be safe over the bathtub, but who wants a medicine cabinet there? You'd probably also be safe on an outside wall, but this is an undesirable location because too much heat would be lost to the outdoors through the cabinet, and the contents of the cabinet might freeze. However, there is no need to rely on guesswork about what goes on in any wall. Drill a small hole or series of small holes and probe with a stiff wire.

Having selected the location, double-check the position of the studs on both sides of the opening you must make. This is best done by drilling small holes close together across one of the studs until the drill misses the stud; then measure 14-3/8 in. across the wall and drill another hole. You should just hit the second stud.

Now with a carpenter's level or plumb line, draw vertical lines on the wall at the drill holes marking the edges of the studs. Determine the height at which the cabinet should be hung, and draw horizontal lines marking the top and bottom. Then carefully cut out the opening. Use a sharp wood chisel on plaster, a saw on gypsum board and other materials.

If you come upon an electric cable in the wall space, staple it to the side of one of the studs. A nonmetallic sheathed cable is thin enough not to interfere with the recessing of the cabinet. But you may have to gouge out a shallow channel for a BX cable.

Set the cabinet into the hole. If it is reasonably snug, secure it to each of the studs with chrome-plated screws. If there's considerable play between cabinet and studs, however, remove it and nail a strip of 1/4-in. plywood or whatever is appropriate to the side of one of the studs; then screw in the cabinet.

Installing a recessed cabinet wider than 14 in. requires opening and then closing a hole that is probably much larger than the cabinet. So I advise against it unless you want to rebuild the entire wall anyway.

UNFRAMED MIRRORS There are two easy ways to hang unframed mirrors of any size in the bathroom or elsewhere in the house.

The usual way is to use plastic clips that are installed around the edges of the mirror. The number needed depends on the size of the mirror; for safety, I recommend one clip every 16 in. across the bottom. They should be positioned over studs and fastened with screws long enough to penetrate the studs. Use half as many clips across the top of the mirror and drive them into the studs, too. One clip on each side is usually enough; since it is unlikely that they can be fastened to studs, they have little strength, but they are needed to keep the mirror from being pushed sideways.

The other way to hang a mirror is with two metal strips cut to the width of the mirror (Fig. 10-9). Screw these securely to the wall at the bottom and top of the mirror. Permanent metal clips are attached to the bottom strap, and the mirror is set into these. Then adjustable clips attached to the top strap are pushed down over the upper edge of the mirror.

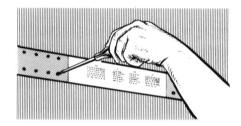

(a)

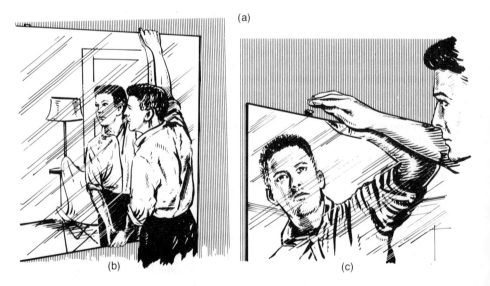

(b)   (c)

Fig. 10-9   Hanging a mirror using metal strips.

INSTALLING CERAMIC TILE...

WALLS This once-difficult job has been made relatively easy by the development of strong, water-resistant adhesives that are used instead of cement to anchor the tiles. Result: You can now add the beauty, practicality, and sales appeal of ceramic tile to any bathroom wall at about one-third of the price you would have formerly paid.

Although ceramic tiles are produced in many sizes and shapes, those usually used in bathrooms are either 4-1/4 x 4-1/4-in. squares or 1-in.-square mosaic tiles that are mounted on a backing and sold, as a rule, in 1-ft. squares. Before ordering either kind, you must decide how high up on the wall the tiles will extend. Over a bathtub they may go all the way to the ceiling or to about 6 in. above the shower head. Elsewhere in the bathroom, use tiles in a wainscot about 4 ft. high.

To estimate the number of 4-1/4-in. tiles you need, mark off a short board in 4-5/16-in. segments (the extra 1/16 in. allows for a joint). Then hold this against the wall and count how many tiles are needed in a vertical row and a horizontal row. Multiply the two answers for the total number of tiles. Then subtract the number of trim tiles needed to trim around the edges of the installation. (The tiles in the main body of the installation are known as field tiles.)

There are several types of trim tile (Fig. 10-10):

1 • Bull-nose tiles which are rounded on one edge. They are used to cap a wall that does not go all the way to the ceiling and also to trim the vertical edges—as, for instance, at the front edges of a tub recess.

2 • Down-angles have two rounded edges forming a corner. Use them to turn the corner when a wall is trimmed at the top and along a vertical edge.

3 • Cove tiles curve outward along the bottom edge and are used at the base of a wall where it meets a tiled floor. Special cove tiles are used at corners.

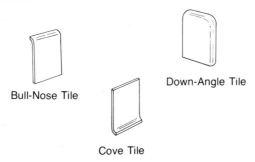

Bull-Nose Tile

Down-Angle Tile

Cove Tile

Fig. 10-10 Ceramic tiles for special situations.

To estimate how many mosaic tiles you need, just determine how many square feet of wall will be tiled and order accordingly. Add the necessary trim tiles. Bull-nose tiles are 1 in. high and come in 1-ft. strips. Down-angles are 1 in. square and are sold by the piece.

You can tile any existing wall that is level, sound, and strong. Patch cracks. Knock out weak or bulging plaster and replace with gypsum board. Remove wallpaper and other coverings. Scrape off loose paint and sand glossy paint. Wash the wall thoroughly.

Over a tub or in a shower stall, prime the wall with a skin coat of tile adhesive and let it dry overnight. Use the smooth edge of your spreader to apply it. Over a tub you should also gouge out a 1/4-in. strip of wall just above the tub rim. This helps to prevent weakening of the wall if water should seep under the tiles.

If you must rebuild a wall in the bathroom or if you are putting up a new one, cover it with 1/2-in. water-resistant gypsum board. You don't have to fill the joints or cover the nailheads. Over a tub or in a shower stall, however, cut edges of the board and nailheads should be coated with a sealer available from the gypsum board maker. Leave a 1/4-in. open space above the tub rim or shower receptor.

To install 4-1/4 x 4-1/4-in. tiles, find the lowest point along the tub rim or floor line with a carpenter's level; place a tile flat against the wall, and mark the wall along the top edge of the tile. (If you are putting in cove tiles, place one of them against the wall, set a field tile on top, and mark the top edge of that.) Then using your level, draw a horizontal line across the entire wall and any adjacent walls that are to be tiled. Nail straight strips of wood end to end just below the line. Let the nailheads protrude so you can later remove the strips.

Now find the center of the wall and mark it (Fig. 10-11). Lay a row of tiles edge to edge from the mark to one end of the wall (it doesn't matter which one). If the space for the last tile is more than 2-1/8 in. wide, strike a plumb line over the pencil mark at the center of the wall. But if the space for the last tile is less than 2-1/8 in. wide, make a new pencil mark exactly 2-1/8 in. to either side of the first mark and strike a plumb line over it. This procedure assures that the tiles at the two ends of the wall will not only be equal in width but also will not be silly looking slivers.

You are now ready to start setting the tiles.

Use an adhesive recommended by the tile dealer and apply it with a notched spreader held at a 45° angle so that the beads of adhesive on the wall will be thick and the valleys between them will be almost bare. Apply the adhesive in horizontal strips over no more than 2 or 3 sq. ft. of wall at a time. Set tiles in the adhesive with a little twisting motion, press them down firmly, and after you have tiled a fairly large area, press the tiles down once more with a board.

Start tiling at the juncture of the horizontal wood strips and the vertical

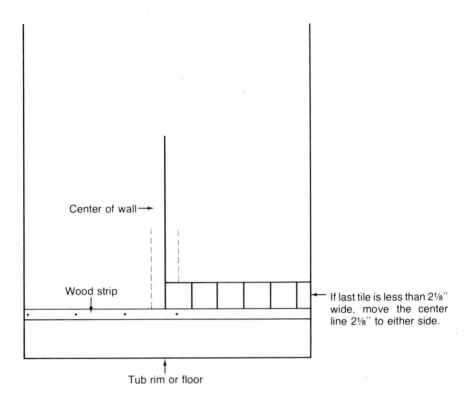

Center of wall⟶

Wood strip

If last tile is less than 2⅛"
wide, move the center
line 2⅛" to either side.

Tub rim or floor

Fig. 10-11 Positioning the first row of tiles from the center of the wall.

line (Fig. 10-12). Lay four or five tiles along the strips (the purpose of which is to keep the tiles from slipping down the wall under the weight of the tiles above). Then lay four or five tiles up along the vertical line and fill in between. The spacing between tiles is automatically determined by the lugs on the edges. If you set them edge to edge, in other words, they will be correctly spaced and should also be in straight horizontal and vertical rows.

After covering the entire wall with field tiles, set the trim tiles. Apply the adhesive directly to the back of each tile, and press it down.

After completing the wall, wait about six hours before prying off the wood strips. Then set the bottom row of tiles. Some of them may have to be trimmed. If you are using cove tiles, set them first along the floor line. Then set the row of field tiles above. Trim these, if required—not the cove tiles.

When tiling two walls at an outside corner, install field tiles on one wall 1/16 in. from the edge of the corner (Fig. 10-13). Use bull-nose tiles on the other wall to cover the edges of the field tiles.

At an inside corner, check the corner first with a plumb line to determine if it's straight. If not, the tiles must be scribed to fit. For how to do this, see the

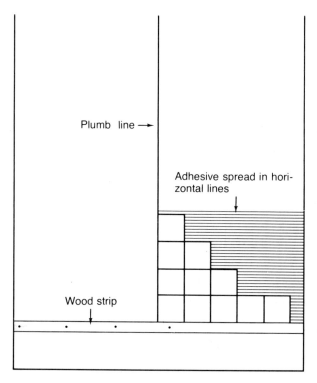

Fig. 10-12 Installing tile from the juncture of the horizontal wood strips and the vertical line.

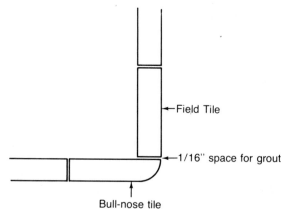

Fig. 10-13 Installing field tiles 1/16" from a corner.

directions in Chapter 5 for scribing resilient floor tiles. The tiles on one wall should extend all the way into the corner. Those on the adjacent wall are butted against the first tiles; however, you must leave a 1/16-in. space to permit grouting.

The easiest way to cut tiles is with a professional tile-cutter which you can rent or perhaps borrow from the tile dealer. But you can also cut them with an ordinary glass cutter. Place the tile face up and lay a yardstick or other straight-edge across it. Hold the cutter vertically between your first and second fingers, with your thumb behind the handle. Press the cutter wheel against the far edge of the tile, and draw the cutter toward you in a smooth, continuous stroke and off the near edge of the tile (Fig. 10-14).

Then slip a large finishing nail under the tile at the scored line, and press down on either side of the line. If the tile doesn't snap in two, deepen the scored line and try again. File rough edges smooth.

If you are trimming off such a thin sliver that you can't break the tile over a nail, use tile nippers (Fig. 10-15) or ordinary pliers and remove the sliver in little bites.

Nippers are also used to cut a tile along an irregular or curved line. Mark the cut on the face of the tile with a pencil. Then, starting at the nearest edge, nibble your way across the tile taking bites no larger than 1/8 in. wide. Smooth the cut edge with a file.

To make a hole in the center of a tile, cut the tile in half with a glass cutter, and then nibble out the hole in each piece.

Tile accessories such as towel-bar holders and paper holders are set last. This means that you must leave spaces for them as you set the field. In fact, you should plan the location of accessories that are recessed in the wall before you even start tiling; otherwise, you may discover that there's a stud or pipe that

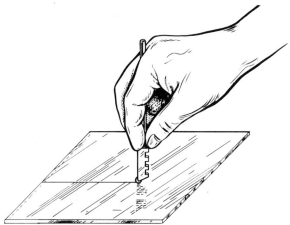

Fig. 10-14 Cutting tile with a glass cutter.

Fig. 10-15 Cutting tile with tile nippers.

prevents installation. Check this question beforehand by drilling a little hole in the subwall and probing with a wire. But don't cut the big holes for the accessories until you are ready to set them. This is because it is hard to establish the precise location of the accessories until the field tiles are in.

To set accessories that are not recessed, just butter the backs with adhesive, push them into the gaps left in the field, and secure them until the adhesive sets with masking tape. To set recessed accessories, butter the backs of the accessories and the edges of the holes.

The final step in tiling a wall is to fill the joints with a grout made of dry, white cement recommended by the tile dealer. This is mixed with water to form a thick paste. Spread it over one wall at a time with a window washer's squeegee or rubber sponge. After working the grout deep into all joints, scrape off the excess and let the joints set for about 15 minutes until they start to dry. Then tool the joints to a concave profile with the end of a rounded toothbrush handle.

As soon as the joints are firm, wash the wall repeatedly with a sponge wrung out in clean water. Then polish with a dry cloth. Spray the wall with a fine water mist twice a day for the next four days. Then let the grout cure for two weeks before taking a shower.

Mosaic tiles are set in much the same way, but instead of working from the center of the wall toward the two ends, start at one end and work straight across to the other (Fig. 10-16). Mark a horizontal line across the wall 1 ft. above the lowest point of the floor or tub rim. Then check the starting corner with a plumb line and if it is not straight up and down, measure out 1 ft. from the widest point and strike a plumb line there. Install the first vertical row of tiles to this line after scribing them to the corner. Install the first horizontal row above the horizontal line. (Strips of wood are not needed because the size of the tile sheets makes slipping unlikely.) Allow space between sheets equal to the spaces between tiles.

As your work proceeds, make sure that the tiles in each sheet line up exactly with those in the adjacent sheets.

Cut the sheets into strips as necessary with scissors. Trim the tiles themselves with nippers.

Do not tool the grouted joints. They are left flat and flush with the surface of the tiles.

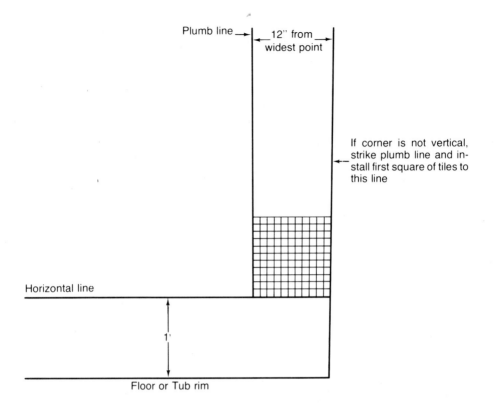

Fig. 10-16 Installing mosaic tiles from the center of the wall.

FLOORS The subfloor on which tiles are laid can be either concrete or wood. A concrete floor need not be smooth, but it should be sound. A wood floor must be firm—not springy—and sound. Nail down all boards securely. Remove old floor coverings and the adhesive under them. Clean thoroughly to get rid of wax, grease, loose paint, dirt, etc. Then check the floor with a straight-edge to determine if it's level. If not, trowel latex or vinyl cement into the low spots, and sand smooth when dry.

If a wood floor is springy, a layer of 3/8-in. exterior-grade plywood must be laid over it. If this is done, however, you will have to tile around the toilet instead of under it. This isn't impossible, but it adds complications to the work.

Before starting to tile, remove the toilet (if you are tiling under it—the best procedure), the pedestal or legs under the lavatory, and the radiator. Also take off baseboards. Either remove the trim at the sides of the door or saw 1/4 in. off the bottom so you can slip the tiles underneath.

The best tile to use on a floor is mosaic. Start at the tub and lay out ten sheets without adhesive. Fit and trim them as necessary. Then cover the area with the adhesive recommended for floor tiles and set the tiles. Press them down well. Avoid walking or kneeling on them; if this is impossible, cover the floor with 2 x 2-ft. pieces of plywood.

Continue thus, laying no more than ten sheets at a time, until the floor is covered. Grout with gray cement. It requires less maintenance than white.

If you tile both the walls and the floor, use cove tiles at the base of the walls. They produce a rounded, easy-to-clean joint around the floor edges. If the walls are not tiled, lay the floor tiles up to within 1/4 in. of the walls and cover the gap with wood baseboards or vinyl cove strips.

When replacing the toilet, you will need four screws 1/4 to 1/2 in. longer than those you took out. You should also use an extra-thick wax ring around the drain.

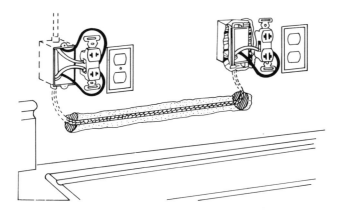

Wiring

It's hard for me to believe that there are today very many houses in the United States with woefully inadequate wiring. Electricity has become as much of a staple as bread and beef. In the late 1930s, when I was junior editor of a trade magazine called *Electrical West*, we marveled at the consumption of electricity by homeowners in Oregon and Washington. They used, as I recall, an average of close to 2000 kilowatt-hours a year, as opposed to the national average of about 500. Today, the average for homes throughout the country is 8150 kw-hr. And needless to say, there are millions of families that use much more.

Despite such figures, however, it is possible that your service entrance may be undersized—only 60 amps. when you need 100, or only 100 amps. when you need 200. Your circuits may be overloaded. You may not have enough convenience outlets where you need them. Your switching may be dated.

There is plenty you can do to correct such conditions—but there are few things you should attempt yourself. Electricity, as you well know, is dangerous. Make one mistake in putting in wiring, and you may have a fire or, worse, a fatality.

INCREASING THE CAPACITY OF YOUR SERVICE...

First of all, if there are only two wires coming into your house from the pole at the street, call up your utility company and ask them to install a three-wire service so you can have 240-volt service to run a range, dryer, large air conditioner, water heater, or electric heater.

Second, hire an electrical contractor to install a new service entrance panel, including the main breaker and circuit breakers. (You can have fuses instead of circuit breakers. They do the same job just as efficiently, though they are more troublesome because when one blows, you must take it out and put in a new one of the same size. But in the eyes of possible buyers of your home, circuit breakers are more modern.)

217

If you already have three-wire service, you may still need to get a contractor to put in a large service entrance. Don't skimp on the capacity. It doesn't cost much more to put in a somewhat larger panel than you presently need, and it's cheaper to do it now than later when your electrical requirements increase (as they probably will after the energy crisis is conquered).

ADDING NEW CIRCUITS...

You can easily tell whether you need more or larger circuits in your house if you keep blowing fuses or don't get top performance out of your appliances. You will also probably need a new circuit if you buy a major appliance, such as a dishwasher, that you haven't owned before.

Adding circuits does not require installation of a new service entrance panel if it has unused capacity. The only way to determine this is to ask an electrical contractor to check. You will need him anyway to install the new circuits.

The type of cable that the contractor installs is limited by your community's electrical code. The size of cable used for individual appliance circuits, such as the range circuit or the automatic washer circuit, and for the small-appliance circuits is also dictated by the code. But when it comes to the general-purpose, or lighting, circuits, you can put in either No. 14 or No. 12 wire. The former is slightly less expensive because it is smaller, and it's completely safe and adequate when fused for 15 amps. But No. 12 wire can carry more current and cannot be overloaded so easily. So it's a better choice.

Running the cable for a new circuit into an existing house is likely to stir up a mess if you have to snake it through walls and ceilings for any distance. Then it becomes necessary to open holes in order to pull the cable through the stud and joist spaces and to get it past the various obstructions created by the house framing. I well remember that, when we remodeled our first kitchen, the plaster ceiling looked like a battlefield after the electrician had installed the wiring for an extensive lighting circuit. But the only way to avoid this is to run the wires through surface-mounted raceways. These are fairly unobtrusive and inoffensive, but I can't say they help the appearance of a room.

REPLACING
KNOB-AND-TUBE WIRING...

If the only wiring you are familiar with is the type that uses large, metal-covered, plastic-covered, or braided cables, you may be frightened out of your wits if you buy a house with knob-and-tube wiring. In this system, there are two small wires that are strung through the house on white porcelain knobs and in white porcelain tubes.

The whole business looks archaic—and is, in fact, the first kind of wiring ever installed. But fear not: Being old doesn't mean it's unsafe. There is no need ever to replace it. But it won't hurt to ask an electrical contractor to check it because it is more readily damaged than newer types of wiring; and, of course, the system very possibly may not have sufficient capacity or enough circuits to satisfy your needs.

ADDING
CONVENIENCE OUTLETS...

BEYOND AN   You can add new electric outlets yourself as well as
EXISTING OUTLET   doing the other jobs described on the following pages.
                       Just be careful.

The way to add a new outlet is to run a cable from an existing general-purpose outlet—not an appliance outlet. Before going to work, however, you must check whether the circuit supplying the existing outlet is large enough to serve another outlet. To do this, plug a lamp into the outlet and turn it on. Then remove the fuses or open the circuit breakers until you hit the one that controls the light. Then go through the house, turning on every light to determine which do not come on and plugging a lamp into every outlet to determine which are dead. Make a list of these, and jot down the wattage of the light or appliance that is normally controlled by each one. For example:

- Master bedroom ceiling light—100 watts
- Master bedroom bedside outlet—lamp, 75 watts; clock, 2 watts
- Master bedroom bureau outlet—2 lamps, 100 watts total

Add the total wattage of the lights and appliances. Let's say it comes to 2500. But it's obvious that you rarely, if ever, have everything turned on at once. So make a rough guess of what things are normally turned on together, and total their wattage. Let's say the figure is reduced to 1500. The new outlet you want to add is to be used for a large color-television set operating at 350 watts. The odds are that you will use it when most everything else is on. So the total normal load on the circuit after you add the outlet will be 1850 watts.

Unfortunately, a 15-amp. general-purpose circuit made with No. 14 wire will not carry a load of more than 1800 watts. On the other hand, a 20-amp. general-purpose circuit made with No. 12 wire will carry 2400 watts. Now, you should find out which type of circuit you have. This is pretty easy. Look at the number on the nose of the fuse or the handle of the circuit breaker. If it's 15, the circuit is very probably made with No. 14 wire. If it's 20, it's probably made with No. 12 wire. (I say "probably" because there is always a chance that somebody at some time put in the wrong fuse.)

Let's say the number is 15. That means that, if you add the TV outlet, you may overload the circuit and blow the fuse frequently. But who knows for sure? In this situation, my personal inclination would be to install the outlet. If the TV set would overload the circuit by more than 50 watts, however, you should investigate the possibility of adding the new outlet to another general-purpose circuit. If this also proves impossible, have an electrician install an entirely new circuit.

The second step to take before running a new outlet from an existing one is to find out whether you can get the latter out of the wall so you can work on it. Make sure the electricity is off. Then remove the outlet cover plate, unscrew the outlet from the steel box in which it's recessed, and pull it out to reveal the inside of the box. If there is a single cable coming into the bottom of the box, it will be possible to take the box out of the wall and add a new cable. But if the cable comes into the box at the top or a side, or if there are two cables entering the box—regardless of their positions—you cannot add a new cable without cutting a big hole in the wall around the box.

On the other hand, if the existing outlet is installed in a baseboard, it makes no difference how many cables come into the box or from what direction; you can get at the box to work on it by pulling off the entire baseboard.

The materials needed to add a new outlet are—

- The outlet itself—The normal type has two receptacles and is known as a duplex outlet. You may put in a triple outlet, however. Modern receptacles have three holes instead of two to allow for grounding.
- A rectangular outlet box with built-in cable clamps—Buy two. They should be 2-1/2 in. deep unless the wall in which they're to be installed is too shallow to take them. In that case, use boxes with a depth of 1-1/2 in.
- Cover plates.
- BX cable of the same size as that used in the existing circuit—It should also have the same number of wires—in all likelihood, two. Three-wire cables allowing for grounding of the circuit are rare in old houses. I recommend BX cable because it is legal to use in virtually all U.S. communities. Nonmetallic sheathed cable can be substituted, but only if the community electrical code permits it.
- Fiber bushings to protect the insulation on the wires in the cable.
- A coil of flat steel wire called a fish wire, or snake.

The procedure for installing the new outlet follows:

1 • Shut off the current to the existing outlet.

2 • Remove the cover plate. Unscrew the outlet, pull it from the box, and detach the wire leads. Then detach the box from the wall. This may be done by removing screws from the brackets at the top and bottom of the box. If there are no screws, look for a nail or screw in one side of the box. A nail can be pried up enough with a screwdriver to allow you to grip and pull it out with pliers, or you can cut off the head with a file or hacksaw blade. Remove a screw with a screwdriver (an offset screwdriver may simplify the operation).

    Finally, take the box out of the wall by pulling straight forward as far as possible and then tipping it to free the cable. Note how the cable is attached to the box. If it is held on the outside of the box by a sleeve with a screw, loosen the flat nut around the cable inside the box with a screwdriver. Discard the box and the connector and replace with a new one. But if the cable is attached by a built-in clamp similar to that in your new boxes, the old box is still usable, and the cable should not be detached.

3 • Find the studs in the vicinity of the new outlet. Ideally, the outlet box should be installed against one of them so it can be attached with a nail or screw. There is no difficulty, however, in anchoring a box in the middle of a stud space with metal box supports.

    If the outlet is installed in a baseboard, it need not be near a stud since the box can be screwed to the baseboard.

4 • Cut a hole in the wall or baseboard for the new box. Figure 11-1 shows the shape of the hole required.

    Cut the round holes in the edges of the opening with a drill; then use a hacksaw blade or keyhole saw to make the straight cuts. However, if the wall is built of plaster on metal lath, you will probably have to cut out the plaster with a chisel and then use tin snips to open the lath.

5 • Run the new cable from the existing outlet hole to the new hole. There are serveral relatively easy ways to do this without damaging the wall.

    One is to remove the baseboard between the holes and gouge a channel in the wall behind it (Fig. 11-2). At the ends of the channel, directly under the outlet openings, drill large holes through the wall. Now, bend a hook in the end of the fish wire, and push it through one of the newly drilled holes into the wall cavity and up toward the outlet opening above. This takes a lot of pushing and pulling and

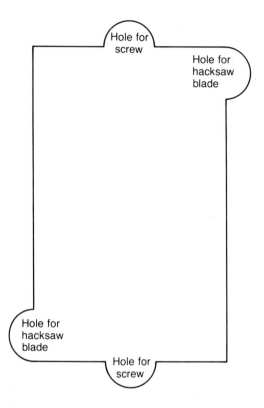

Fig. 11-1   Hole for electrical outlet box.

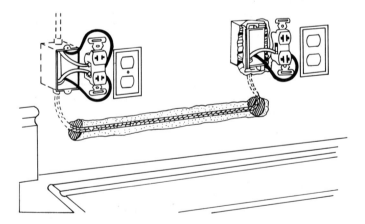

Fig. 11-2   Running cable from one outlet to another.

wiggling. If you have trouble finding the outlet opening, cut off a short length of fish wire, make a hook in the end, and reach down through the outlet opening until you engage the hook on the first wire. Then pull the first wire out of the outlet opening a short distance, attach the wires in the BX cable to it, and pull the fish wire and cable down through the wall and out of the hole at the bottom.

Extend the cable to the other outlet opening and work it up through the wall and out of the opening with your fish wires. Then fit the cable into the channel and fasten it with electrician's staples or nails. Finally, cut the cable to the required length. It should have plenty of slack at both ends.

If there's a door between the two outlet openings, it's still possible to conceal a cable behind the baseboards. Simply remove the trim from the sides and top of the doorway and run the cable around it in a channel or in the gap between the door jambs and framing (Fig. 11-3).

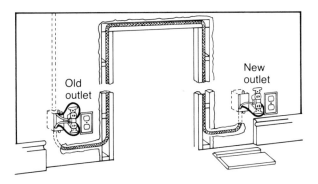

Fig. 11-3   Running cable around a door.

A second way to run in a cable if the existing and new outlets are on the first floor over a basement or crawl space is to drill holes through the floor into the stud spaces containing the outlets. Then with a fish wire, pull the cable down from one outlet opening, run it across the basement ceiling, and fish it up into the other outlet opening (Fig. 11-4).

A comparable procedure may be followed to run a cable between outlets on the first or second floor if there is an attic directly overhead. Drill down from the attic into the stud spaces, and run the cable through the attic.

6 • Remove 8 in. of the spiral-wound steel sheath from each end of the BX cable [Fig. 11-5(a)]. To do this, cut more or less at right angles across one of the twists of steel with a hacksaw. Be careful to cut

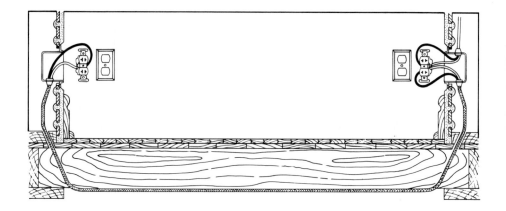

Fig. 11-4   Running cable through a basement or crawl space.

just through the steel—no further. Bend the cable sharply to complete the break. Then pull off the short length of armor to expose
the bare steel bond wire and the paper-wrapped insulated wires.
Smooth the raw edge of the armor with a file. Then strip the paper
off the insulated wires; slip a fiber bushing around them, and push
it down into the armor to protect the insulation [Fig. 11-5(b)].

Cut off all but 3 in. of the bond wire, and remove 1/2 in. of
insulation from the ends of both insulated wires.

7 • If you can keep the existing outlet box, remove the rounded
knockout tab in the bottom next to the incoming cable. This is done
by inserting a screwdriver blade through the slot in the tab and
bending outward.

If you replace the existing outlet box, remove both tabs in the
bottom of the new box.

Remove one tab in the bottom of the box for the new outlet.

8 • Insert the new cable in the boxes. (You may also have to insert the
old cable if the old box has been replaced.) Push it into the
connector clamp as far as possible. Loop the bond wire around the
screw in the clamp, and tighten the screw until the cable is secure
[Fig. 11-5(c)].

9 • Push the outlet boxes into their respective holes in the wall. The
rims of the boxes should be a slight fraction of an inch below the
wall surface. Adjust the depth as necessary by loosening the brackets
on the top and bottom of each box.

To fasten a box to a stud, hammer one or two nails diagonally
through the holes in the side. You will need a nailset to drive them
in all the way. The alternative is to make holes in the stud with an

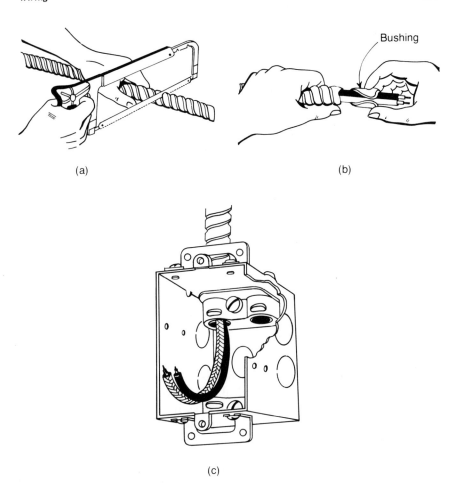

(a) (b)

(c)

Fig. 11-5 Attaching cable to the outlet box.

awl and drive in screws. As noted earlier, an offset screwdriver is easier to use than a conventional screwdriver.

To install a box between studs calls for two metal box supports. These resemble a pair of Ts with the crossbars joined at the end (Fig. 11-6). After setting the box in the hole, slip the crossbar of one support through the crack at one side of the box, pull the crossbar tight against the inside surface of the wall, and fold the legs of the support back inside the box, tight against the side. Install the second support on the other side of the box in the same way.

To install a box in a baseboard or a wood-paneled wall, drive short screws through the holes in the top and bottom brackets.

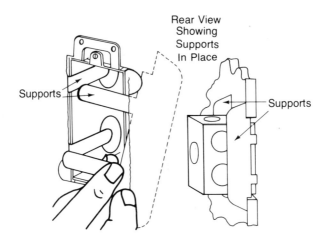

Fig. 11-6   Installing metal box supports.

   10 • Attach the outlets to the insulated wires in both boxes, screw the
          outlets into the boxes, and install the cover plates. For how to do
          this, see "Replacing Outlets" below.

FROM A JUNCTION BOX   A junction box is a shallow box with a solid metal
                          cover attached by two screws. It is usually octagonal,
and is usually found in the basement or attic. Its purpose is to joint together
several different runs of cable within the same circuit.

   A good way to install a new outlet is to run a cable from a junction box
that is surface-mounted on a ceiling or wall. It must have an unused knockout
tab in one side; otherwise, it will have to be replaced with a larger box.

   The method of checking whether the new outlet will overload a circuit,
snaking the cable through walls, and installing the outlet box and outlet is
similar to that just described.

   To connect new BX cable at the junction box, remove a knockout tab
with a screwdriver and hammer. After taking 8 in. of armor off the end of the
cable and exposing the wires, remove the locknut from a BX cable connector
and slip the connector down over the wires onto the end of the armor. Tighten
the set screw and wrap the bond wire around it securely.

   Slip the insulated wires and the threaded end of the cable connector
through the knockout hole in the junction box. Screw the locknut onto the
connector, and turn it tight by pushing the teeth on the rim with a screwdriver
[Fig. 11-7(a)].

   Remove the wire nuts or electrical tape from the old wiring in the junction
box. Scrape the bare wires bright if they have been taped. Then wrap the new

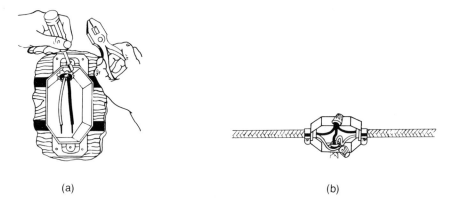

Fig. 11-7   (a) Tightening the locknut; (b) Covering bare wires with wire nuts.

black wire around the old black wires, the new white wire around the old white wires. Secure them with wire nuts. The nuts should completely cover the bare wires [Fig. 11-7(b)]. If they don't, remove them, snip a bit from the ends, and try the nut again. The alternative is to wrap black cellulose electrical tape over the wires and nuts.

Seal the box with a cover plate. The plate must be left exposed. Plastering over it or permanently covering it with any other material is illegal.

The same method is used to run a new outlet from a basement or attic ceiling light that is operated by a pull chain.

BY CUTTING A CABLE   The cable must be part of a general-purpose circuit and must be live at all times (not controlled by a switch). In addition, it should be exposed—as in a basement or attic—and should have sufficient slack so you can splice the wires after cutting the cable.

Sever the cable and remove 8 in. of armor from the end of each piece. Mount a 4-in. octagonal junction box on the ceiling, wall, or attic floor with nails. Remove three of the knockout tabs. Install the ends of the cut cable through two of them and secure them with cable connectors. Install the new cable that runs to the new outlet in the third hole. Then splice the three black wires and the three white wires with wire nuts. Cover the box.

Installation of the new cable and outlet is made in the manner previously described.

REPLACING OUTLETS...

From the standpoint of delivering power to a light or appliance, an old outlet is as good as a new one. The only reason for replacing an outlet, therefore, is because it is defective. That, of course, is a very good reason.

Shut off the current, and remove the cover plate; unscrew the outlet from the box, pull it out, and detach the wires. If the wires are so dirty that you can't be sure of their color, make careful note of the color of the screws to which they are attached. Black wires are "hot" wires and must be connected to gold screws; white wires are connected to silver screws. If there is a colored ground wire (highly unusual in an old house), it is connected to a colored grounding screw.

Modern outlets with three holes in each receptacle are grounded outlets, but they can be used equally well in an ungrounded system. To install one, wrap the black wire clockwise around the gold screw and the white wire clockwise around the silver screw; tighten the screws (Fig. 11-8). Fasten the outlet in the box, and apply the cover plate.

If there are two black wires and two white wires in the box, use either of the two gold screws on the outlet for either of the black wires, and use either of the silver screws for either white wire.

Many outlets can also be attached by straightening the bare ends of the wires and trimming them to 1/2 in. in length. They are then stuck into holes in the back of the outlet. The holes for the black wires are adjacent to the gold screws; those for the white wires are adjacent to the silver screws. Before placing the outlet in the box, pull the wires to make sure they are secure. (The outlet can be removed at any time by inserting a small screwdriver blade into a slot next to each wire. This frees the wire.)

REPLACING SWITCHES...

Whether you have antique button switches or noisy toggle switches, replacing

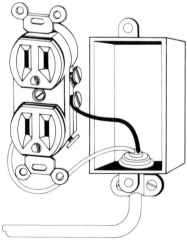

Fig. 11-8   Attaching electric outlets.

them with modern silent switches makes a surprisingly big change in a house at a modest price.

The best of the silent switches are mercury units that must be installed with the end marked "top" upward. Other switches are a little less silent and a little less durable—but otherwise thoroughly satisfactory and considerably cheaper. They can be installed with either end up.

To remove an old switch, shut off the current. Remove the switch plate and then the screws holding the switch in the box. Detach the wires, and scrape the ends bright if they are corroded.

A single-pole switch with two terminals may be wired in two ways. If a single cable enters the box, the black wire is connected to the gold screw, the white wire to the silver screw [Fig. 11-9(a)]. But if two cables enter the box, the white wires are spliced together with a wire nut (don't bother these when replacing the switch). The two black wires are attached to the screws. It doesn't make any difference which wire you attach to which screw [Fig. 11-9(b)].

In a three-way switch with three terminals, the black wire is connected to the single gold screw, the other wires to either of the side-by-side silver screws.

Wire a four-way switch with four terminals in the same way you find it. If you're afraid you won't remember which wire goes to which terminal, tie tags to them.

In all cases, the wires should be wrapped clockwise around the screws. Modern switches, like modern outlets, can also be connected by inserting the wires in holes.

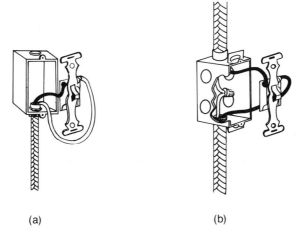

(a)   (b)

Fig. 11-9 Wiring a single-pole switch (a) if a single cable enters the box and (b) if two cables enter the box.

12

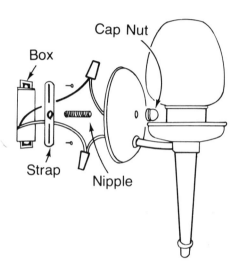

Box

Cap Nut

Strap

Nipple

Lighting

The first thing Elizabeth and I did when we bought our present old house was to hire a general contractor to get started on the renovation while we were selling and cleaning out our home at the other end of the state.

The second thing we did was to visit our favorite electrical store and buy new fixtures for every light in the new house. The old ones were gruesome. No, gruesome is the word I reserve for those dreadful fixtures you see in the big, glass-walled, two-story lighting emporiums which seem to be springing up in shopping areas everywhere. The fixtures in our house were just tired. Some were broken or discolored. All were of 1930 or 1940 vintage.

Although our purpose in replacing the fixtures was simply to get rid of ancient eyesores, other even more important reasons for rejuvenating the lighting in a house are to help you see better, to make the house brighter, and to use light to accent the colors and textures of furnishings and building materials. It's possible that you can achieve these aims just by changing fixtures, but improbable. All depends on whether your house has enough lighting outlets in all the necessary places; and this is rarely true in houses built in the past—particularly in the 1920s and 30s. So you may have to put in additional lights or at least newer, more efficient kinds of light.

THE BASICS
OF GOOD LIGHTING...

I am well aware that the term "good lighting" means different things to different experts. I have never known a decorator who defined it like an architect, or an architect who defined it like an illuminating engineer. All have sound arguments to support their opinions. Still and all, people with the Illuminating Engineering Society, General Electric, Westinghouse, and Sylvania make the most sense. Their basic beliefs can be summarized as follows:

- Residential lighting must provide ample light so you can see what you're doing without straining.

- At the same time, it must be glareless and more or less uniform throughout a room. Sharp contrasts between dark areas and light areas cause eyestrain.

- With few exceptions, all lights must be shielded so you do not look directly at the bulbs.

- There should be a choice of methods for lighting the living room, dining room, family room, study, and bedrooms. Thus, you can suit the lighting to your needs and moods.

- The lighting system should be a combination of general and local lighting. General lighting provides the overall, or background, light that lets you see and move around. Local lighting is needed for specific tasks such as reading, sewing, and cooking.

- Finally, it must be remembered that the colors and to some extent the textures used in the house have a major bearing on the efficiency of the lighting and the way it affects people. Reflecting surfaces, in short, must not be too dark. Ceilings should always be very light colored; walls, only a little darker; floors, no darker than cocoa color.

DESIGNING
YOUR LIGHTING SYSTEM...

Exactly how you get this highly desirable kind of lighting in your home is not for me to say. There are many means to the end.

GENERAL LIGHTING   General lighting is most inexpensively done with surface-mounted or suspended ceiling fixtures with diffusing bowls. In rooms of under 250 sq. ft., one central fixture is enough; in larger rooms, use two. In all cases, provide one watt for each square foot of floor space.

Recessed ceiling fixtures and surface-mounted fixtures that direct all light downward are less effective because they don't spread the light; consequently, you need two or three times as many fixtures.

Fluorescent wall valances installed over windows and extending for much of the length of the wall are excellent general lighting units because they throw light up on the ceiling and down on the draperies. Thus, they give much the effect of natural daylight. In addition, they bring out the beauty of the draperies. Fluorescent wall brackets that are installed on inside walls can be used in the same way but do not blend into all rooms as easily as valances.

Luminous ceilings are the newest and most dramatic type of general lighting unit, and give the highest level of illumination because they cover a large area—sometimes an entire ceiling.

Local lighting is usually done with portable lamps, but it is also done with built-in fixtures that concentrate light on specific areas. For example, small fluorescent brackets may be used over the heads of beds as reading lights. A downlight mounted on the ceiling may be used to light a desk or sewing machine. A directional fixture recessed in the ceiling may be used to light a piano or bookshelf.

Although an illuminating engineer would take me to task for saying so, the design of the lighting for the living room, dining room, family room, study, and bedrooms is less crucial than that for the kitchen and bathrooms. This is not to say that you don't need plenty of good, even, glareless light plus assorted types of local lighting. But in the kitchen and bathrooms a very high level of illumination in very specific locations is essential.

KITCHEN LIGHTING General lighting in the kitchen should be about twice as intense as in other rooms. This is why a luminous ceiling is particularly desirable. Surface-mounted fixtures, however, are effective if they are lamped at two watts per square foot of floor area.

All counters should be lighted with 20-watt fluorescent fixtures installed on the bottoms of the wall cabinets above. Use one fixture every 4 ft.

Over the sink, recess fixtures in the ceiling close to the wall or mount them on the ceiling and shield them with an 8-in. board. Use either two 25-watt fluorescents or two 75-watt incandescent flood-lamps. (Use the same type of lighting for counters that do not have wall cabinets above.)

To illuminate the range (don't depend on the built-in light, because it is inadequate in all ranges except those with an oven above the surface burners), use a 25-watt fluorescent under a wall cabinet, and shield it with a board. Or mount the fluorescent in a wall bracket 58 in. above the floor.

BATHROOM LIGHTING If bathrooms have luminous ceilings, no other lighting is required. The alternative is to mount fixtures on either side of the mirror over the lavatory. They should be 30 in. apart and centered 5 ft. above the floor. Ideally, a third fixture should be installed on the ceiling 12 to 18 in. out from the wall. All the fixtures should be lamped either with one 60-watt incandescent bulb or with one 20-watt fluorescent tube.

If you have an unusually wide mirror above the lavatory, mount two rows of fluorescent tubes on the ceiling 1 ft. from the wall. The fluorescents should be as long as the mirror.

INSTALLING LIGHTING...

There are many lighting jobs you can do yourself, although some may prove a little difficult. These are discussed below. If it's necessary to add new wiring circuits to serve the lighting outlets, however, get an electrical contractor.

REPLACING   Shut off the current at the fuse box or circuit
CONVENTIONAL   breaker, and loosen the nuts or screws fastening the
FIXTURES   light to the outlet box in the wall or ceiling. Then
                              separate the small fixture wires from the heavy wires
in the box. They may be connected by wire nuts or by solder overwrapped with
electrical tape. To break a soldered joint, snip the heavy wires and then cut back
the insulation on the ends a little.

Incandescent fixtures   Attach a new incandescent fixture by twisting the
                              black fixture wire around the black circuit wire in the
box, the white fixture wire around the white circuit wire. Then screw on wire
nuts until the wires are secure and the bare copper is completely covered. If the
copper sticks out from the nuts, remove the nuts, shorten the wires slightly, and
replace the nuts. (Note that wire nuts make a strong enough splice for you to let
a small fixture dangle as you work on it. But have someone support a heavy
fixture.)

Finish the job by pushing the wires into the box and fastening the fixture
to the box. The last step sounds easy but often is not because the new fixture is
designed differently from the old one and may not be immediately adapted to
the box.

In the simplest ceiling installation, the fixture is screwed directly to screw
holes provided on flanges on the rim of the box. But if the screw holes in the
fixture are not spaced like those in the box, you need a mounting strap [Fig.
12-1(a)]. These are designed in different ways but are really nothing more than a
thin strip of steel with various holes and slots. The strap may be attached to the
screw holes in the box, or it may be pushed up on a large threaded stud that is
found in some boxes, and bolted to the stud. In either case, the fixture is then
bolted to the strap.

Hanging and very heavy, surface-mounted ceiling fixtures must be bolted to
a stud in the outlet box [Fig. 12-1(b)]. The device used to join the stud with the
fixture is a U-shaped gadget with threaded bolts in the uprights. It is called a
hickey.

Wall fixtures are usually fastened by a headless bolt called a nipple [Fig.
12-1(c)]. The nipple is screwed into a strap fastened to the outlet box. A hole in
the center of the fixture is then slipped over the nipple, and a bolt is screwed on
the exposed end of the nipple.

Fluorescent fixtures   To install a fluorescent fixture (Fig. 12-2) you must
                              first open the long metal box, called a channel,
containing the wiring and ballast. Determine the best position of the light and
then open the knockout tab in the channel that will be closest to the outlet box.
If the box contains a stud, attach a hickey to it and then attach a hollow nipple.
Insert the wires in the box through the hickey and nipple. Then insert the nipple

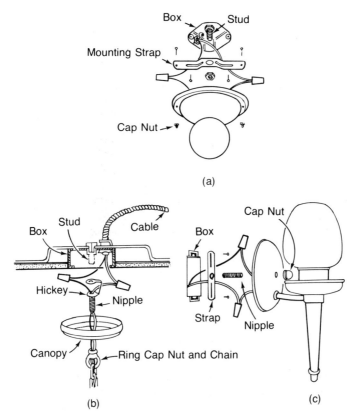

Fig. 12-1   Hanging incandescent fixtures.

through the hole in the channel, and attach the channel to the box with a lock nut. This should conceal the box. If the fluorescent fixture is small, no additional support is necessary. But if the fixture is large, drive one or two screws through the back into the studs, or install toggle bolts or hollow-wall screw anchors.

Now, connect the black fixture wire to the black circuit wire and the white fixture wire to the white circuit wire with wire nuts. Replace the cover on the channel. Plug in a starter if required. (A starter is a small metal canister that is installed through a hole in the channel cover.) Then plug in the tube and cover it with the shielding (if part of the fixture).

An additional point to remember when installing fluorescent fixtures is that they must never be placed directly against a wall or ceiling made of wood, fiberboard, or other combustible material. Slip asbestos or asbestos-cement board underneath. The alternative is to provide a 1/2-in. air space between the channel and wall. This will necessitate pulling the outlet box out from the wall 1/2 in.

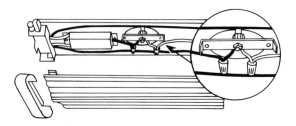

Fig. 12-2   Hanging fluorescent fixtures.

INSTALLING A NEW   Because of the difficulties of snaking cable through
CEILING FIXTURE   the walls and ceilings without breaking holes in them,
                             you should attempt this project only if there is an
attic above the room in which you put the light.

First, make sure that the light will not overload the circuit to which it is
added. Run the cable to the light from an outlet that you can pull out of the
wall. (See Chapter 11.) A single-pole switch should be installed on the cable 4 ft.
off the floor.

The installation procedure follows:

1 • Cut a hole in the wall for the switch box. It should be adjacent to a
     stud to which the box can be nailed or screwed.

2 • Drill a large hole through the plate at the top of the wall space. Push
     a length of BX cable down through it to the opening for the switch.
         Drop a second length of BX cable down through the switch
     opening to the bottom of the stud space. Tie something on the free
     end so it won't fall into the wall.

3 • Shut off the current and pull the outlet out of the wall. Remove the
     knockout tab in the bottom of the outlet box next to the existing
     cable. Then fish the cable from the switch opening out of the wall,
     and after removing an 8-in. length of the armor, insert it in the
     knockout and secure it to the box with the connector clamp.
         Let the new cable loop down inside the wall space so it has
     plenty of room to make the turn up to the switch. Replace the
     outlet box in the wall. Then attach the wires to the outlet and
     replace it in the box.

4 • Remove the two knockout tabs from the bottom of a new switch
     box. (The same kind of box is used for an outlet.) Take some of the
     slack out of the cable running up from the outlet, but don't pull too
     hard. Then cut off what you don't need, and strip the armor from
     the end. Insert it through one of the knockouts in the box and
     secure it.

Strip the armor from the end of the cable coming down from the attic, and attach the cable to the box through the other knockout. Letting the cable loop down inside the wall, set the box in the wall opening and fasten it to the stud.

5 • Remove the insulation from the ends of the four wires in the switch box. Twist the two white wires together and apply a wire nut. Then screw one of the black wires to either of the switch terminals, and screw the other black wire to the other terminal. Fasten the switch in the box.

6 • Two types of box can be used to mount the light fixture on the ceiling. One is a shallow octagonal box about 4 in. wide attached under a steel hanger bar that is nailed to the sides of the joists [Fig. 12-3(a)]. Ask for a box with a "new work" hanger. The other is a solid, round disk that is screwed to the bottom of a joist [Fig. 12-3(b)]. It is called a pancake box.

If you want the light in the exact center of the room and a joist happens to be at that point, use a pancake box. But use an octagonal box if the center of the room is between joists.

7 • To install an octagonal box, cut a hole of the same size and shape through the ceiling. Work from below rather than from the attic so you don't damage the surface of the ceiling.

Then climb up into the attic, set the box in the opening with the rim slightly above the ceiling surface, and nail the hanger bar to the joists on either side.

Remove a knockout tab in the top of the box. Cut the cable running from the switch to the proper length, and remove the armor from the end. Fasten the cable to the box with a BX cable connector and locknut. Join the circuit wires with the fixture wires. And hang the fixture from the box with the appropriate mounting straps or studs.

8 • Almost all the work involved in the installation of a pancake box is done in the room being lighted.

After cutting a hole for the box directly below a joist, pull the cable running through the attic down through the hole and cut it off about a foot below the ceiling. Remove 8 in. of armor from the end.

Hold the box with its flat back facing the ends of the insulated wires, and stick the wires through one of the four connector holes in the box. Wrap the bond wire around the adjacent set screw and tighten the screw to secure the cable in the box. Then push the cable up through the hole and anchor the box with a couple of screws. Attach and hang the light.

9 • Turn on the current. You're in business.

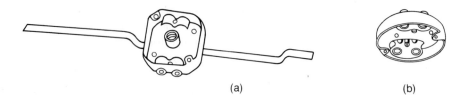

(a)   (b)

Fig. 12-3 Two types of outlet boxes for light fixtures.

Note that power for the light can also be drawn from a junction box in the basement, but fishing the wire up through the wall to the switch is more difficult.

If power is taken from a junction box in the attic, it's easier to put in a fixture with a pull-chain than to install a separate switch. But it's perfectly feasible to have the convenience of a wall switch by attaching a second cable to the box containing the ceiling fixture and running it across the attic and down through the wall to the switch.

In the ceiling box, connect the black wire from the junction box to the white wire running to the switch. Connect the white wire from the junction box to the white wire on the light. Connect the black wire on the light to the black wire running to the switch (Fig. 12-4).

At the switch, connect either wire to either screw. Then paint the white wire at the switch and the same wire in the ceiling box black so you will know that it is hot.

INSTALLING A NEW WALL FIXTURE   This is essentially similar to installing a ceiling light. Take the power for the light from an outlet directly below or from a junction box in the basement. Mount the fixture on a pancake box screwed to the front of a stud or on a rectangular outlet box. For maximum security, the latter should be nailed or screwed to the

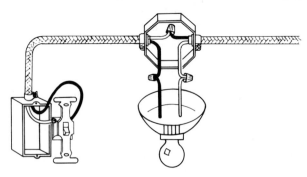

Fig. 12-4 Adding a wall switch to control a ceiling light at the end of the run.

side of a stud, but it can be installed with metal box supports if the fixture is not large or heavy.

A wall switch is unnecessary if the fixture has a built-in switch. Both of the switch wires are black, and both of the light wires are white. Attach one of the switch wires to the black circuit wire, the other switch wire to one of the light wires, and the other light wire to the white circuit wire.

If you want a wall switch even though the fixture has its own switch, don't connect the wires of the switch in the fixture to anything.

The easiest place to install a wall switch is in the stud space with the light and cable running to the light. In this situation, the cable from the power source runs to the switch and a second cable runs from the switch to the light. Hook up the switch in the manner described in Step 5 under "Installing a New Ceiling Fixture".

If you want to control the light from another part of the room, extend the cable from the power source directly to the fixture and run a second cable from the fixture to the switch. This second cable can be installed by dropping it down through the stud space, hiding it behind a baseboard, and pulling it up through another stud space to the switch. Or if there is an attic overhead, you can run the cable through that. Hook up the fixture and the switch according to the directions for running power from an attic junction box to a ceiling fixture.

INSTALLING RECESSED CEILING FIXTURES When selecting recessed fixtures, you must first determine the depth of the joist space in which they will be mounted. This is usually 8 in., which is deep enough for the majority of fixtures. But some fixtures require a depth of 10 or 12 in.

The fixtures are connected directly to the cable supplying power. The best modern fixtures are then mounted in a metal frame that grips the edges of the hole cut in the ceiling.

BUILDING IN FLUORESCENT LIGHTS 1 • Use 24, 36, and 48-in. fluorescent channels. These take tubes of 20, 30, and 40 watts respectively.

2 • If there is more than one channel in a fixture, use fluorescent tubes of the same color and same diameter in all. The best tube size, labeled T-12, has a diameter of 1-1/2 in.

3 • If you want a light to come on almost instantly after you flip the switch, use a "trigger start" ballast for 24-in., 20-watt fixtures; a "rapid start" ballast for 36-in., 30-watt and 48-in., 40-watt fixtures. If you don't mind a slight delay in starting, use a conventional ballast with a separate starter.

4 • When you install several channels in a straight row, remove the knockout tabs in the ends of adjacent fixtures and fasten the fixtures together with a BX cable connector and locknut or with a threaded hollow nipple and two locknuts. The cable supplying power is connected to one fixture, and insulated wires are then run through the fixture to the other fixtures. All black wires are connected to black wires, all whites to white.

5 • If several channels are installed in parallel rows, connect them with short lengths of BX cable secured in knockouts in the sides of the channels. Bring the power to one fixture and tie the others to it—black wires to black wires and whites to whites.

6 • When a channel is furred out from a wall or ceiling, the cable supplying power can be attached directly to it with a BX connector and locknut. But when the channel is installed directly on a wall or ceiling, the cable should be connected to an outlet box recessed in the wall behind the channel.

7 • For maximum light and minimum color distortion, paint all inside surfaces of a fixture flat white. (I once ignored this rule and left the back of the shielding board on a wall bracket unpainted. As a result, the white wall behind the fixture turned pale brown when the light was on.)

8 • Note again that a fluorescent channel must never be mounted directly on a combustible surface.

Valance lights   A valance light consists of a single long row of fluorescent channels mounted on a wall above a window and shielded from view by a board that usually has returns at the ends to conceal the ends of the fixture. Light is directed upward and downward.

The top of the fluorescent channel and the top edge of the shielding should be at least 10 in. below the ceiling to keep the ceiling from being objectionably glary. If the space is less than 10 in., the top of the valance is closed.

The shielding board should be a minimum of 5 in. wide [Fig. 12-5(a)]. Allow a 2-in. space between the back of the board and the center line of the fluorescent tubes. And allow at least 3 in.—preferably 4 in.—from the center line of the tubes to the drapery track. The last requirement means that the channel must be furred out from the wall with blocks of wood.

If the shielding board isn't very long, it can be hung securely with a single angle iron at each end. Attach the irons to the returns with screws and to the wall with screws or toggle bolts. A long shielding board, however, requires some intermediate support. This can be provided with large angle irons screwed to the

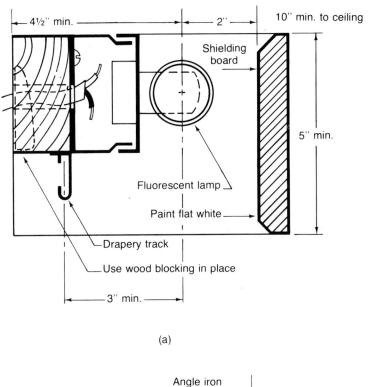

(a)

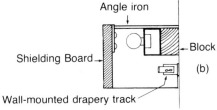

Fig. 12-5   Installing a valance light.

tops of the blocks supporting the fluorescent channels and to the back of the shielding [Fig. 12-5(b)].

Wall brackets   A lighted wall bracket is built and installed like a valance light except that the fluorescent channels are attached directly to the wall if it isn't combustible.

Brackets that are used for local lighting—over the head of a bed or a desk, for instance—are mounted much lower on the wall than those used for general lighting; consequently, you must test the position of the shielding board in relation to the light before installing it. For instance, if the bracket is mounted, say, 54 in. off the floor, the shielding must be extended several inches above the top of the channel to conceal the tube from a person standing. It might also have to extend well below the channel to conceal it from a person sitting. Diffusing glass or plastic is sometimes used as a top for a low-mounted wall bracket to shield the tube and at the same time to serve as a shelf for ornaments, plants, etc.

Cornice lights   A cornice light is a long strip of fluorescents mounted on a ceiling close to a wall and shielded from view by a board with returns at the ends. It is used for general lighting of a room—but since all the light is directed downward on the wall, it provides a somewhat lower level of illumination than a valance light or wall bracket.

The front side of the fluorescent channel should be at least 6 in. out from the wall they parallel (Fig. 12-6). If there are windows in the wall, the distance from the center line of the fluorescent tubes to the draperies should be 3 in. To install the lights, mark their location on the ceiling; then nail 1 x 3-in. blocks of wood back of this line and screw the channels to them. Nail the shielding board, which should be at least 6 in. wide, to the front edges of the blocks.

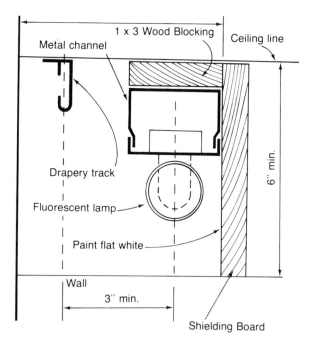

Fig. 12-6   Installing a cornice light.

Cove lights   Because a cove light (Fig. 12-7) directs all light
                         upward on to the ceiling, it provides little illu-
mination and is not recommended except for its decorative value.

A single row of fluorescents is set in what amounts to a trough built along
a wall. The top of the channel and the shielding board should be at least 12 in.
below the ceiling. The board is usually slanted outward to improve the
appearance of the cove; it need not be more than 5 in. wide.

The channels are furred out from the wall on wood blocks to which the
bottom of the cove is also attached. The space from the wall to the center line of
the tubes should be no less than 4-1/2 in. And the space from the center line of
the tubes to the shielding board should be no less than 2 in.

Soffit lights   Soffit lights are similar to cornice lights but in-
                         corporate two or three parallel rows of fluorescent
tubes with diffusing glass or plastic or metal grilles underneath. They are used
for local lighting to give a high level of illumination on surfaces directly below.
Common installations are over the kitchen sink and over built-in dressing tables.

The channels are mounted on the ceiling close to a wall and behind a front
shielding board 8 to 12 in. wide (Fig. 12-8). The diffuser rests on small moldings
attached to the wall and the back of the shielding board so it can be easily
removed. Two rows of fluorescents are normally installed in soffits less than 18
in. wide, three rows in those up to 24 in. wide.

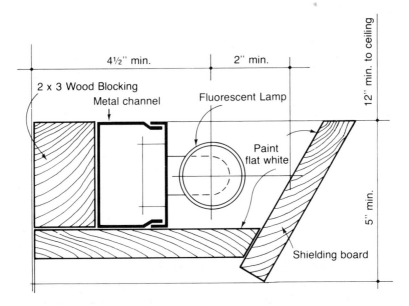

Fig. 12-7   Installing a cove light.

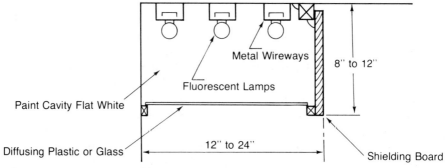

Fig. 12-8   Installing a soffit light.

When a soffit is used in the bathroom or bedroom as a grooming light, it should be made shallow and wide (with three rows of lights) to light the person as well as the mirror. On the other hand, a deep, narrow soffit is best for concentrating light on a surface such as a sink or counter. When very high intensity light is required from this type of soffit, use fluorescent channels equipped with polished metal reflectors; they have almost twice the output of standard channels.

Luminous ceilings   You can buy packaged luminous ceiling assemblies, but it's just as easy to construct your own. In order to plan the installation, you must understand certain points about this excellent kind of light fixture:

1 • Fluorescent tubes—usually 4-footers—are mounted end to end in parallel rows on the ceiling or between the ceiling joists. If on a ceiling, the tubes produce a large panel of light broken only by the framework that supports the diffusing panels or grilles. But if the tubes are installed between joists, they produce 14-in.-wide strips of light divided by the black lines of the joists.

2 • To achieve uniform lighting and to prevent the tubes from showing as bright streaks through the diffusing panels or grilles beneath them, the spaces between the rows of tubes and between the tubes and diffusers must be calculated carefully. As a rule, the tubes should be spaced no more than one-and-a-half times their distance from the diffusers. In other words, if the distance from the center line of the tube to the upper surface of the diffusing panels is 10 in., the distance from the center line of one row of tubes to the center line of another should be no more than 15 in.

3 • Testing and experience have proved that the ideal space from tube to diffuser is 10 to 12 in. This means the rows of tubes would be spaced 15 to 18 in. apart.

4 • The diffusing panels should not be less than 7 ft., 6 in. above the floor—and it is far better if they are at least 8 ft.

5 • All surfaces within the light fixture must be painted flat white.

What does all this add up to?

If you want to create a large, unbroken panel of light, the ceiling must be at least 8-1/2 to 9 ft. high so you can mount the tubes directly on it. Hang the diffusing panels a foot below the tubes in the same type of metal framing used for suspended ceilings. (See Chapter 4.)

If the ceiling is less than 8-1/2 ft. high, you can use it as a light fixture only by knocking it out and installing the fluorescent tubes on asbestos-cement board which is nailed to the subfloor between the joists. If the joist spaces are 8 or 10 in. deep, you need two rows of tubes in each to give uniform light without bright streaks. If the joist spaces are 12 in. deep, however, one row of tubes is sufficient. The diffusing panels below the joist spaces should rest on moldings or metal strips attached to the bottoms of the joists.

One problem with all joist-space installations is that whatever bridging crosses the tubes must be torn out; otherwise, it will create black lines. This, in turn, takes some of the stiffness out of the floor above.

There are no rules to help in determining the size or shape of a luminous ceiling. Here you're on your own. Generally a panel that covers the entire ceiling is most effective in appearance and certainly in light output. But unless you are lighting a bathroom (which is small) or a kitchen (where you need lots of light), such a wall-to-wall installation is more expensive than it's worth.

Hard-and-fast rules about the selection of diffusing panels or grilles for a luminous ceiling are also lacking. This is unfortunate because the materials to choose from are almost without number. The main points to consider are the amount of light transmitted by the diffuser, how easy it is to take down and put up, and whether it holds its color. Generally, plastic is preferred over frosted, textured, or patterned glass because it is lightweight and unbreakable. The best type of plastic is acrylic because it transmits light well and doesn't change color. Always use a rigid plastic, not a flexible type that will move in the framework when a breeze blows through the room.

Grilles should not be used unless you hang a diffuser above them; otherwise, when you look up, you can see the tubes. However, grilles are often more attractive than diffusers because of their texture.

INSTALLING LIGHTS AT A DISTANCE FROM THE HOUSE I am not sure that this comes under the heading of renovating a house, but I guarantee that if you have a detached garage, it's improved by the installation of a light. And if you have a fairly long front walk, your home will appear more inviting and the walk will be safer if you put in a post-light next to it.

Both installations require you to run a cable from the house to the light fixture. In most localities, the best type to use is a relatively inexpensive underground feeder (UF) cable that is insulated with tough plastic. Some communities, however, stipulate that the cable must be put in a rigid conduit, which makes the cost prohibitive.

Run the UF cable through a hole in the basement wall if that is made of easily drilled concrete block; otherwise, run it through the sill. From the house to the garage or walk light, lay the cable in a trench. In lawn areas, this need be only 6 in. deep, but in shrubbery borders, flower beds, and wherever else you may dig, it should be a foot deep.

When installing a walk light, start the cable at a first-floor outlet or junction box in the basement, and run it to a new single-pole switch near the front door. Then run it down into the basement and out to the light. Wire the switch according to Step 5 under "Installing a New Ceiling Fixture".

A garage light, to be of maximum utility, should be controlled by three-way switches in the house and garage (Fig. 12-9). At the house, run a two-wire cable from the power source to the switch. From the house switch to the garage switch, use a three-wire UF cable. Then from the garage switch to the light, use a two-wire cable.

At the house switch, connect the two white wires with a wire nut, and connect the two black wires to either of the side-by-side terminals. The red wire goes to the single terminal.

The garage switch is wired in similar fashion. At the light, connect the two black wires and the two white wires separately.

INSTALLING A
DIMMER SWITCH
Dimmer switches to control incandescent lights are easily installed—but those for fluorescent lights are too tricky to play with.

An incandescent dimmer can be substituted for a conventional switch in any switch box that is 2-1/2 in. deep. Simply shut off the current, remove the old switch, and wire the new switch black wire to gold screw and white wire to silver screw. Secure the switch to the box, and pull off the control knob. Then attach the switch plate and replace the control knob, which is large enough to conceal the rectangular slot in the plate.

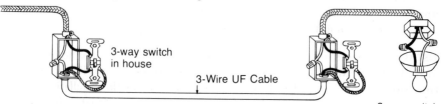

3-way switch
in house
3-Wire UF Cable

3-way switch and
light in garage

Fig. 12-9   Installing a garage light controlled by three-way switches.

13

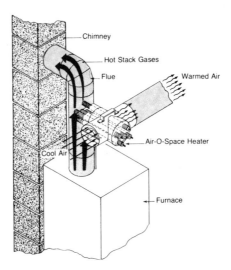

Chimney

Hot Stack Gases

Flue

Warmed Air

Air-O-Space Heater

Cool Air

Furnace

Heating and Cooling Systems

Rejuvenating a house by remodeling the heating system or installing a cooling system is mainly a subject for *discussion*. You should be aware of what can be done—but there is precious little you should try to do yourself.

REMODELING
THE HEATING SYSTEM...

Just because a house is old doesn't mean the heating system is poor. It needs attention only (1) if you have a hand-fired coal furnace or boiler, (2) if the furnace or boiler is on its last legs, (3) if it makes the house very dirty, (4) if it doesn't heat the house adequately, (5) if it is very expensive to operate.

The first four faults are easy to spot. But while the fifth may seem obvious, you can't be sure the cost of heating is exorbitant unless you compare your figures with those of other families living in similar houses and operating their heating systems in the same way you do—and even this isn't a very reliable indicator. A better way to find out if the system is costing too much to operate is to ask your local weather bureau station for the number of degree-days in each of the preceding four or five years. Then find out from your fuel supplier or your own records how many gallons of oil, therms of gas, or kilowatt-hours of electricity you used in each of the same years. Divide the number of degree-days for each year by the fuel consumption figures for the corresponding year.

If the answers you come up with show no more than a 5 per cent variation, you can be sure that, while your heating costs may be higher than they should be, nothing has gone wrong with the system in recent years. But if there is more than a 5 per cent difference between the figures, take warning. There may be a simple explanation. For example, it may be that in the year the figure shot out of line, an elderly parent who likes a very warm house was living with you. But if you can't find such an explanation, it means that the system should get a going over.

INSTALLING A NEW　　Since a heating plant cannot last forever, it has to be
BURNER, FURNACE,　　replaced now and then—but happily, not very often.
OR BOILER　　When the time comes, a heating contractor can do the
job with comparative ease. Complications arise, however, if the doors into the basement are too narrow to admit the new equipment (unless it is disassembled) or if the new equipment cannot be accommodated in the existing arrangement of flues, ducts, or pipes. We face both of these problems in our house, and there has been a good deal of head-scratching about what to do when the boiler gives up the ghost. But no one doubts that an answer will be found.

REPLACING A　　Warm air heating is dirtier than hot water or steam
DIRTY SYSTEM　　heating, although it needn't be. If you have a forced
warm air system, you can quickly make your home cleaner by cleaning or replacing the filters at the furnace. This also increases the efficiency of the system. A two-stage electronic air cleaner gives infinitely cleaner air than you get with ordinary filters, but it costs around $500 to put in.

If you have an old-fashioned gravity system, however, the only answer is to have it replaced with a new forced system. This involves running new supply and return ducts throughout the house. The supplies radiate out from the furnace to the outside walls; the returns go through the interior walls. Placing ducts in the walls can be done only by opening the walls, which is a major undertaking. The alternative is to run the ducts through closets or through the rooms themselves. In the latter case, they should be boxed in with boards.

IMPROVING COMFORT　　There are various minor things you can do to make a
IN THE HOUSE　　heating system somewhat more efficient. They include the following:

- Have the heating plant inspected, cleaned, and adjusted annually.
- Paint radiators to match the walls. Metallic paint reduces heat output as much as 15 per cent.
- Remove radiator covers.
- Insulate heating pipes and ducts.
- Repair broken insulation on furnaces and boilers.

These are all little jobs you can do yourself—but major improvements in efficiency call for an expert.

One simple thing that can be done in a forced warm air system is to have the blower adjusted so that it operates continuously when the outdoor temperature is low. While this increases your consumption of electricity a little—but not much—it makes for more even, comfortable conditions in the house and usually results in some fuel saving.

Similarly, if you have a forced hot water system, the pump should be operated continuously.

Adding new radiators or changing the locations of radiators and registers also makes a house feel more comfortable. But here again you face the necessity of opening up the walls or running the new pipes or ducts up through rooms and boxing them in.

ADDING AUXILIARY   Sometimes a simpler way to get more heat into a
HEATING UNITS   room or section of the house is to leave the present
                        system as is—or perhaps shut it off entirely in the
cold area—and install auxiliary heating units. This sounds more expensive than it often is.

Electric heating units are readily installed, highly efficient, and not too costly to operate if you put in adequate insulation. Baseboard units are most popular—partly because they are simply substituted for wooden baseboards—but recessed wall heaters and ceiling coils that turn an entire ceiling into a radiant panel are widely used. All are controlled by individual room thermostats. They require 240-volt wiring circuits.

If you prefer gas to electricity, you can put in individual room heaters or a single large wall furnace that can heat as much as 1000 sq. ft. of floor space. The room heaters are small boxy units that are placed in the outside wall. They take in fresh outdoor air, heat it, and blow it indoors. Wall furnaces are tall, slim devices that are either recessed in or set against an inside wall in the center of the space to be heated. Cold air enters at the bottom; heated air comes out at the top (Fig. 13-1). The best units have blowers. To assure that heat is distributed throughout the area, you must either install ducts to the distant rooms or build grilled openings above the doors.

Heat-pump room conditioners resemble ordinary room air conditioners and are installed in the same way. However, they not only cool the room in summer but also heat it in winter. Heating is done by extracting heat from the outdoor air and pumping it indoors. In relatively mild climates the heated air costs little or nothing; the only cost is for the electricity powering the unit. In colder climates, however, it is necessary to supplement the heat extracted from the air by turning on resistance heaters in the unit. This raises operating cost.

Heat-pump room conditioners are made in a wide range of sizes so that you can heat anything from a single small room to several large rooms that open into one another. A 240-volt circuit is required for each conditioner. For a permanent installation, the conditioner should be placed in an opening cut through an outside wall above a door or window so that it doesn't obstruct the view through a window or interfere with the decoration of the room.

A final method of heating an underheated space is to install a new device, called an Air-O-Space heater, that is designed to capture some of the heat that

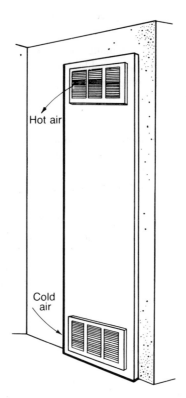

Hot air

Cold air

Fig. 13-1   Wall furnace.

normally escapes up the furnace flue and to use it to heat the basement or other cold area in the house (Fig. 13-2). Connected to the flue just above an old oil-fired furnace or boiler, the heater can recover as much as 10,000 BTUs per hour—enough to heat an area of up to 200 sq. ft. of floor space all by itself. The only moving part is a blower that sucks in clean air from the basement, passes it over pipes heated by the flue gases, and blows it into the basement or through a duct (no more than 20 ft. long) into rooms upstairs. Most people who have put in the device so far use it to heat the basement and, thus, indirectly to raise the temperature in the rooms above.

HEATING AN
EXPANSION ATTIC OR
ADDITION

Generally, if the builder of a house puts in an attic or other space for future expansion, he installs a furnace or boiler with sufficient capacity to heat the space. But you can't count on this. So before you start to expand your house, you must call in a heating contractor to look over the heating system. If it has capacity, it is an easy matter to add the pipes or ducts and radiators or registers needed in the expansion space. But if the system is too

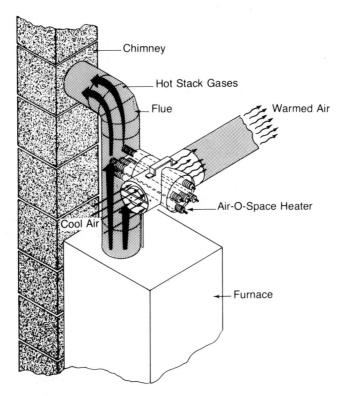

Chimney

Hot Stack Gases

Flue

Warmed Air

Air-O-Space Heater

Cool Air

Furnace

Fig. 13-2   Air-O-Space heater.

small, you must either put in a larger one or install auxiliary heating equipment such as electric baseboards, gas heaters, heat-pump room conditioners, etc.

The heating of an addition is handled in the same way. First, find out whether your present furnace or boiler is large enough to serve the addition. You may be happily surprised to find that it does. But if not, there are many alternatives.

REPLACING RADIATORS   This seemingly simple job of substituting small, modern radiators for enormous, old fashioned units is full of complications.

Buying a new radiator of the proper size isn't a problem. Just measure the old radiator, count how many rows of tubes it has, and let a heating dealer determine what you should replace it with.

Removal of the old radiator isn't a problem either. All you need is a big wrench to unscrew the nut or nuts attaching it to the pipes.

But—If you have a one-pipe steam system, you will find when you put in the new radiator that there is a much wider gap between it and the wall than there was with the old radiator. This spoils the appearance of an otherwise attractive installation, and the only thing you can do about it is to have a plumber cut a hole in the floor and change the piping in order to move the radiator closer to the wall.

You run into the same problem with radiators that have two pipes. In addition, since the new radiators are shorter than those they replace, you must extend one of the pipes.

COVERING RADIATORS   Covering a radiator reduces its heat output. But if this doesn't bother you as much as the appearance of the radiator, go ahead and cover it.

The cover should stand on legs so that the bottom edges are 2 to 4 in. above the floor. For maximum efficiency, cover the entire front (except for the framework) and top with perforated metal. If you build the front and top of plywood, leave a 2-in.-high slot across the front just below the top, and make a similar slot in the top along the back edge. If you prefer a completely solid top, fasten a sheet of aluminum to the wall behind the radiator and curve it over the top of the radiator so that heat is funneled through the slot in the front.

REPLACING A   Until recently, replacement of an old, possibly
THERMOSTAT   worn-out thermostat was done only by professionals. But now thermostat manufacturers are beginning to recognize that the high cost of this practice is limiting replacement sales; consequently, many now are publishing clear directions for the do-it-yourselfer. Ask for these directions and follow them carefully. The work is not difficult—mainly involving making a few simple electrical connections—but it varies with the brand and type of thermostat.

INSTALLING
CENTRAL AIR CONDITIONING...

Of course, you can cool your house with room conditioners. But while they make you more comfortable on sultry days, they do not add to the value of the house as central air conditioning does; and in the aggregate, they don't cost a great deal less.

The first step in putting in central air conditioning is to find two or three reputable, experienced air conditioning contractors, and ask them to make a survey of your house in order to give you an estimate of what a system will cost. To prepare an estimate, a contractor must consider the total area of the house; the width, depth, and height of each room; the number, dimensions, and types of windows; the construction of the exterior walls and roof; the direction the house faces; the extent to which the house is shaded by trees, hills, and other buildings; and the mean temperature of the community. In addition, he must consider the number of people in the family and the extent to which they entertain guests and visitors.

When he submits his bid, a contractor should tell you the cooling load of the house and the capacity of the air conditioner he recommends. The two figures should be almost identical. Putting in a system that is too large for a house is just as bad as putting in an undersized system.

In comparing bids of several contractors, take note of whether they have figured more or less the same cooling load for the house. If one is much higher or lower than others, you had better drop that contractor from consideration. However, if you want to check into things, your local electric utility company may send around a representative to look over the house. Or you can call in an independent heating engineer.

The chances are that all the contractors will recommend installation of the same type of system; but if they don't, you shouldn't be surprised: There are various ways to air condition a house.

If you have forced warm air heating, the cooling system will usually utilize the existing blower and ductwork. It may be either a split system or a single-package system. In a split system, the cooling coils are at the furnace and the compressor and condenser are outside the house on a concrete slab or in the foundation wall. In a single-package air conditioning system, on the other hand, all the parts of the conditioner are contained in one unit that is placed close to the furnace and tied in with the ductwork through a separate connecting duct.

If your house does not have forced warm air heating, it is still possible to have central air conditioning. Either a split or a single-package system can be used.

In a one-story house with an attic, the air conditioner is installed on the attic floor and cool air is carried to the rooms below by a simple layout of ducts and ceiling registers. In a house without an attic, the air conditioner is installed high in an outside wall and feeds air into the rooms through ducts suspended just below the ceiling and through registers placed high in the interior walls.

In a two-story house, the second story is cooled from the attic. The first floor can be cooled either by installing a separate ceiling system like that for a one-story house without an attic, or by installing a separate system in the basement and ducting the air into the rooms through floor registers.

INSULATING THE HOUSE...

Insulation not only reduces the cost of heating and cooling a house but also adds to your comfort by stopping air leaks through outside walls, roof, and floors over unheated spaces.

Over the past 30 or 40 years so much attention has been given to the value of insulation that almost all old houses incorporate some. But the fuel crisis has intensified interest in insulation, and experts now generally agree that even if a house has some insulation, it should probably have more.

The optimum amount needed is stated in terms of the insulation's resistance, or R, value.

Insulation in a roof or top-story ceiling should have an R value of 19. This is equivalent to about 6 in. of fluffy fiberglass or mineral wool insulation.

The R value for exterior walls is 11—equal to 2 to 3 in. of fiberglass.

The R value for floors over unheated spaces and for concrete floors laid on the ground is 13—equal to 3 in. of fiberglass.

Homeowners can usually install insulation in all locations except the exterior walls and inaccessible spaces under the roof. In the latter cases, you must hire an insulating contractor who will remove the siding or roofing, cut holes into the spaces between studs or rafters, and blow in loose fill material. He will then cover the holes so they are watertight and invisible.

The easiest way to insulate an attic floor is to use a loose fill of fiberglass or mineral wool, and pour it into the joist spaces until you have a depth of 6 in. Use a rake to level it, or if this is too heavy to handle in tight spaces under the eaves, nail a strip of lath at right angles to the end of a long 3/4-in. quarter round.

An attic roof is insulated with batts or rolls of fiberglass with a paper vapor barrier on one side. Push the fiberglass into the rafter spaces up against the roof deck and staple the paper flanges to the sides of the joists (Fig. 13-3).

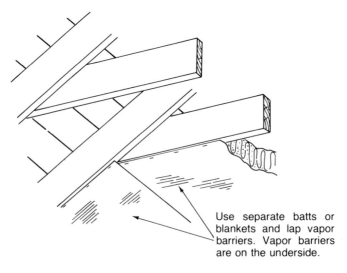

Use separate batts or blankets and lap vapor barriers. Vapor barriers are on the underside.

Fig. 13-3   Stapling batts to the attic roof.

If an attic roof is already insulated with, say, 3- or 4-in. batts, push additional 3- or 2-in. batts, respectively, into the rafter spaces over them, and staple the flanges to the bottoms of the rafters.

Floors over a crawl space, porch, or other unheated space are insulated by pushing fiberglass batts up between the floor joists and letting them rest on chicken wire or single wires nailed in large diamond patterns to the bottoms of the joists (Fig. 13-4). Use batts that have a vapor barrier on one side, and install them with the barrier next to the floor.

If your house is built on a concrete slab, you can take the chill out of the slab by digging a trench around the entire house and covering the edges of the slab with rigid urethane or polystyrene insulating boards. Use 1-in. boards in mild climates, 2-in. in intermediate climates, and 3-in. in very cold climates. The boards should extend from the top of the slab to at least 2 ft. below the grade level. Stick the boards to the concrete with roofing cement.

Insulating the walls of an unheated basement helps to make the rooms overhead warmer, but the job is so time-consuming and expensive that it's probably smarter simply to insulate the ceiling with batts resting on wire. Another even simpler possibility—if you have an oil-fired heating system—is to install an Air-O-Space heater on the flue.

INSTALLING STORM
DOORS AND WINDOWS...

Storm doors and windows add further to your fuel savings and comfort. But while they may add to the value of your home, they detract from its beauty.

The only good looking storm windows have an ordinary single-pane sash made with insulating glass (two sheets of glass sealed together around the edges and separated by an air space in the center). If you are feeling flush, you should substitute such sash for old single-pane sash with a single thickness of glass. For how to do this, see Chapter 6.

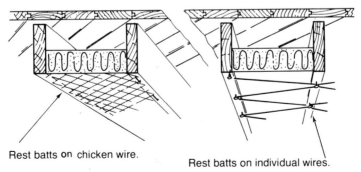

Rest batts on chicken wire.

Rest batts on individual wires.

Fig. 13-4   Two ways of installing batts in a crawl space.

I have no enthusiasm, however, for this type of insulating window sash on houses that look best with multi-pane windows. Reason: Insulating glass is not made in small sizes for multi-pane windows. Consequently, you must buy single-pane windows and place snap-in mullions against the inside surface. These are supposed to make the panes look as if they were a number of small panes. I emphasize "supposed". The fact is that from outside the house the windows are an obvious phony—and a very expensive phony at that.

The alternative, alas, is no better—but it is a lot cheaper: Cover the windows with aluminum combination storm sash and screens. Order the units through a local dealer, and let him measure your window frames so that if the delivered units do not fit properly, he will be responsible for replacing them. Be sure also (1) that the combinations he gives you have frames with a baked enamel finish because they are more attractive and more durable than unfinished frames, and (2) that the crossbars of the combinations line up with those of the windows.

If you have the dealer install the storm windows, there is an extra charge for each unit—but you can install them yourself perfectly well.

1 • Make certain that you have the correct sash for each window. In an old house especially, there are fractional differences in the size of window openings—and if the dealer does his measuring job properly, he will note these differences and order the combinations accordingly.

2 • Depending on the design of the window frame, some storm windows are set inside the frame and are screwed to the stops (the wood strips holding the window sash in the frame); others are installed just outside the frame and are screwed to the window trim. In either case, apply a thick bead of polysulfide rubber caulking compound to the top and side window edges to which the storm window is screwed. This helps to prevent air leakage.

3 • Drill screw holes through the flanges of the storm window. They should be about 1/4 to 3/8 in. in from the edges, depending on how far the flanges overlap the stops or window trim. For the average storm window, you should make two holes in the top flange and two or three holes in each side flange. No screw holes are bored in the bottom flange, which simply rests on the sill. Note that in better storm windows, the bottom flange is partially covered with a tight-fitting, envelope-like sleeve. The purpose of this is to permit a tight fit in the frame window's frame in the event that the storm window is slightly shorter than the window opening.

4 • If the storm window is light enough to handle, *do not remove the black metal clips that temporarily hold the sash rigid in the frame.*

Carry the sash to the window, center it, and press it into place against the window frame. Push it up to the top of the frame as far as possible. Make sure it is still centered. Then drive an awl through one of the screw holes, make a hole in the frame, and drive in a screw. (Phillips-head screws come with storm windows.) Since the storm window tends to slide around on the caulking compound, check again whether it is centered and perpendicular. Then install the other screws around the frame. Finish the job by pushing the sleeve at the bottom of the storm window down on the sill. And later, when you're inside the house, seal the joint between the sleeve and sill with caulking compound. But leave a couple of 1/4-in.-wide gaps in the caulking strip so that any moisture accumulating inside the storm window can leak out. Finally, pry off the clips.

5 • If a storm window is too large and heavy to handle with the sash in place, or if you are installing the window on the second floor, removal of the black metal clips before making the installation permits you to take out one or both of the sashes. This makes it lighter and easier to handle. But take care not to warp or bend the storm window frame when you install it. The sash can be replaced from inside the house once the storm window frame is screwed tight.

CONTROLLING CONDENSATION...

If you live in a cold climate, it is very possible that you already have trouble with condensation. If you don't, adding insulation and storm windows will probably tip the scales against you. But don't let this turn you against the insulation or storm windows. Condensation control is not difficult. The following steps should be taken:

1 • Prevent leaks in basements and crawl spaces by the methods covered in Chapter 4.

2 • Cover the ground in crawl spaces with heavy polyethylene film. Use a single big sheet if possible; otherwise, overlap the edges of smaller sheets 1 ft.

3 • Install a large, ducted ventilating fan in the kitchen, and vent the dryer to the outdoors with a duct. (See Chapter 9.) If you have heavy condensation in a bathroom, it's a good idea to install a small ventilating fan in the outside wall or ceiling.

4 • Install fixed screen ventilators high in the walls of all crawl spaces, and keep them open the year round. The same type of ventilators may be needed in the attic.

5 • Prevent the water vapor in the indoor air from penetrating exterior wall, joist, and roof spaces by installing vapor barriers on the warm side of all exterior walls, roofs, top-story ceilings, and floors over unheated spaces.

Wherever you install insulating batts or blankets with paper vapor barriers on one side, no additional protection is required. Elsewhere, however, the easiest kind of vapor barrier to use is simply a couple of coats of alkyd or latex paint applied to the inside surfaces of exterior walls and top-story ceilings. On wood floors over unheated spaces, apply two coats of gym seal or urethane varnish. Other excellent vapor barriers are vinyl wall covering and resilient flooring.

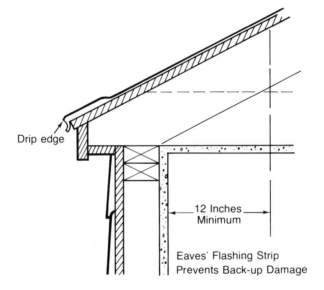

Drip edge

12 Inches
Minimum

Eaves' Flashing Strip
Prevents Back-up Damage

The House Exterior

As long as the exterior walls and roof of an old house are sound, most families worry first about renovating the interior. But sooner or later their attention shifts outdoors—and for an obvious reason: Anyone who cares enough to make over the inside of a house also cares about the face the house presents to the world.

PAINTING THE EXTERIOR...

Nothing makes as big a change in the appearance of a house as a new coat of paint. And there are few improvements that yield larger savings if you do the painting yourself.

The work can be done whenever the weather is dry, the temperature ranges from $50°$ to $80°$, the winds are subdued, and the bugs are relatively quiet. Autumn usually offers ideal conditions.

PREPARING TO PAINT   The care with which you prepare the job has as much to do with the attractiveness and durability of the painted surfaces as the choice of finish and its application.

Remove shutters, screens, and storm sashes first.

Wash dirty surfaces and those streaked with brown rust or green copper stains with trisodium phosphate. Wash off mildew with diluted chlorine bleach, and use the bleach almost full strength to remove moss from brick and other masonry surfaces. If you live near the seacoast, hose the entire house down with fresh water to remove salt crystals.

Scrape off loose and powdery paint. If the paint is alligatored or wrinkled in small areas, brush on a paste-type paint remover; let it stand for about 15 minutes until the finish is soft, and scrape hard. If the paint is defective over large areas, however, you will save time and energy with an electric paint remover. Use a heavy-duty extension cord made with No. 12 or No. 14 wire if you are working far from an outlet. Hold the paint remover flat on the surface until the paint has softened; then quickly scrape it off with a stiff putty knife or wall scraper. If the paint is not too thick, the heat will soften it so rapidly that you can keep moving the remover along in a straight line with the scraper right behind. When all the paint is off, sand the surface smooth.

Blistered areas may require special attention once the paint has been removed. If the blisters are concentrated around windows and doors, check and renew the caulking around the frames. If the blisters are under the eaves, make sure your gutters are in good condition. You may also need to install drip edges (see below). But if the blisters are widespread, the odds are that you have a condensation problem that must be brought under control by the measures outlined in the preceding chapter.

Seal knots that have bled through the old paint with a stain-killer. Countersink rusty nailheads, brush on a rust-inhibiting primer, and cover them with putty. If galvanized steel gutters are rusty but still sound, sand thoroughly and prime with a rust-inhibitor. Treat rusty ornamental ironwork in the same way.

Fill holes and splits in wood with putty or spackle made for exterior use. Renew bad putty around window panes. Replace dried-out caulking compound with polysulfide rubber caulking. Scrape out and replace loose and crumbling mortar in masonry walls with latex cement or a mixture of 1 part masonry cement and 2-1/2 parts sand.

Cover foundation plantings with drop cloths, and pull vines off the house if you want to paint the walls underneath. (Be sure to scrape off the holdfasts that some vines use to fasten themselves to walls.)

SELECTING A FINISH   The best paint for use on wood, plywood, and hardboard siding is an exterior alkyd. Latex has been highly touted in recent years but has not been perfected to the point that it can be trusted. Alkyd should also be used over any painted surface—regardless of the material underneath—that is chalking or very dirty.

Use an exterior alkyd trim enamel on all trim, doors, windows, shutters, screen frames, gutters, leaders, and ornamental ironwork.

Exterior latex paint is preferred for masonry and asbestos-cement surfaces. Unlike alkyd, which must be applied only to a dry surface, latex can be used on slightly damp surfaces.

Both latex and alkyd paints are available in so-called one-coat formulations. But these should be used only if the existing paint is sound and fairly thick—and even then they are not needed since one coat of ordinary paint usually gives adequate coverage. On worn or unpainted surfaces, however, always use an ordinary latex (apply two coats) or an alkyd primer followed by alkyd finish paint.

Another type of finish for wood or plywood is an exterior oil stain. There are two kinds.

1 • Transparent stains change the color of wood without hiding the grain or texture. They should be used only on walls and woodwork that have never been finished or that have been previously treated with a transparent stain or water repellent.

2 • Opaque stains contain insoluble pigments that give wood a thin paint-like finish. They are used on walls that were finished previously with opaque or transparent stain. And they can also be used on old painted surfaces, provided the paint has worn away almost completely and the stain is of approximately the same color.

PAINTING   No matter what the finish, all houses are painted in the same way. To avoid working in the sun on a hot, glary surface, paint the west and south sides in the morning; the east and north sides in the afternoon. Paint the eaves, rakes, and cornices first; then the siding; then the trim, windows, and doors; and finally—before you rehang them—the shutters, screens, or storm sashes. Generally, it is best to start at the top of a wall and work across it in a deep band before you do the lower part—but you don't have to be a slave to this idea. For example, if you can't finish a wall, end each day's work next to a break in the wall such as a door or window. This helps to conceal the lapped edges between the second day's work and the first.

On all except very rough siding, such as uneven or porous masonry, I find it saves time to apply paint with a roller and finish the spots the roller misses with a wide brush. I also roll paint on wide board trim and then smooth the entire surface with a brush.

It's better to apply oil stains with a brush, however, since you should work them into the wood as much as possible.

RESURFACING
EXTERIOR WALLS...

There is rarely anything so bad about the old siding on a house that you need to replace it. Simple repairs and a coat of paint are all that's necessary to give the house a new lease on life.

This is not to say that there are not houses with ugly exterior walls. Fifty years ago, when stucco was popular, a number of contractors succeeded in building some truly monstrous walls—but the houses themselves were so monstrous that nothing would be gained by recovering the walls today. This is also true of other ugly walls.

To be sure, homowners have for a long time been under pressure from remodeling contractors to alter the exterior walls of their houses; but the goal is not to improve the appearance, durability, and weather-resistance of the walls. In the early 1930s, asphalt roll siding was touted as a way to fireproof the home; however, the idea got nowhere—which was a blessing because asphalt siding is one of the surest downgraders of a home I can think of. Then asbestos-cement shingles were given a play—mainly on the grounds that they require little maintenance. And today all attention is on aluminum and vinyl siding.

Just an hour ago, in fact, my phone rang and the man announced that he was calling for the PQR Company. It happened that the PQR Company advertises extensively on the morning news program we listen to, so I had an idea what was coming.

"We're making a survey, Mr. Schuler. Do you own your home?"

"Yes, but I'm not interested."

He was too fast for me: "Do you have modern siding?"

"Not your kind," I said. "And I'm not about to."

I hung up.

I'm not really opposed to aluminum or vinyl siding. On the contrary, I'm frank to admit that they require little or no maintenance for many years; and if that't what you want, fine. But they are no more modern than any other siding. They are not as attractive as the wood they imitate. And I very much doubt that they are essential to the renovation of more than one out of every 100 houses they cover.

But enough's enough.

If the exterior walls of your house are really in a condition beyond simple redemption, by all means have them resurfaced with a modern siding such as wood, brick, plywood, hardboard, asbestos-cement, aluminum, or vinyl. But let an expert do the work. In most cases the new siding is installed over the existing siding; but in some cases, the existing siding must be completely removed. It's a big job either way.

PUTTING NEW
LIFE IN AN OLD ROOF...

You can do this to all roofs, except those covered with wood shingles or shakes, provided they have not deteriorated badly or begun to leak. But the treatment should not be considered as a substitute for new roofing. It simply adds several years to the life of a roof, while improving its appearance.

The material used is a paint-like coating. On roofs made with asphalt you can use a black or aluminum-colored asphaltic coating containing asbestos fibers or other minerals. The aluminum-colored type also contains aluminum flakes that reflect heat from the roof and increase the life of the coating.

On other types of roof—as well as those made with asphalt—you can use a colored aluminum coating made with a variety of colored pigments, aluminum flakes for reflectance, asbestos fibers for body, and an asphalt, resinous, or synthetic rubber vehicle.

Before treating a roof, clean it thoroughly, remove loose gravel and mineral particles, and patch holes with fibered asphalt roofing cement. The roof must be dry. Application is made with a paint brush or long-handled roof brush. Start at the top of the roof and work down. Let the coating dry for the time recommended by the manufacturer before you inspect the roof to make sure you have covered every inch.

It takes approximately 2 to 4 gal. of asphalt-fibered roof coating to cover 100 sq. ft.; 1 to 2 gal. of colored aluminum coating to cover 150 sq. ft. Coverage is greater on smooth surfaces such as metal, less on very rough surfaces such as tar-and-gravel.

RESURFACING A ROOF...

ASPHALT SHINGLES   Asphalt shingles are the most popular roofing material because they are inexpensive, long-lasting, fire-resistant, available in many colors, and easily installed by anyone who feels secure working on a roof. They can be used only on roofs that have a pitch of 4 in. or more per foot. The temperature at time of installation should be over 40°.

Estimating your needs   Buy shingles with square tabs. They should weigh 230 lb. or more per square (a square has an area of 100 sq. ft). The shingles are sold in bundles covering approximately 25 to 33 sq. ft. To determine how many bundles you need, find the square foot area of the entire roof, and divide by the square foot coverage of the bundle. Add 15 per cent for waste if the roof is cut up, 10 per cent if it is a smooth expanse broken only by a chimney.

The application instructions accompanying each bundle indicate how many galvanized roofing nails are required.

Preparing the roof   If the roof deck is sound and strong and is covered with only a single layer of old roofing, you can lay the new shingles right over it. Old asphalt shingles that are curled or loose should be cut out or nailed down tight. Remove all protruding nails. On old roll roofing, cut through bulges and nail them down.

If you're laying the new roof over wood shingles, remove loose nails, split and nail down curled shingles, and replace missing shingles. Completely remove all shingles within 6 in. of the eaves and rakes, and fill in the gaps with 6-in.

boards. Then nail beveled wood feathering strips under the butts of each course of shingles to provide a smooth deck (Fig. 14-1).

Always sweep the roof clean before starting installation of new shingles.

Nail L-shaped aluminum drip edges over the edges of all eaves and rakes to force water to drip off straight into the gutters or to the ground (Fig. 14-2). The drip edges are installed with the wide flanges on the roof, the narrow flanges pointing down. Put about three nails through the wide flange of each drip edge.

In cold climates water running down the roof often forms ice dams along the eaves. Heating cables can be installed in the gutters, as shown in Fig. 14-3(a). In the alternative, lay along each eave a flashing strip made of smooth roll roofing 3 ft. wide. The bottom edge should overhang the drip edge at least 1/4 in. The upper edge should extend up the roof far enough to cover a point at least 1 ft. inside the interior wall line of the house [Fig. 14-3(b)]. If a 3-ft. strip is not wide enough to span this space, lay a second strip above it, overlap the edges 3 in., and glue them with asphalt roofing cement.

Laying the shingles   The first row of shingles is a concealed row laid along an eave with the tabs facing up the roof. Cut 3 in. off the end of the first strip. The smooth bottom edges of the shingles should align with the bottom edge of the flashing strip or, if there isn't a flashing strip, they should overhang the drip edge 1/4 in.

Exposed courses of shingles are laid with the tabs facing down the roof (Fig. 14-4). Work from the most visible rake toward a valley, a wall, or the rake at the opposite end of the roof. If both rakes are equally visible, you can start in the center of the roof and work toward them; but before doing so, make sure

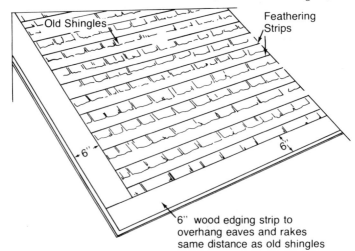

Fig. 14-1   Nailing feathering strips under old shingles to provide a smooth deck for new shingles.

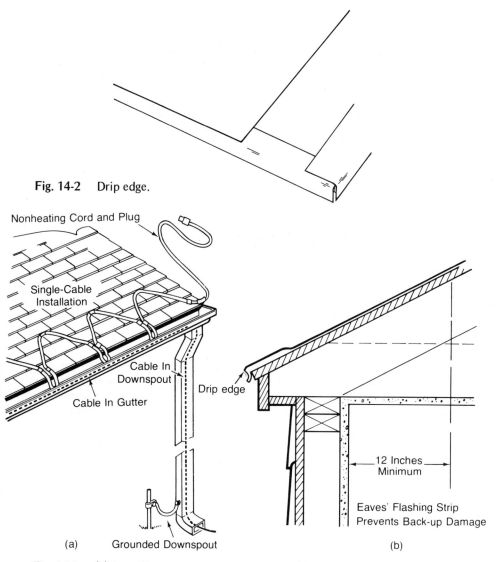

Fig. 14-2 Drip edge.

Nonheating Cord and Plug

Single-Cable Installation

Cable In Downspout

Cable In Gutter

Drip edge

12 Inches Minimum

Eaves' Flashing Strip Prevents Back-up Damage

(a)   Grounded Downspout

(b)

Fig. 14-3 (a) Installing heating cable in gutters; (b) Protecting eaves with a 36-in. flashing strip.

that you do not wind up at the rakes with very narrow tabs that can be ripped off by high winds.

If you start at the end of the roof (as is usually the case), start with a full shingle strip in the first row. Align the bottom edge with the bottom edge of the concealed starter course, and let the end overhang the rake at least 1/4 in.

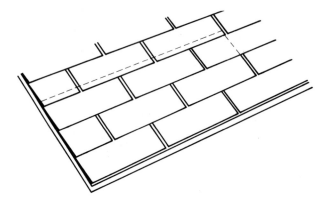

Fig. 14-4   Laying the shingles with tabs facing down the roof.

For the second course, cut the first tab on the starting strip in half. Thereafter all odd-numbered courses start with a full-width tab; all even-numbered courses, with a half-width tab. Thus, the cutouts (slits between tabs) in alternate courses are staggered.

To assure that each course is level and straight, snap chalk lines the length of the roof to mark the position of the tabs. In most installations, the exposed height of the tabs is 5 in.; but if you live in a very windy location, reduce the exposure to 4 in., or follow the directions of the shingle manufacturer.

When reroofing over old asphalt shingles or roll roofing, use 1-1/2-in. galvanized roofing nails. Over old wood shingles, use 1-3/4-in. nails. On a new roof or one with the old roofing removed, use 1-1/4-in. nails. For 5-in. exposure, use four nails per shingle strip (Fig. 14-5). These are placed 5/8 in. above the tops of the cutouts, or 5-5/8 in. above the bottom edges of the tabs. Center one nail above each cutout, and drive one nail 1 in. in from each end. For 4-in. exposure, use six nails located 4-5/8 in. above the bottom edges of the tabs. Place the nails 1-1/2 in. in from the ends of the strip and 1-1/2 in. to each side of the cutouts. In all cases, nail the strips from one end to the other—don't nail the ends and then the middle. Drive the nails flush with the surface—don't embed them.

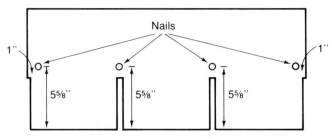

Fig. 14-5   Nailing shingles.

In windy locations, spot asphalt roofing cement under each tab to keep it from curling. The alternative is to buy shingles that have self-sealing tabs.

Nails should never be driven through flashing. Hold the shingles down with fibered roofing cement instead.

When laying shingles around chimneys and vents, place them over or under the flashing in the same way the old shingles were laid.

Where the rake of a roof abuts a vertical wall, install an 8-in.-wide strip of smooth roll roofing up and down the old roof hard against the wall. Nail it along each edge at 4-in. intervals. Cement the new shingles over the strip.

Over valley flashing, clip 1 in. diagonally off the upper corner of each new shingle; then align the ends with the old shingles. Bed the shingles in roofing cement.

To cover roof ridges and hips (Fig. 14-6), cut the shingle strips into three 1-ft. lengths. Center the pieces over the ridge or hip, and bend them down on either side (but don't crease them so hard that you crack the surface). Each piece should be exposed 5 in. to the weather and secured with a single nail on each side. The nails should be 1 in. in from the side edges and 5-1/2 in. back from the exposed ends. On a ridge, start laying the shingles at one end of the roof and proceed to the other end. On a hip, install the shingles from the bottom up.

CEDAR SHINGLES   Cedar shingles are made in 16-, 18- and 24-in. lengths. The size you use depends on the effect you wish to achieve. The shorter the shingle, the less it is exposed to the weather.

The minimum roof pitch is 3 in. in 12 in. If your roof has a pitch of 3 to 5 in., expose 16-in. shingles 3-3/4 in., 18-in. shingles 4-1/2 in., and 24-in. shingles 5-3/4 in. If your roof has a pitch in excess of 5 in., expose 16-in. shingles 5 in., 18-in. shingles 5-1/2 in., and 24-in. shingles 7-1/2 in.

Estimating your needs   To figure how many shingles you need, calculate the square foot area of the entire roof and divide by 25 if the roof has a pitch of 5 in. or more. (Regardless of length, a bundle of shingles covers 25 sq. ft. on a roof with this pitch.) But if the pitch of the roof is less than 5 in., divide the roof area by 25, and then increase the number of bundles by one-third. In all cases, add an extra bundle for each 25 running feet of hips and ridges.

Preparing the roof   You can install new cedar shingles directly over an old roof of cedar or asphalt shingles or roll roofing, provided it is reasonably sound and only one layer thick; otherwise, the old roofing should be ripped off down to the deck. Remove the ridge strip of shingles and replace it with beveled siding boards laid with the thick edge

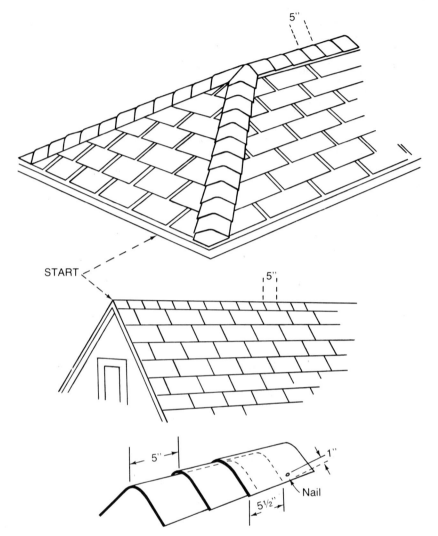

Fig. 14-6   Covering roof ridges and hips.

pointing up. Cut out the first course of shingles at the eaves and fill the gap with 1-in. boards. Cut the shingles back 6 in. along the rakes, and replace them with boards.

Flashing strips for drip edges and eaves are normally not used with cedar shingles, although they are just as useful here as they are on asphalt roofs.

Laying the shingles   The shingles in each bundle are of varying widths; consequently, the joints in the roof follow no

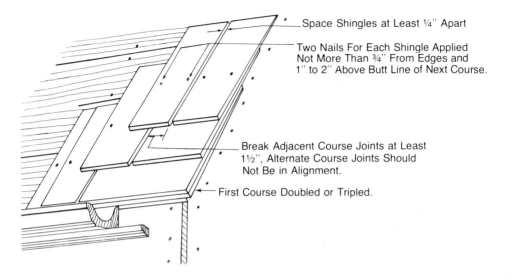

Space Shingles at Least ¼" Apart

Two Nails For Each Shingle Applied
Not More Than ¾" From Edges and
1" to 2" Above Butt Line of Next Course.

Break Adjacent Course Joints at Least
1½", Alternate Course Joints Should
Not Be in Alignment.

First Course Doubled or Tripled.

Fig. 14-7 Making and placing joints in the roof.

pattern. But you must be careful how you make and place them (Fig. 14-7). All joints should be 1/4 in. wide; they must be offset at least 1-1/2 in. from one course to the next; and they must not be in an exact line between one course and the second next above.

Lay shingles from one rake to another or to a side wall. But if a roof section terminates in a valley, start at the valley and lay toward the rake. This permits you to select wider shingles for the valley area.

The first courses at the eaves should be two shingles thick and should overhang the eaves 1 in. A similar overhang is provided at the rakes.

Lay all subsequent courses to chalk lines.

Use 1-3/4-in. galvanized shingle nails. Secure each shingle, regardless of its width, with two nails. These should be driven at least 3/4 in. above the butts of the shingles in the next higher course and no more than 3/4 in. in from the sides of the shingle. However, to avoid driving nails through flashing, it is usually necessary to locate one of them much closer to the center of the shingles. In some cases, in fact, you may have to drive one nail directly above the other (Fig. 14-8).

If specially fabricated V-shaped "shingles" are available, use them to cover ridges and hips. Otherwise, lay ordinary shingles lengthwise on each side of the peak. Shape and butt the edges carefully to make a tight joint (Fig. 14-9). Allow the same exposure as that for the rest of the shingles.

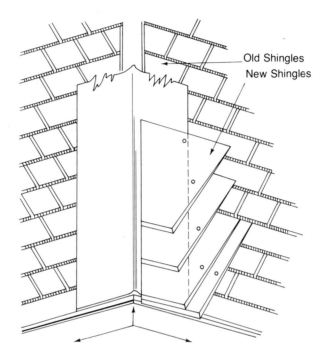

Fig. 14-8   Nailing shingles in a valley.

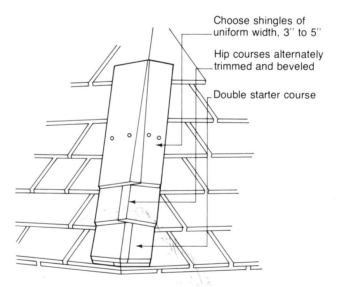

Fig. 14-9   Butting shingles on a hip or ridge.

REPLACING
GUTTERS AND LEADERS...

Although gutters and leaders are made of various materials, you will be well advised to stick to aluminum with a baked-on finish. They're durable, inexpensive, and easy to hang if you have a helper.

A complete gutter and leader assembly is made up of a variety of pieces. The principal items are the gutter troughs and leader pipes—both sold in 10-ft. lengths—which can be cut with a fine-toothed hacksaw or tin snips. Other items you may need are the following:

- Hangers—Use T-bar strap hangers if there is no fascia board below the eaves. Use L-shaped hangers where there's a fascia board no more than 2 in. back from the eaves' edge.
- End caps to close the gutters at the ends—You need right-end and left-end caps.
- Corner troughs—One type for an inside corner, another type for an outside corner.
- Gutter connectors—These are used to join the trough pieces end to end.
- Gutter outlets for connecting the gutters to the leaders—You need one for each leader.
- Leader elbows—Unless a roof has almost no overhang, two elbows are used to connect the gutter outlet to the top of the leader. The top elbow bows outward; the bottom, inward. A third elbow is commonly installed at the bottom of the leader to conduct water away from the foundation walls. A standard elbow is creased across the wider side. A side elbow is creased across the narrow side and is used to shift a leader to the right or left of the gutter outlet.
- Leader straps—These are flat straps used to hold a leader against the house wall. You should install two on each 10-ft. length of leader.

Before hanging new gutters, install drip edges along the eaves so that roof water will drop straight into the gutters.

You should put in one leader for each gutter up to 35 ft. long. It can be placed at either end of the gutter or anywhere in between. Whatever its location, slope the gutter toward it at the rate of 1/16 in. per foot. If a gutter is over 35 ft. long, install two leaders. If they are at the ends of the gutter, slope the gutter from the middle toward them.

Because the various pieces of gutter are very difficult to join, I long ago gave up trying to put them together while standing on a ladder. Now I assemble them on the ground and have someone help me hang them. Each joint is made with a gutter connector (Fig. 14-10). First, squeeze silicone caulking compound into the connector sleeves; then push the gutter troughs, drop outlets, or corners into the sleeves. To strengthen the joint so it cannot come apart when you hang the gutter, you can then drill holes through the sleeves and drive in short, aluminum sheet-metal screws. Use four screws per connector.

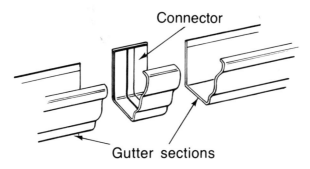

Fig. 14-10 Connector joints.

Gutter hangers are installed at 3-ft. intervals. To install a T-bar hanger, drill holes through the front and back top edges of the gutter, and bolt the rigid crossbar hanger to them (Fig. 14-11). Then bend the flexible strap on top of the crossbar backward, and nail it to the roof. Put a spot of asphalt roofing cement under the hanger strap to prevent leaks through the nail hole.

When hanging a gutter with T-bar hangers, nail down the strap at the high end of the gutter first, the strap at the gutter outlet next. Then, using a carpenter's level, adjust the pitch of the gutter, and nail down the intermediate straps.

When hanging a gutter with L-shaped hangers (Fig. 14-12), strike a chalk line the length of the fascia board to establish the position of the gutter. Then

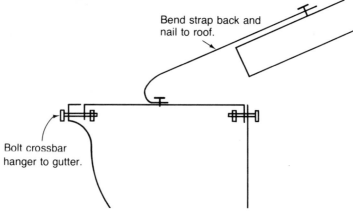

Fig. 14-11 Installing T-bar gutter hangers.

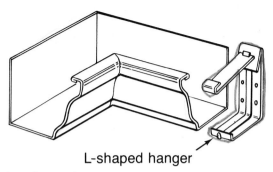

L-shaped hanger

Fig. 14-12 L-shaped gutter hanger.

nail the hanger brackets to the fascia board just below the line. Insert the hanger straps under the front lip of the gutter. Set the gutter into the brackets, and hook the straps to the brackets.

Install the end caps on the gutter [Fig. 14-13(a)]. Then seal all joints at the end caps and connectors with additional caulking compound.

Slip an elbow up over the gutter outlet, slip a second elbow up over the base of the first, and then slip a leader pipe up over the bottom elbow. No caulking is needed. Bend the leader straps [Fig. 14-13(b)] tightly around the leader at top and bottom, and nail them to the house wall. Add a second length of leader pipe, if necessary, by crimping the bottom end of the top length slightly and slipping the lower length up over it.

Ideally, the leader should be connected into a 4-in. drain pipe that carries the water well away from the house. (See Chapter 4.) If this is not done, crimp

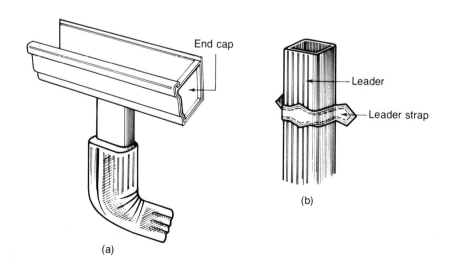

Fig. 14-13 (a) Gutter with end cap and leader; (b) Leader and leader strap.

the bottom end of the leader, and slip an elbow up over it. Point the elbow away from the house, and place a concrete or plastic drainage trough on the ground under it.

Foundation Planting

Charlie and Cary Hull hadn't been in their new old house more than two days before Charlie got out his axe and chopped down several large hemlocks that jostled against the walls. In spite of the many other major and minor improvements they have since made, this one simple act (which startled the previous owners out of their wits) did more to improve the place than anything else. The effect was that of the rising sun. Dark gloom gave way indoors to cheerful brightness.

Whenever I visit a strange community, I am always struck by the number of houses that are swathed—like the Hulls'—with dense shrubs and trees. Whatever is attractive about the houses is lost from view. The planting itself is dreary and often hideous because of inappropriate pruning. And even though I may never enter a single house, I know that it has a general resemblance to Mammoth Cave.

A cave is not what a house should be.

THE WHATS AND WHYS
OF FOUNDATION PLANTING...

Foundation planting consists of the shrubs, trees, vines, groundcovers, ferns, and flowers that are planted close to the four walls of a house. The principal purpose of the planting is to conceal unattractive foundation walls, basement bulkheads, areaways, and electric meters. In addition, it helps to tie the house to the ground and may soften or change the lines of the house. The thing it is *not* meant to do is to block off windows, doors, and porches.

There is no rule that a house must have foundation planting. Neither are there any hard-and-fast rules about how it should be used. The following suggestions, however, serve as useful guidelines that have pretty well withstood the test of time:

- Put the plants in beds that are distinct from the lawn. If this does nothing else, it greatly simplifies lawn mowing, and makes it easier to keep weeds and stray grass plants out of the foundation planting.

- Shape the border to accommodate and complement the plants in it and the house, and to blend with the contours of the land. It can be straight, curved, scallopped—whatever looks best. In depth it can range from 1 to 6 or even 8 ft.
- Avoid arranging the plants in a neatly spaced row unless you want a crisp, hedge-like effect.
- Don't alternate high and low plants from one end of the house to the other.
- Use only a few varieties of plants over and over again. If you use too many varieties, the whole thing is a hodge-podge.
- Use low, spreading plants to accent the horizontal lines of a house; tall, slim plants to accent the vertical lines. Reverse the procedure to change the lines of a house.
- Use low plants under windows.
- Use tall plants at the corners of a house if you want to frame it and tie it to the ground.
- Use rather tall, compact plants to call attention to a door.

CHANGING THE
FOUNDATION PLANTING AROUND
AN OLD HOUSE...

I do not know just why homeowners hesitate to change their foundation planting, even when it is obviously detracting from the appearance and livability of their homes. Do they hate to destroy plants that have taken years to grow? Do they dislike spending money to replace the plants? Or is it that they just don't know what to do once the plants have been taken out?

I'm curious—but no explanation is really necessary. The important point is that, if your foundation planting is overgrown, something drastic must be done about it.

If the offending plants are trees, the best solution is to chop them down to the ground and dig out as much of the root system as you can. Pruning them back to manageable size is almost impossible; and anyway, there are very few trees that belong in a foundation border.

A number of overgrown shrubs should be treated in the same way simply because they are varieties that either do not deserve the prominence they receive in a foundation planting or grow too large and too fast to be readily manageable. The weeping variety of forsythia, mockoranges, bridal wreath, and *Rhododendron maximum* are examples.

Other shrubs and vines, however, should be given more kindly treatment. Try pruning. If you go at it carefully, the plants should respond well. By "carefully" I do not mean taking your shears and chopping the tops of the plants back to a lower level the way Marine barbers cut a new recruit's hair. You should, instead, reach into the hearts of the plants and cut out the over-long branches at their starting points. If you do this on a selective basis over a period of two or three years, injury to the plants can be minimized and their natural shapes will be retained.

PUTTING IN NEW PLANTS...

Once you have ripped out the undesirable plants and started trimming back the others, you're ready to fill in the gaps—as necessary—with new plants. The best planting time is in early spring. For fastest results, buy large specimens with soil around their roots. These may be wrapped in burlap or growing in metal or plastic cans. If you are pressed for funds, however, buy smaller plants and give them a little extra fertilizer and water for the first couple of years.

Following is a list of the choicest plants for foundation planting. Note that the heights given are the maximums attainable. All the tall plants, such as American arborvitae and firethorn, can be kept low by judicious annual pruning.

EVERGREENS...

ANDROMEDA, JAPANESE   (Pieris japonica)

8 ft. Broadleaf evergreen. Broad and rounded. Panicles of creamy white flowers in spring. Sun or partial shade. Temperate climates.

ARALIA, JAPANESE   (Fatsia japonica)

8 ft. Broadleaf evergreen. Upright. Enormous leaves shaped like many-pointed stars. Shade. Tropical climates.

ARBORVITAE, AMERICAN   (Thuya occidentalis)

60 ft.—but can be kept much, much lower. Columnar. Sun or partial shade. Cold and temperate climates.

ARDISIA   (Ardisia crispa)

3 ft. Broadleaf evergreen. Spreading. White flowers in spring, followed by red berries in fall. Sun or shade. Warmest climates.

AZALEA HYBRIDS

Among the many outstanding evergreen azaleas are the Indian, Kurume, and Glendale hybrids. Sizes and growth habits vary, but all are beautiful. Best in partial sun. Temperate and warmest climates.

BAMBOO, HEAVENLY (*Nandina domestica*)

8 ft. Broadleaf evergreen. Looks like an open, upright bamboo. White flowers in summer; red berries in fall. Sun or partial shade. Warm climates.

BARBERRY, WINTERGREEN (*Berberis Julianae*)

6 ft. Broadleaf evergreen. Turns reddish in fall. Sun. Temperate climate.

COTONEASTER, PYRENEES (*Cotoneaster congesta*)

3 ft. Broadleaf evergreen. Rounded and dense. Red berries in fall. Sun. Temperate climates.

CYPRESS, HINOKI (*Chamaecyparis obtusa filicioides*)

8 ft. Upright and slender. Fern-like foliage. Sun. Temperate climates.

FIRETHORN (*Pyracantha coccinea Lalandi*)

20 ft. Broadleaf evergreen. Can be trained as an espalier against the house wall or allowed to develop as a low, mounded shrub. Brilliant orange-red berries in fall. Sun or partial shade. Temperate climates.

GOLD-DUST PLANT (*Aucuba japonica variegata*)

6 ft. Broadleaf evergreen. Leaves are splattered with gold markings; red berries on female plants if you also put in a male plant. Partial shade. Temperate climates.

GRAPE HOLLY, OREGON (*Mahonia Aquifolium*)

5 ft. Broadleaf evergreen. Yellow flowers in spring; edible blue fruits in summer. Bronze-red or purple holly-like foliage in fall and winter. Partial shade. Temperate climates.

HAWTHORN, YEDDO (*Raphiolepis umbellata*)

10 ft. Broadleaf evergreen. Compact. Dense, glossy foliage; fragrant white to red flowers in winter and spring, then blue fruits. Sun. Tropical climates.

HOLLY, BURFORD *(Ilex cornuta Burfordii)*

> 8 ft. Broadleaf evergreen. Rounded. Large, red berries in fall and winter. Sun. Temperate climates.

HOLLY, CONVEX JAPANESE *(Ilex crenata convexa)*

> 6 ft. Broadleaf evergreen. Superb plant resembling a large boxwood. Sun or partial shade. Temperate climates.

HOLLY, HELLER'S *(Ilex crenata Helleri)*

> 4 ft. Broadleaf evergreen. Rounded plant with leaves like boxwood. Sun. Temperate climates.

JUNIPER, CREEPING *(Juniperus horizontalis)*

> 18 in. or less. Spreading, prostrate groundcover. Bluish foliage. Sun. Grows almost everywhere.

JUNIPER, MEYER'S *(Juniperus squamata Meyeri)*

> 12 ft. Upright but slightly spreading. Blue foliage. Sun. Temperate climates.

JUNIPER, PFITZER *(Juniperus chinensis Pfitzeriana)*

> 10 ft. Wide-spreading, flat topped. Bright blue berries in winter. Sun. Cold and temperate climates.

LEUCOTHOË, DROOPING *(Leucothoe fontanesiana)*

> 6 ft. Broadleaf evergreen. Arching branches. White flowers hanging in clusters underneath branches in spring. Sun or partial shade. Temperate climates.

MYRTLE *(Myrtus communis)*

> 8 ft. Broadleaf evergreen. Compact and upright. Aromatic leaves. Sun. Warmest climates.

PACHYSANDRA *(Pachysandra terminalis)*

> 9 in. Broadleaf evergreen. Outstanding groundcover. Shade or partial sun. Temperate climates.

PERIWINKLE   (*Vinca minor*)

9 in. Broadleaf evergreen. Another excellent groundcover. Blue flowers in spring. Partial sun or shade. Temperate climates.

PINE, MUGO   (*Pinus Mugo mughus*)

8 ft. Spreading but with upright branches. Some varieties resembling a groundcover; others are bushy and tall. Sun. Cold and temperate climates.

PITTOSPORUM   (*Pittosporum tobira*)

10 ft. Broadleaf evergreen. Upright. Fragrant, white spring flowers. Sun or shade. Warmest climates.

PRIVET, JAPANESE   (*Ligustrum japonicum*)

10 ft. Broadleaf evergreen. Rounded and upright. Waxy leaves; white flowers in spring. Sun or partial shade. Warmest climates.

RHODODENDRON HYBRIDS

Try the Catawba, Dexter or Griffithianum hybrids. They're all beautiful. Sizes, habits, and climate requirements vary. Best in partial sun. Temperate climates.

VIBURNUM, SANDANKWA   (*Viburnum suspensum*)

6 ft. Broadleaf evergreen. Spreading. Pinkish-white flowers in winter and spring; red berries in fall. Partial shade. Tropical climates.

YEW, HICKS'   (*Taxus media Hicksii*)

8 ft. Columnar and dense. Sun or shade. Temperate climates.

YEW, JAPANESE   (*Taxus cuspidata expansa*)

5 ft. Flat and wide-spreading. Dark green needles; red berries in fall. Sun or shade. Cold and temperate climates.

DECIDUOUS PLANTS...

AZALEA HYBRIDS

The best include the Mollis, Ghent, Knapp Hill and Exbury hybrids. Gorgeous flowers. Sizes and habits variable. Sun for part of the day. Temperate climates.

COTONEASTER, SPREADING   (*Cotoneaster divaricata*)

5 ft. Mounded plant with arching branches. Red berries in fall. Sun. Temperate climates.

ENKIANTHUS, RED-VEIN   (*Enkianthus campanulatus*)

15 ft. Upright, narrow, with many stems. Pinkish-white flowers in spring; bright red fall foliage. Sun. Temperate climates.

LILAC, LITTLELEAF   (*Syringa microphylla*)

5 ft. Spreading. Fragrant, pale-lilac flowers in spring and sometimes again in the autumn. Sun. Temperate climates.

LILAC, PERSIAN   (*Syringa persica*)

7 ft. Rounded. Fragrant, lilac flowers in spring. Sun. Cold and temperate climates.

LILAC, SWEGIFLEXA   (*Syringa swegiflexa*)

9 ft. Upright. Beautiful, fragrant, pink flowers in spring. Sun. Temperate climates.

VIBURNUM, BURKWOOD   (*Viburnum Burkwoodii*)

6 ft. Rounded. Fragrant pinkish-white flowers in spring; red to black berries in fall; purple-red fall foliage. Sun. Temperate climates.

VIBURNUM, FRAGRANT SNOWBALL   (*Viburnum carlcephalum*)

7 ft. Rounded. Big, fragrant, pinkish-white flowers in spring; red and black berries in fall; red fall foliage. Sun. Temperate climates.

VIBURNUM, KOREAN SPICE   (*Viburnum Carlesii*)

6 ft. Rounded. Fragrant, pinkish-white flowers in spring; black berries in fall. Sun. Temperate climates.

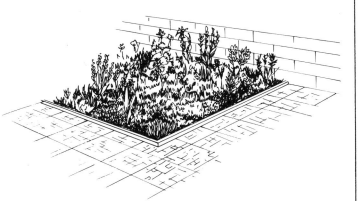

Terraces, Decks, and Porches

Is there a specific place outside your house where your family can sit and enjoy the beauties of nature while they talk, read, eat, entertain, play, and generally relax?

Many old homes had porches; and if yours is one of these, the only thing you have to worry about is whether the porch is in good shape. But lacking a porch, something else is needed because no home today can be considered modern if it doesn't provide a place for outdoor living.

Usually this something else is a terrace, but frequently it's a deck—which is really nothing more than a porch except that porches usually have roofs whereas decks usually do not.

TERRACES...

Old houses were not restricted to porches. Some had—and have—terraces; and these often need to be rejuvenated. But since this rejuvenation process usually calls for nothing more than simple repairs, I skip it here. The discussion below on designing and building a brand new terrace should contain the information you need for making repairs, too.

PLANNING A TERRACE Planning a terrace calls for as much thought as you give to any room in the house. The fact that a terrace has few, if any, walls and maybe no ceiling means nothing. You live there many hours of the day, many days of the year; therefore, it must be attractive and comfortable.

The questions you must ask, the steps you should take in planning a terrace, are as follows:

What do you want the terrace for?

Just sitting outdoors? Sunbathing? Eating? Entertaining? Playing adult and/or children's games? Dancing? Sheltering house plants in summer?

The odds are that you will use the terrace in a number of ways. But it's important to identify them before you build because they affect the design and construction.

Should you have just one terrace or perhaps two or three?

I don't want to belabor this question because it is slightly extraneous in a book of this kind. On the other hand, you shouldn't ignore it.

Most people get along perfectly happily with only one terrace. We did in our last house. Now, we have three next to the house and a fourth at the swimming pool. We use them all, and we wouldn't give one of them up because they not only give us a pleasant change of outlook and surroundings but also—more importantly—serve different purposes.

For a larger family, two or three terraces would be even more useful because they eliminate conflict. For instance, someone can sunbathe in privacy while the rest of the family plays games.

What is the best location for the terrace?

This is influenced by many things:

1 • The purpose of the terrace—For example, if it is strictly for eating, it should be near the kitchen or dining room. But if it's a sort of general-purpose terrace, it probably should be off the living room or family room.

2 • The plan of the house—Here you run into many complications, and the worst is usually the back door. Most houses have only two doors—one in front and one in back. Since most people want a terrace in the backyard or sideyard, the back door becomes the entrance to it. This doesn't mean the terrace must be close to the door, but it generally is because we want it to be as accessible as possible to the interior of the house. But do you like always walking through the kitchen to get to the terrace? Probably not.

The point I am trying to make is this: There's no reason why your back door should saddle you with the location of your terrace. It's usually easy enough to put in another outside door directly to the terrace from, say, the living room or dining room.

Having at least semi-disposed of this problem, you still must cope with others raised by the plan of your house. For example, you want the terrace to open off the living area—but suppose the living area is in front of the house, and the back is taken up with bedrooms. Suggestion: Don't rule out the possibility of putting the terrace in the front yard, and building a wall around it.

Another point to consider is that, if your house is L-shaped or

U-shaped, it's usually desirable to locate the terrace in the L or U. This gives it greater privacy and more protection from sun and wind.

Yes, a house plan may complicate terrace location. All you can do is weigh this against that and come out with a compromise.

3 . The sun also influences where you put your terrace. The sun is both friend and foe. You want it sometimes, and you don't want it other times.

Locating a terrace on the west side of a house is asking for trouble, unless you have some way to screen it from the setting sun, because it is blistering hot and blinding at the very time you most want to use it. An east terrace is much better: not too hot in the morning, shaded in the afternoon. But on certain days it may also be too cool in the afternoon.

In hot climates, a north terrace is excellent. It is also good in colder climates in mid-summer because it receives more sun during the middle of the day than you might expect; but in the spring and fall, it's usually too cold for comfort.

This leaves the south terrace. It's the best of all in most areas. There's sun the year round—but not the long low rays that dazzle you with their heat and brilliance. To be sure, it can get pretty hot in the summer, but you can protect yourself against the worst by a roof or other shade-maker. In winter, the terrace dries off quickly after rain or snow, and it is often warm enough for a quick after-noon siesta.

4 . The wind is another matter. A strong prevailing wind makes a terrace uncomfortable regardless of where you live, but especially in cool climates. On the other hand, in a hot climate, a steady whisper of a breeze is a delight.

5 . Finally, you should consider the view and the shape and contours of your lot. A good view has a positive effect on your choice of terrace location because it's something you want to take advantage of. But the shape and contours of the lot have more of a negative effect because, if they are unusual, they may force you to put the terrace in a second-choice location.

How big should the terrace be?

People are strange. Two years ago we went to a large outdoor cocktail party. The terrace was about the size of a postage stamp but was surrounded by a big, smooth, level lawn. The hosts obviously thought there was plenty of room for the gathering. But everybody crowded onto the postage stamp, and it was about as uncomfortable a party as I have ever attended.

The moral is that, if you do a lot of big entertaining, you need a big terrace—15 x 30 ft. or more. But there's no point in spending the money for such an expanse otherwise. One hundred fifty square feet of space is ample for most families in most situations.

How should the terrace be shaped?

You can't go wrong with a simple square or rectangle (unless the rectangle is so narrow that people can't move around readily). They require no design skill, and they conform with the straight lines of the house.

But sometimes the shape or contours of the space selected require a terrace of unusual shape. And sometimes you want a rounded or irregular terrace for a special effect. In such cases, use a really flexible, light-colored garden hose to help you design it. String the hose out on the ground where the terrace will be, and move it around until you hit on the perfect shape. Then, to double-check, spread newspapers on the ground within the hose, and cut those on the perimeter to follow the lines of the hose. This helps to clarify the shape of the terrace because the papers have the same kind of artificiality as the ultimate terrace paving.

What should the elevation of the terrace be?

If it's on almost the same level as the room off of which it opens, it is easy to walk out on, and this gives it somewhat greater attraction. In addition, if there are large sliding glass doors between the room and terrace, the terrace becomes a visual part of the room, makes the room feel larger, and brings the outdoors indoors—all of which are very good reasons for having a contractor install such doors.

But if your house is raised off the ground—as many old ones are—raising the terrace increases its cost; and building a deck instead of a terrace doesn't alter the situation. So it may be preferable to build the terrace at ground level, provided you don't have to go down too many steps to reach it and provided that, if you roof it, the roof doesn't make the room too dark.

Should there be a wall or hedge around the terrace?

A high wall, fence, or hedge is needed to screen the terrace from nearby neighbors and vice versa. (Oh, yes, your neighbors may find your unscreened terrace more objectionable than you do.) You may also need such screening to keep off the wind. But there isn't any point in it otherwise.

The main purpose of a low wall is to keep people from falling off a raised terrace. Here it's a necessity. But if a terrace is at ground level, the only reason for a low wall or hedge is to define the terrace—separate it visually from the rest of the yard. This is sometimes desirable. On the other hand, both hedge and wall tend to discourage further expansion of a terrace that turns out to be too small. And they keep a crowd from spilling over on to the surrounding lawn. (Despite my experience at the overcrowded cocktail party, people do not always feel restricted to a terrace. At one of the last parties we had, in fact, they stood on the lawn as much as on the terrace.)

BUILDING A TERRACE   Building a terrace is largely a paving project; and even if it weren't, your choice of paving and the way you put it down have much to do with your enjoyment of the terrace.

Here are some things to think about when selecting the paving:

- It should be in harmony with the house.
- It should be reasonably skidproof.
- It should be durable.
- If there's a lot of sun on the terrace, a medium color is best. A light color is glary; a dark color soaks up heat and becomes uncomfortable underfoot.
- The rougher the paving, the more difficult it is to sweep and the harder it is on children's knees.
- The more porous a material, the more it soaks up stains.
- If it's an unbroken material such as concrete, tree and shrub roots underneath will be deprived of water and oxygen, and the plants are likely to die.
- The least expensive material—concrete—is one of the few you shouldn't try to put down yourself.

The following is a detailed rundown on the best of the paving materials and how they should be installed. The directions assume that the terrace is at ground level. It it's raised, you must build a retaining wall around it first; then pour in coarse fill topped with gravel and sand to serve as the base for the paving. The installation of the paving is made in the way described below.

Brick   I admit to being very partial toward bricks. They make a beautiful terrace floor. The color is soft, the patterns you can create are interesting, and you can buy bricks not only in rectangles but also in hexagons, octagons, squares, etc.

More than that, brick paving is pretty durable, water sinks through to the plant roots if you lay the bricks in sand, and installation can be made by anyone.

On the other hand, brick paving is not as easy to keep clean as some other materials, and it stains readily (although this can be largely prevented if you coat it with a penetrating masonry sealer). Weeds and grass come up through the joints. And when laid in shade, the bricks acquire a coating of moss that makes them very slippery when damp.

Bricks are often laid in mortar on a concrete slab, but the 1/2-in. joints that are required spoil the appearance of the paving to some extent. When bricks are laid in sand, the joints are minimized, and the pavement lacks the rigidity it has when concrete is used. This contributes to its beauty.

Laying a brick terrace is easy, but it takes time. If you rush the job, you'll be unhappy with the results.

Since the top of the bricks should be a fraction of an inch above the surrounding ground, dig out the ground to a depth of 6 in. or a bit more. To allow water to run off the terrace, slope the excavation away from the house at the rate of 1/8 in. per foot. Firm the ground well. Then pour in a 3-in. layer of gravel or crushed rock, and after tamping, add 1 in. of sand. This cushion not only provides a solid base for the bricks but also helps to protect them against frost-heaving. The top of the bricks, which are 2-1/4 in. thick, will be at about the right level.

Order gravel and sand by the cubic yard. Measure the area of the terrace in square feet and divide by nine to give you the area in square yards. One cubic yard of gravel yields a 3-in. cushion covering 12 sq. yd. A cubic yard of sand yields a 1-in. cushion covering 36 sq. yd. Thus, if your terrace measures 10 x 15 ft. (17 sq. yd.), you need 1-1/2 cu. yd. of gravel and 1/2 cu. yd. of sand.

Order bricks by the unit. To find how many will be needed along the outer edges of the terrace (see below), measure the total length of the outer edges in inches and divide by 2.25. For the bricks in the center of the terrace, measure the length and width of the area inside the outer edges in inches, multiply the numbers, and divide by 30 (the square-inch area of a common brick).

Stretch strings between stakes to mark the edges of the terrace. Pull them tight so they serve as elevation lines. Measure carefully from one to the other to avoid unnecessary cutting of the bricks. To make sure you have 90° corners, measure 3 ft. in one direction from a corner and 4 ft. in the other direction. Measure from point to point. If the space is exactly 5 ft., the corner is square. If the space is more or less, the corner must be adjusted.

Lay the bricks around the edges of the terrace first (Fig. 16-1). If one edge is hard against a wall, the bricks in that row are laid flat, like those in the center of the terrace. But bricks along the outer edges—the edges next to grass and garden beds—should not be laid flat because they tend to twist when people step on them. These are laid vertically in a trench, with the exposed top perpendicular to the terrace. Pack soil around them.

Lay the center bricks across the terrace—not lengthwise. This is not essential if the terrace is less than 16 ft. long, but it simplifies installation. Cut a 2 x 4 the width of the terrace and notch the ends to fit over the edging bricks, as shown in Fig. 16-1. The notches should be 2 in. deep; thus, the center of the timber hangs 2 in. below what will be the top of the terrace. The timber serves as a sand-leveler.

Dampen the sand a little, rake it level, and firm it—but not too much—with a tamper. (If you can't rent a steel tamper, make one by nailing two foot-long pieces of 2 x 12 or 2 x 10 together and attaching them to a handle.) Then lay your sand-leveler across the terrace, and draw it forward 12 to 15 in. to level the base perfectly. If there are hollows, fill them with additional sand; tamp and level again.

There are innumerable patterns for brick paving, but the running bond is most widely used (Fig. 16-2). The bricks go down quickly, fit tightly together, and create an attractive effect. In this pattern, the vertical joints at the ends of the bricks fall midway between the ends of the bricks in the adjacent rows.

Start the first row with a half brick, and then lay whole bricks to the end of the row. Start the second row with a whole brick and finish at the other end with a half brick. Then repeat the process again and again until the terrace is completed. Set all bricks snug to the adjacent bricks—don't leave spaces.

To cut a brick, use a mason's wide chisel or an ordinary cold chisel. Score the brick on opposite sides; then place the chisel on one of the lines, and give it a sharp rap with a hammer.

When each row of bricks is laid, set your sand-leveler on top of it, and pound it down until the ends touch the edging bricks. If any bricks seem loose or wobbly after leveling, pick them out, shovel in more sand, and replace them.

After putting down three rows, check with a carpenter's square to make sure they are perpendicular to the edges. Then tamp and level another 12 to 15 in. of sand, and lay another three rows.

When the entire terrace is paved, sweep dry sand over it. Work as much as possible into the joints. Then spray with water to settle the sand, and sweep up the excess when dry. You may have to repeat this step after a week or so if the joints appear open and the bricks are a little loose.

Concrete   You can color and texture ordinary concrete, but it still doesn't make a very pretty terrace. Furthermore, it stains badly and keeps moisture and oxygen from reaching plant roots underneath. On the other hand, it makes the strongest, most durable terrace floor.

To give concrete—especially a large expanse—a smooth, level surface takes more experience than the homeowner has—so hire a mason. The slab he gives you should be 4 in. thick and slightly sloped for runoff of water. If your soil is porous, the slab can rest directly on it; otherwise, it should be dug out to a depth or 8 to 10 in. and filled with 4 to 6 in. of gravel. Be sure to settle with the mason beforehand what sort of final finish you want.

Exposed-aggregate concrete   This is an ordinary concrete slab covered with marble chips, granite screenings, or other rock materials that project slightly above the matrix. It is usually put down in large squares separated by pronounced open joints or by redwood 2 x 4s.

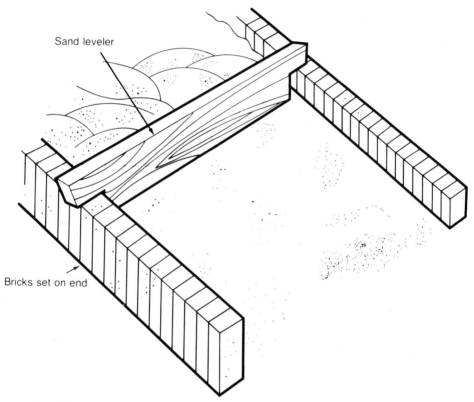

Sand leveler

Bricks set on end

Fig. 16-1   Building a brick terrace.

Fig. 16-2   Running bond.

The effect depends on the aggregate used, but in most cases, the paving is very handsome. It is also durable and nonglary; and if it becomes stained, you can't tell it. On the negative side, however, it may be a bit uncomfortable to walk on—especially if you're going barefooted. Water runoff is a little slow, and none percolates down to plant roots.

An exposed-aggregate concrete terrace is built like an ordinary concrete terrace. Give the job to a mason. The slope should be increased slightly for better drainage.

Concrete patio blocks   These are 1-1/2-in.-thick concrete "tiles" sold in large rectangles, squares, hexagons, and several special shapes. Some have the texture of ordinary building blocks; others are covered with stone chips or pebbles. Various colors are available. Half blocks of the special shapes are available so you can square off the terrace edges.

The blocks are easy to install and economical; and unlike other concrete pavings, they let water and oxygen through to the soil beneath. But they stain readily and are less durable than other block and slab materials.

If you pave the entire terrace with squares or rectangles of the same size, it's easy enough to determine how many you need by dividing the square-inch area of the terrace by the area of the blocks. But if you're going to use a mixture or squares and/or rectangles or special shapes, let the dealer figure your needs.

Lay the blocks slightly above ground level on a base made with 3 in. of gravel or crushed rock topped with 1 in. of sand. The base should have a slight slope to provide drainage. After raking the sand level, dampen and tamp it; then level it with a 2 x 4.

If you take pains to provide a full, deep sand and gravel base along all outer edges of the terrace, the edging blocks will be as firm as those in the center. However, if any blocks abut a planting bed, it's a good idea to install a vertical metal or wood curbing to keep them from sliding sideways into the beds (Fig. 16-3).

Allow 1/8- to 1/4-in. spaces between blocks, and fill them with coarse sand when the terrace is completed. To make sure the paving is level, check it frequently with your 2 x 4 and a spirit level.

Cut stone blocks   Cobblestones come under this heading. There are also rectangular and square blocks in other rather small sizes. They are heavy and durable, and make a beautiful but somewhat rough pavement. I particularly like the very small (about 3-in.-square) blocks. Use them alone or in combination with bricks. Install the blocks like bricks.

Flagstones   Here's another handsome, durable paving material. The stones are large, flat slabs of various colors— mainly in grays and blues. They have enough texture to provide skidproof

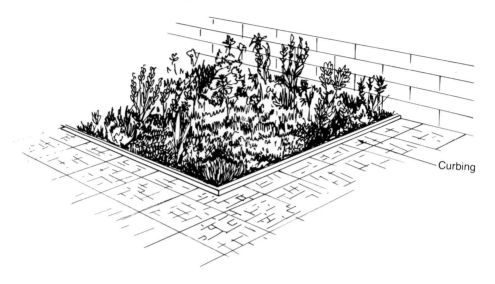

Curbing

Fig. 16-3 Edging around concrete patio tiles.

footing; yet they are not too rough for children's knees or for easy sweeping. Staining can be minimized by applying a penetrating masonry sealer.

Flagstones are cut into squares and rectangles of numerous sizes, and you can also have them cut to special shapes. Irregular shapes are available, too, but they don't make a good-looking paving. The effect is rather like that of a windshield that has been shattered by a rock.

If you stick to flagstones of one size, it's no problem to figure out how many you will need. But if you use squares and rectangles of several sizes, let the masonry supplies dealer work out a numbered plan for you. This will add to the cost of the stones, but it will save time and labor and will eliminate waste of stone. When placing your order, if you want all the stones to be of approximately the same color (the paving looks better if they are), be sure to say so; otherwise, you may get a mixture.

The best thickness to use is 1-1/2 in., but you can get by with 1 in. Lay the stones like concrete patio blocks.

Slate   Slate is an excellent substitute for flagstone and very
                                         much like it in all respects. It has, however, a
tendency to spall in cold weather.

Use squares and rectangles, not irregular pieces. All should be of the same color; but beware the very dark shades—which are common in slate—on a sunny terrace. I know of a magnificent, sun-swept terrace outside Chicago that is paved in black slate. It cost a small fortune and is an absolute misery because it stores up so much heat.

Have the dealer make a numbered layout for you if you put down slates of different sizes.

Tiles   Quarry tiles are heavy-duty ceramic tiles in many
                                         shapes and sizes. Besides the familiar red, they come
in colors ranging from off-white to blue-green. There are also tiles with fired-in designs. All make a beautiful, durable, stain-resistant, easy-to-clean terrace floor that is smooth enough to do ballroom dancing on, but slippery when wet.

Since tiles should be set in mortar on a strong concrete base, you should have the terrace built by a tilesetter.

Wood blocks   Of all terrace paving materials, wood blocks are the
                                         best underfoot. They are delightfully resilient, quiet,
and cool. And they blend beautifully with the landscape. But they are treacherously slippery when wet (especially if used in the shade); and even though you have them cut from redwood, cypress, or cedar, they will eventually rot.

Some people use rounds of wood to pave a terrace, but this results in large gaps that must be filled somehow—probably with sand or gravel, which makes sweeping almost impossible. Square blocks are better because they can be set so snug that the joints are almost invisible.

Install the blocks like bricks on a sand-gravel base.

Combinations of materials   There are so many ways you can combine paving
                                         materials I won't even start to suggest them. Just
remember that it is much harder to design an attractive floor this way.

BUILDING A   Building a raised terrace isn't any harder than
RAISED TERRACE   building one on grade. It just takes longer because
                               more is involved. For one thing, you must make sure
that where the terrace abuts the house it is not in direct contact with any wood; otherwise, termites will soon attack the house.

For another thing, you must pile in fill to raise the terrace to the desired height. This can be done partly before the retaining wall is built, but the work cannot be completed until the wall is high enough to hold the fill in place. Give the fill at least a month to settle before you add the gravel and sand base for the terrace floor.

Finally, you must build a wall around the outer edges of the terrace. Because of the pressure exerted on it by the fill and paving, this should not be more than 3 ft. high from ground level to the top of the terrace floor. However, there is no limitation on the height of the wall above the floor.

You can build the wall of brick, concrete block, or stone.

Concrete block   I start with concrete block because it's the easiest
material to work with. But it certainly isn't the
prettiest.

The length of the wall should be an exact multiple of 16 in. with the
blocks laid out in a running bond in which the vertical joints in adjacent courses
are staggered. Make a sketch of the wall on graph paper to determine exactly
how many full-size (8 x 8 x 16 in.) blocks and how many half-size blocks you
need. (If you used nothing but full-size blocks, it would take 113—plus one sack
of masonry cement and two sacks of sand—to build 100 sq. ft. of wall.) The half
blocks and a few of the full-size blocks should be corner blocks with flat ends.

Build the wall up from a concrete footing laid in a trench. The bottom
should be at least 18 in. below ground level; and in very cold climates, it should
be below the frost line. Make the footing 16 in. wide and 8 in. deep. Use greased
boards that are well braced to form the sides, and strike the top of the concrete
off flush with the edges of the boards. You'll save much work if you have
ready-mixed concrete delivered in a truck. If you mix your own, the proportions
should be 1 sack of portland cement (a sack is equal to 1 cu. ft.), 2-3/4 cu. ft. of
builder's sand, and 4 cu. ft. of coarse aggregate (clean pebbles and stones
between 1/4 and 1-1/2 in. in diameter). If the pebbles and sand are dry, use
6-1/4 gal. of water for each 1-sack batch. Decrease the water to 5-1/2 gal. if the
pebbles and sand are wet. When the footing is hard, you can start laying up the
blocks.

Build from the two ends toward the center. Stretch a cord between the
end blocks to assure that the wall is straight and level (Fig. 16-4). Raise the cord
for each course. Until you get the knack of setting blocks, check each one with a
carpenter's level to make sure it is level from front to back. Also check the entire
wall repeatedly with a level or plumb line to make sure it is straight up and
down.

The mortar, made of 1 part masonry cement and 2-1/2 parts sand, should
be plastic but not soupy. Lay the first course of blocks in a 3/8-in.-thick bed of
mortar spread on the footing. To set succeeding courses, trowel strips of mortar
on the front and back edges of the blocks previously laid. Then trowel strips of
mortar on one end of the new block (Fig. 16-5); set it into place on the row
below and against the end of the block just previously laid. Tap it down firmly.
The horizontal and vertical joints should be 3/8 in. thick. Scrape off the excess
cement, and return it to your mortar box. After the joints have set awhile, tool
them with a grooving tool or piece of pipe drawn from end to end (Fig. 16-6).

Don't spread mortar for more than one block at a time. If you have to
remove a block because it isn't set properly, scrape up the mortar, throw it back
into the box, and apply new mortar. If the mortar in the box stiffens, retemper
it with a little water. At $80°$ or less, the life of mortar is 3-1/2 hours; at $90°$ it's
only 2-1/2 hours.

Workman is tapping block into place with end of handle of trowel.

←—Cord

Fig. 16-4 Laying concrete blocks to a line.

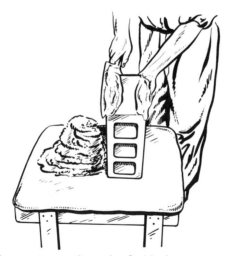

Fig. 16-5 Buttering mortar on the ends of a block.

Cover the wall at the top with solid cap blocks. When the mortar has set four or five days, you can give the wall a couple of coats of exterior latex paint.

If you build walls around several sides of the terrace (as is usually the case), build both sides of each corner at the same time. (But you should complete only one wall at a time.) Interlock the corner blocks so that the block

Fig. 16-6 After the block is laid and leveled, scrape off excess mortar with trowel. When joints have set, tool them with a pipe to a concave contour (as shown in the lower courses).

in the first course runs lengthwise of, say, the end wall; that in the second course runs lengthwise of the front wall; and so on up to the top of the walls.

Because the terrace floor is laid on sand, water falling on it seeps down into the ground underneath; consequently, you don't have to provide weep holes in the terrace wall. If the floor were laid in mortar, however, weep holes would be needed at frequent intervals along the floor line.

Brick   A brick wall around a terrace should be two tiers thick—made of two bricks laid flat, side by side, to give a total wall thickness of 8 in.

Lay the bricks upon concrete footings like those for a concrete block wall. Work from the corners toward the middle of each wall. Use a taut cord to keep going straight. Build one course at a time (except at the ends of the wall) and one tier at a time. After completing the two tiers in a course, slush concrete down into the joint to tie them together (Fig. 16-7). But a better tie is effected by laying five stretcher courses and then a single header course. A stretcher course is made with bricks running lengthwise of the wall; a header course has bricks laid at right angles to the wall (Fig. 16-8).

The mortar is made of 1 part masonry cement to 3 parts sand. Hose the bricks down thoroughly or soak them in water for an hour before starting construction.

Fig. 16-7 Build the wall one course at a time except at the ends. Put down a ribbon of concrete no more than two feet long and make a slight furrow down the center.

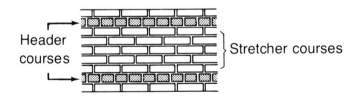

Fig. 16-8 Stretcher and header courses in brick walls.

Spread an even ribbon of mortar no more than 2 ft. long over the bricks previously laid, and make a slight furrow down the center with the point of your mason's trowel as shown in Fig. 16-6. Butter one end of the brick being laid with mortar. Then set the brick squarely—without twisting—on the mortar bed and against the end of the previous brick, and tap it into place. All joints should be about 1/2 in. thick. Scrape off excess mortar. Take care not to smear it on the face of the bricks. When the joints have set, tool them smooth. Remove mortar stains with a weak solution of muriatic acid a fortnight after the wall is completed.

Stone   Building a stone wall is a challenging project which I highly recommend. It isn't easy. It takes a long time. But when you're finished, you should have a wall you can point to with pride for the rest of your life.

The best stones to work with are flat rectangles—but they are not easy to come by in every part of the country. So you may have to use whatever you can lay hands on. Happily, a wall made of an assortment of flat, round, and irregular stones in many sizes often turns out to be the handsomest of all.

You may be able to build a wall as little as a foot wide if you have a good supply of flat stones; but 18 in. is a more likely average. It should rest on a footing—at least 18 in. below grade—that is twice the width of the wall and as high as the wall is wide. The footing is usually made of stones that are not good enough for the wall.

Remove all dirt from the stones with a hose or brush. To cut or trim them, use a hammer and cold chisel; this is likely to be a painfully slow process. For mortar, use 1 part portland cement and 3 parts sand. The joints should be at least 1/2 in. thick, and many will be much thicker.

Build the wall to a taut string from the ends toward the center. When you get above the terrace floor, use two parallel strings. Put down only enough mortar for one stone at a time. If possible, butter the end of the stone with mortar as in setting concrete blocks and bricks, but this is feasible only when you're working with rectangular stones. As a rule, it is necessary to trowel mortar down around the ends and backs of stones after they have been set firmly in a mortar bed.

Setting stones is pretty much of a trial-and-error process. First, put each one in position without mortar. Some stones fit better across the wall; others are laid lengthwise. Generally, if a wall has pronounced horizontal lines, it looks wrong to set an occasional stone in a vertical position; but when the texture of the wall is uneven, you can position stones however they fit best.

ROOFING THE   In my opinion, the best way to shade a terrace is to
TERRACE TO PROVIDE   plant trees. But trees, alas, do not grow into
SHADE   shade-makers overnight. That is one good argument
                             for building a sun-shade of some sort over a terrace. Another argument is that a man-made structure can be designed to give more controlled shade. In addition, it does not drop leaves, twigs, or fruits.

A roof that is built strictly for shade is really a filter, not a roof, because it is made with openings that let in a certain amount of sunlight and air. It is built in countless ways. Egg-crates and louvers are among the most popular designs but also among the most difficult to create because, in order to keep out the sun when you don't want it and let it in when you do want it, you must have sound knowledge of the angles at which it strikes your particular corner of the earth in different seasons of the year. For this reason, you will be well advised to stick to a simple "lath" roof. This is made of 1 x 2-in. boards (not real laths) laid parallel and spaced 1 in. apart for deep shade, 2 in. apart for half shade and half sun. As a rule, they should run from north to south so that the pattern of sun and shade on the terrace changes constantly.

The roof can be sloped or flat, whichever looks better. If the terrace adjoins the house, nail a 2 x 6-in. ledger strip to the house to support the rafters. Install the strip horizontally, 8 to 10 ft. above the floor, with spikes driven through the siding into the studs. At the opposite side of the terrace, the rafters rest on a 2 x 6-in. beam notched into the top ends of vertical 4 x 4-in. posts. Use redwood or cypress for the posts, or make them of any other suitable wood that is treated with wood preservative. To prevent lateral movement, set the bottoms of the posts about 20 in. into the ground, and pour concrete around them in a cone-shaped or pyramidal footing 8 in. wide at the top and twice as wide at the bottom. The top of the footing should be just below the bottom of the terrace paving. Space the posts no more than 10 ft. apart, center to center.

Use 2 x 6s for the rafters and space them 2 ft. apart. The length of the rafters from ledger strip to beam should not exceed 12 ft.—in addition to which they may extend beyond the beam about 2 ft. Toenail them to the top of the ledger strip and beam with 5-in. galvanized nails. Use 3-in. galvanized nails to fasten the laths to the rafters. When the roof is built in this fashion, the laths will parallel the house wall.

If you want the laths to be perpendicular to the house, install 4 x 4-in. posts in the same way, but connect each one to the ledger strip with 2 x 6 beams (Fig. 16-9). Attach the beams to the side of the ledger strip with patented metal hangers, or stirrups, and notch them into the posts. The beams should be no more than 10 ft. long, plus 2 ft. for an overhang. Space them no more than 10 ft. apart. Install 2 x 6-in. rafters between the beams and perpendicular to them. At the open edge of the roof, nail the rafter to the ends of the beams. Nail the next rafter to the posts. Hang the remaining rafters, up to the ledger strip, in metal hangers. Space the rafters 2 ft. apart.

ROOFING THE TERRACE TO KEEP IT DRY For this purpose, of course, you need a solid roof sloping away from the house. Build it of translucent fiberglass-reinforced plastic panels or of the same roofing material used on the house.

The plastic panels are available in a number of colors and are usually corrugated. I dislike them because they do nothing for the appearance of a house, because when you look up at them from underneath you can see a murky outline of every leaf and other particle on them, and because they let in a certain

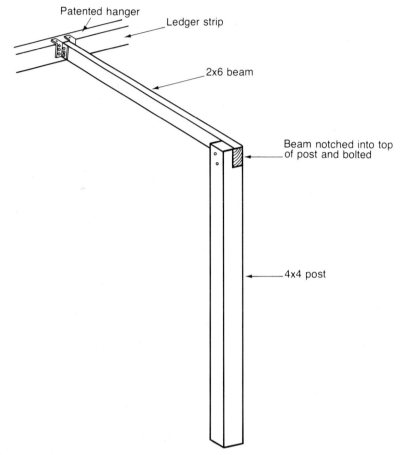

Fig. 16-9   Installing a terrace roof with laths perpendicular to the house.

amount of light without admitting air and therefore make the terrace hot. But they are strong, durable, relatively inexpensive, and easy to work with.

The framework for the roof should be built much like the first of the two just described. Nail a ledger strip to the house. Notch a beam into the front edges of posts spaced no more than 12 ft. apart. Fasten 2 x 6-in. rafters to the sides of the ledger strip and beam with metal hangers. The spacing between rafters should equal the width of the plastic panels used minus 2 in. (Fig. 16-10). For example, if you use 26-in. panels, space the rafters 24 in. on centers.

Cross blocking is required between rafters for all panels except 26-in. widths up to 10 ft. long. Use 2 x 6s or 2 x 4s, and toenail them to the sides of the rafters midway between the ledger strip and beam.

To cut the plastic, use an old crosscut saw with fine teeth. Brace the panels well to keep the saw from binding.

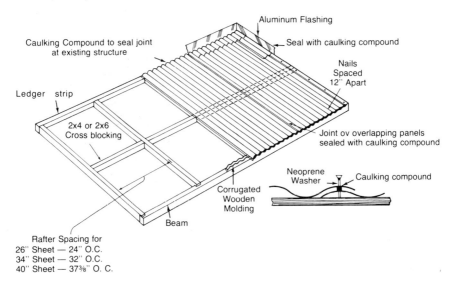

Aluminum Flashing

Caulking Compound to seal joint
at existing structure

Seal with caulking compound

Nails
Spaced
12" Apart

Ledger   strip

2x4 or 2x6
Cross blocking

Joint ov overlapping panels
sealed with caulking compound

Neoprene
Washer   Caulking compound

Corrugated
Wooden
Molding

Beam

Rafter Spacing for
26" Sheet — 24" O.C.
34" Sheet — 32" O.C.
40" Sheet — 37⅜" O. C.

Fig. 16-10 Installing a roof of plastic panels.

Install the panels with the corrugations running up and down the roof. Overlap adjacent panels 1-1/2 in., with the open edge pointing away from the prevailing wind. Seal the joints with caulking compound provided by the panel dealer. Then drill holes through the joints into the rafters, and nail the panels down with aluminum or galvanized screw nails. To prevent leaks, fit neoprene washers under the nailheads. Space the nails 12 in. apart.

Use at least three screw nails in the ends of the panels. In the best construction, a corrugated filler strip of rubber or wood is placed under the panel ends.

Standard panel lengths are 8, 10, and 12 ft., though other sizes are sold. If your terrace roof is more than 12 ft. deep, the panel at the high end of the roof should overlap that at the low end by 3 in. The joint should be made directly over a beam or cross block, and should be sealed with caulking.

The last step in building the roof is to install aluminum flashing across the upper end. If the wall of the house is covered with shingles or beveled siding, try to slip the top edge of the flashing under them. If this is impossible, nail the flashing tight to the wall, and seal it with caulking compound. Also apply caulking between the bottom of the flashing and the plastic.

If you use wood or asphalt shingles on a terrace roof (Fig. 16-11), the roof must be sloped at least 3 in. in every foot. Use 4 x 4s for the posts, and space them no more than 10 ft. apart. On the tops of the posts nail a beam made of two 2 x 8s nailed securely together. Use a 2 x 6 for the ledger strip.

Make the rafters of Douglas fir. If you use 2 x 6s spaced 24 in. on centers, the span from the ledger strip to the beam should not exceed 12 ft. If you use 2

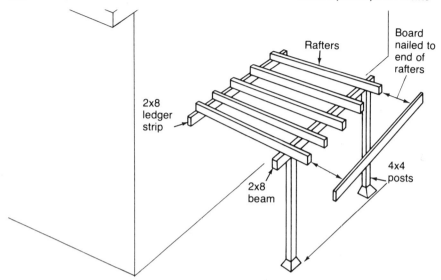

Fig. 16-11 Installing a roof covered with shingles.

x 8s, the span can be increased to 16 ft. If you use 2 x 10s, it can be 20 ft. If the spacing between rafters is reduced to 16 in., you can increase the span 2 ft. for each timber size.

The rafters can overhang the beam as much as 2 ft. Nail them to the top of the ledger strip and beam with 5-in. galvanized nails. To help hold them upright, nail a board or timber the width of the rafters to the lower ends.

Nail 3/4-in. exterior-grade plywood to the rafters to form the roof deck. For appearance's sake, the bottom side of the plywood should be free of knot holes and other flaws. The deck can also be made of 1 x 8-in. boards.

For how to apply asphalt and cedar shingles, see Chapter 14. To prevent the points of the nails ordinarily used in roofing from coming through the underside of the deck, use 1-in. galvanized nails.

Flash the joint between the upper end of the roof and the house wall with an aluminum strip 12 in. wide. If possible, force the upper edge of the strip under the siding; otherwise, nail it securely to the siding, and seal the edge with caulking compound. Fasten the lower edge of the flashing to the roof with fibered asphalt roofing cement.

DECKS...

As I indicated earlier, a deck is really nothing but a modern version of the old-fashioned porch. Unlike a porch, it usually has no roof; and because of this, the floor boards are spaced about 1/4 in. apart to provide rapid drainage. The entire structure is normally stained or allowed to weather naturally.

The purpose of a deck is to provide level outdoor living space on a sloping terrain. Most decks are connected to the house at the first-floor level, but some are built at a distance from the house.

If you can build a terrace roof, it would seem logical to think that you can build a deck because the method of framing is similar. However, a deck must bear a much heavier load—not just a static load but also a live load—and this means it should be designed and built by professionals.

When adjacent to the house, a deck is supported on a ledger strip attached to the house wall and a series of large posts built up from masonry piers that extend below the frost line. The posts are connected with beams that, in turn, support the joists. Bridging between joists stiffens the deck floor, while timber cross-braces are used to strengthen the entire structure. The flooring is normally made of 2 x 4s or 2 x 6s, but it can be made of 1 in. boards if the joists are closely spaced. A railing should be built around the open sides of any deck that is raised more than 10 in. off the ground.

PORCHES...

WOOD FLOORS   A board that is badly splintered, worn, or rotten should be cut out between the joists by boring holes next to the joists and sawing the boards with a keyhole saw (Fig. 16-12). Nail 4-in. boards to the sides of the joists close up against the bottom of the floor. Then cut a new board to fill the gap and nail it to the cleats.

If a floor simply needs repainting, use the best oil-base deck paint you can buy.

If wooden steps are weak, tear them out and buy a pair of notched stringers from a lumberyard (Fig. 16-13). Cut them to fit between the sidewalk and the joist or header at the front of the porch. Notch the upper ends to rest on a ledger strip nailed to the face of the joist or header, flush with the bottom edge. Saturate the stringers with pentachlorophenol wood preservative before nailing them to the porch.

Cut boards for the risers to the height of the notches in the stringers. Cut boards for the treads to overhang the risers and sides of the stringers about 1 in. Saturate all the pieces with preservative before nailing them to the stringers with galvanized nails.

Rebuilding an entire porch gets to be a sizable undertaking if you have to replace joists that are showing signs of rot. But if the joists are sound and only the floor boards are gone, rip off the boards and replace them with yellow-pine boards with square edges (so water will drip through). Use 3-in. galvanized annular-ring nails. Spot-prime knots with stain-killer to prevent bleeding. Then apply a primer followed by two coats of deck paint.

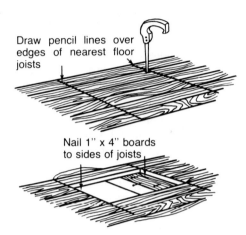

Draw pencil lines over
edges of nearest floor
joists

Nail 1" x 4" boards
to sides of joists

Fig. 16-12   Replacing floor boards in a porch.

A more attractive, more durable porch floor is made with 3/4-in. exterior-grade plywood covered with silicone traffic topping—an abrasion- and skid-resistant material available in several colors.

Lay the plywood parallel with the joists. The long edges must bear directly on the joists. Blocks cut from 2 x 4s must be installed between the joists under the short edges of the plywood panels. Nail the plywood with 3-in. galvanized annular-ring nails or screw nails spaced 8 in. apart around the perimeter and along the intermediate joists.

Leave a 1/4-in. space between the plywood panels. When the subfloor is completed, vacuum out the dust and debris in the joints, and stick masking tape on the plywood surface 1/16 in. back from either side of the joints. Install 3/8-in. polyethylene-foam rods in the joints 1/8 in. below the surface. Prime the edges of the joints with the primer supplied by the traffic topping dealer, and let it dry for an hour. Then fill the joints solidly with silicone sealant, strike the top off level with the plywood, and take up the masking tape before the sealant dries.

After the sealant has cured for at least eight hours, clean the plywood thoroughly, dampen it slightly with clean water, and roll on the traffic topping primer. Let this dry until it is no longer tacky.

Add curing agent to the traffic topping, and blend thoroughly for about four minutes. Immediately pour small amounts of the topping on the plywood, and spread it evenly over the floor with a notched spreader with 3/16-in. notches. Smooth the topping with the smooth edge of the spreader. Finish smoothing by going over the topping within five minutes of spreading with a short-napped paint roller moistened with just enough mineral spirits to keep it from sticking. The finished surface should resemble smooth concrete.

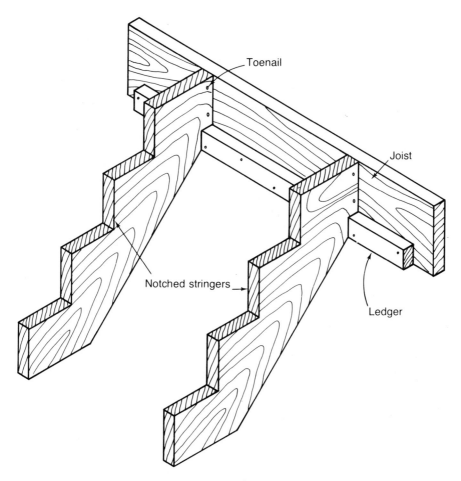

Fig. 16-13 Replacing outside steps.

In 70° weather, the traffic topping should be dry enough to walk on in about 16 hours. To protect the topping at the outer edges of the porch, screw flat aluminum bars measuring 1 in. wide and 1/4 in. thick to the edges flush with the surface of the topping. The bars are sold in hardware and building supplies stores.

CONCRETE FLOORS Cut open cracks and fill them with epoxy or latex cement. If the edges of the porch or porch steps are worn, brace a lightly greased board against the edge, and fill in behind it with the same cement. Then paint the floor with deck paint.

SCREEN PORCHES A screen porch is a delight, provided it does what it's supposed to do: Keep out bugs. Unfortunately, old porches often fail to do this because the huge screens are usually left up the year round; consequently, they are exposed to much more wear and moisture (and resultant corrosion) than window screens. In addition, the screen frames may rot out.

When the screen cloth goes, replace it with new aluminum or fiberglass screening. The latter lasts longer and, after a few years, looks better because it does not corrode; but aluminum is more resistant to distortion when it is struck, pushed, or scratched.

To remove the old screen cloth, take down the screen and lay it flat on the porch floor; then pry off the moldings around the edges of the cloth. Remove all tacks or staples.

Tack or staple the new screen cloth to the top rail of the frame. You can use aluminum tacks for both aluminum and fiberglass cloth, steel staples for fiberglass. Space tacks and staples about 2 in. apart. Then stretch the cloth tight—taking care not to distort it—and tack it to the bottom rail. Then fasten it along the side rails.

Replace the moldings with small aluminum or galvanized brads, and countersink the heads. Then with a sharp knife, cut off the screen cloth extending beyond the moldings.

If screen frames are wobbly at the joints, brace them with angle irons set into or over the corners. If a frame is rotted out, build a new frame with wood of the same size. Make half-lap joints in the four corners, and secure them with resorcinol glue and short aluminum or brass screws. Join the cross-brace near the middle of the screen to the side rails with middle lap or dado joints. Treating the frames with a paintable wood preservative will add years to their life.

RIPPING OFF
AN OLD PORCH
Maybe the appearance of your house is spoiled by an old front porch. If so, it won't be the first house to suffer this indignity. Countless houses built in the simple Colonial and Federal styles of architecture had porches that detracted from their lines and that were accordingly removed.

Admittedly, it takes some courage to rip from a house anything as permanent looking as a porch. It also takes some foresight and understanding of architecture to visualize how a house will look without its porch. For these reasons, you may wish to pay an architect for his opinion before you move into action. But you have no other grounds for hesitancy.

Removing a porch generally is not difficult work. Just start on the roof and work down. When everything is gone, there will probably be gaps in the siding left by the porch roof and floor. Cover them with building paper before filling them in with new siding. To avoid a patchwork effect, don't fill the gaps exactly as you find them, but remove additional siding around them so that the joints will be staggered. For example, if you tear out a half-round porch column, don't fill in the space it leaves with a straight row of, say, shingles because the lines of joints on the sides of the row will stand out like a sore thumb. Instead, you should pry out a number of the shingles on either side of the space and nail in new shingles of assorted widths (Fig. 16-14).

Removal of a porch usually requires construction of new steps to the front door. This calls for a mason to build the steps of bricks, flagstones, slates, or perhaps marble. In many houses, especially those in cities, steps are built in a simple, straight flight up from the front walk. But you will create a more inviting, accommodating, and safer entrance by making the top step just below the threshold a deep, wide platform on which several people can stand. The steps below this can be the same width or narrower, but they should not be less than 3 ft. wide. The treads should be a minimum of 11 in. deep; risers, a maximum of 7-1/2 in. high.

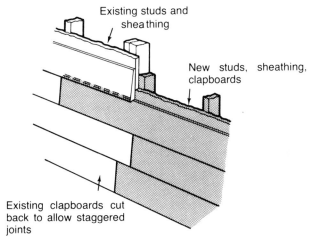

Existing studs and sheathing

New studs, sheathing, clapboards

Existing clapboards cut back to allow staggered joints

Fig. 16-14 Filling in siding with new boards.

17

Garages and Carports

One of the most glaring inadequacies of old homes is lack of garage space. Some never had any at all. Others had space but lost it when it was made over into a family room or workshop. Still others have space that is much too small. This is even true of moderate-cost homes that were built only yesterday.

GARAGES...

ENLARGING AN EXISTING GARAGE This isn't a simple job. For one thing if the garage was built before the local zoning code was enacted and if it is now nonconforming, you may not be allowed to enlarge it in its present location. This is a point you must check with your town building department.

For another thing, you may not be able to enlarge the garage without violating setback rules.

Finally, the present garage may be designed in such a way that you cannot add to it attractively except by tearing it down and building anew.

All of this sounds very negative, but it shouldn't discourage you from trying to enlarge an old garage or building a new one. In any home building operation there are usually several solutions to every problem—and that's the case here. For instance, if you can't build a garage that's two cars wide, maybe you can build it for two cars in tandem. Or maybe if you add a deck to a hillside house, you can fit your cars underneath. Or maybe if you cannot enlarge a one-car attached garage, you can build an additional one-car detached garage in the backyard where it will also serve as a tool shed or pool house. Or maybe instead of struggling to enlarge an existing garage, you can build a totally new garage, and convert the old one into a family room or bedroom. Or maybe if you live in a community that permits building up to the lot lines, you can surround your front yard with walls, build a garage in one corner, and use the rest of the area as an attractive automobile courtyard.

BUILDING A   Finding the right place and space to build a garage
NEW GARAGE   can prove very difficult when a house has already
                    been built and the lot already developed.

If you want to connect the garage to the house—the ideal arrangement—there must be enough space at one side to accommodate the garage
without violating the zoning code that requires a minimum setback from the side
lot lines. Similarly, you cannot put the garage in front of the house if it would
extend over the front setback. Of course, you probably wouldn't run into
setback problems if you place the garage behind the house—but this would mess
up the backyard, and you might have to face the garage doors away from the
street, thus requiring an enormous turn-around behind it.

These are not the only problems with an attached garage. You must also
consider how it will affect the lines of the house and whether it can be attached
so you can go to and from it without tramping through the main living area or
even through the bedrooms.

A detached garage avoids the last two problems. In addition, it should cost
less to build. On the other hand, there's no certainty you won't run into setback
snags or that you won't chop up the yard. And you can look forward to many
wet, cold trips between the house and garage.

Garage dimensions   Even if you're a confirmed user of compact cars, you
                          should not build a garage strictly for them because
the person who wants to buy your home may be a confirmed user of big cars.
For this reason, don't build a one-car garage smaller than 10 x 22 ft., or a
two-car garage smaller than 20 x 22 ft. These are minimum dimensions. They
allow just enough space for you to park the largest car on the road and to
squeeze in and out of the doors on either side.

The dimensions, however, are not realistic. In the 1970s, it is folly for a
homeowner to build anything less than a two-car garage that is large enough to
accommodate—in addition to the cars—a power mower, a leaf shredder, a
wheelbarrow, several bicycles, a snowmobile, and vast amounts of terrace
furniture. In other words, realistic dimensions for today's garage are 23 ft. wide
by 25 ft. long.

Garage construction   Leave this to professionals. Masonry footings should
                          be built below the frost line to protect the floor and
above-ground structure against frost action. For the floor, put in a 6-in. base of
gravel or crushed rock. Cover this with polyethylene film if you think you might
some day convert the garage into living space. Then put down a 4-in. slab of
reinforced concrete. The top should be an inch or two above ground level to
keep out water and about 6 in. below the level of an adjoining house floor to
keep dirt and fumes out of the house. Slope the slab slightly toward the entrance

or provide a drain in the center. The drain should be connected to a dry well, not to the city sewer or a septic tank.

The apron is an extension of the garage floor but usually poured separately from it. It is 2 to 3 ft. deep and is usually flared slightly to the sides. The slope is somewhat greater than the floor slope.

The walls and roof of the garage are, as a rule, similar to those on the house. In many communities, the door and wall between an attached garage and the house must be fire-resistant. If a garage is built under the house, the ceiling should be fire-resistant.

Minimum width of a single-car garage door is 8 ft., but a 9-ft. size is worth the extra cost because you can drive in and out more easily. The extra width is especially valuable if you must turn to enter the garage. For a two-car garage, two single doors are more convenient and easier to operate than a double door, but the latter is less expensive. It should be 16 ft. wide.

For car washing and other purposes, install a cold-water faucet with hose thread. A laundry tub below the faucet is a very useful extra. It can be drained directly to the driveway or garden.

If the garage is used primarily for car and other storage, install two 100-watt incandescent lights in a one-car garage, three in a two-car garage. In the former, mount the lights on the ceiling on either side of the car 7 ft. from the back wall. In a two-car garage, mount the third light between the cars 3 ft. from the front wall. The lights should be controlled from a switch in the garage and another in the house.

Install at least one duplex outlet midway along a side wall 3 to 4 ft. above the floor.

Heating an entire garage is impractical. However, if you use the garage as a laundry, workshop, etc., it's a good idea to take the chill off the work area by installing electric baseboards or recessed wall heaters or by putting heating coils in the ceiling.

REPLACING A
GARAGE DOOR
If an existing garage has an overhead door that has seen better days, buy a new door of the same construction and replace it, using the old hardware. But if you don't like the way the old door operates or if you have rickety hinged doors, buy a new door with a new track and all new hardware. Follow the manufacturer's installation directions; there's too much variation between different types and makes of door to give directions here.

The sectional door with curved tracks is the most popular because it gives a tight seal against the weather, dust, and sand; it is reliable and fairly easy to operate; and it can be opened even when snow drifts high against it. Rigid, one-piece doors are less expensive but don't fit or operate quite as well.

Roll-up doors are made of wood, hardboard, fiberglass, steel, or aluminum.

Those of wood are the least durable and require the most maintenance, but I feel they are the most attractive.

CARPORTS...

A carport cannot be considered a really good substitute for a garage. It protects automobiles against sun and precipitation—though not completely. It allows you to climb in and out of the cars without getting wet—though here again it isn't perfect. But I have never seen a carport that provided enough space for storing the countless things that people store in a garage. And as a concealer of automobiles and clutter, it is flop unless it faces away from the street and is enclosed on three sides.

In other words, carports do not contribute to the value of a property to the same extent as garages. Nevertheless, many homeowners have built them because they are less expensive. Perhaps you will, too.

CARPORT DIMENSIONS Minimum dimensions for a single-car carport that is open at both ends and both sides are 8 x 20 ft.; for a two-car carport, 17 x 20 ft. If there's a wall at the back end, add 2 ft. to the length; if there's a wall at one side, add 2 ft. to the width; if there's a storage wall at the end or along one side, add 5 ft.

BUILDING A CARPORT Let a mason put in the floor. But you should be able to build the rest of the structure if you keep it simple. Construct the roof in the same way you roof a terrace. (See Chapter 16.) For how to build a stud wall, see Chapter 4.

The simplest way to build a large storage closet in a carport is to cement a rectangle of bricks the size of the closet to the carport floor. Attach the closet floor, made of 3/4-in. plywood sheathing, on top of the bricks with screws driven into lead anchors. Then build the walls up from the floor with 2 x 4s, as in Chapter 4. You may omit the sole plates, however, and fasten the studs directly to the floor with angle irons. Space the studs 24 in. on centers. Close in the walls with a 1/2-in. plywood siding. Make the doors of the same material, and reinforce them with 1 x 2s nailed around the perimeter and diagonally across the middle. The closet can be extended all the way to the carport roof or can be topped off with a plywood ceiling 12 to 18 in. below the roof.

DRIVEWAYS...

Your driveway should be straight and direct, with a slope of no more than 1-3/4 in. in a foot. It should enter the street at an angle as close as possible to $90°$, and the corners should be flared back sharply so that you don't have to swing wide to enter or leave the street.

A 10-ft. width is adequate for a one-lane driveway, but all driveways really should be wide enough at some point to allow two cars to pass. For two lanes you need no less than 14 ft.; 16 ft. is a better width. All turns should have an inside radius of 20 ft. If two cars are to pass on a turn, the outside radius should be 40 ft.

If possible, provide a turn-around space in front of the garage so you don't have to back into the street. This also increases off-street parking space.

The garage or carport should be slightly higher than the driveway so water will drain away from it. If the garage is at the foot of a slope, the apron in front of it should slant away from it 5 or 6 ft. to form a little valley to catch the water. Install a drain in the bottom.

Index